The Nature
of Adolescence

The Nature
of Adolescence

John C. Coleman

METHUEN
LONDON and NEW YORK

*In memory of Sonya Coleman,
and for her grandchildren
Christopher and Nicholas.*

First published in 1980 by
Methuen & Co. Ltd
11 New Fetter Lane, London EC4P 4EE
Reprinted 1982

Published in the USA by
Methuen & Co.
in association with Methuen, Inc.
733 Third Avenue, New York, NY 10017

© 1980 John C. Coleman

Phototypeset in V.I.P. Sabon by
Western Printing Services Ltd, Bristol.
Printed in Great Britain by
Richard Clay (The Chaucer Press) Ltd
Bungay, Suffolk.

British Library Cataloguing in Publication Data
Coleman, John C
   The nature of adolescence. – (University paperbacks).
   1. Adolescence
   I. Title
   301.43'15   HQ796   79–42946

   ISBN 0–416–72620–8
   ISBN 0416–72630–5 Pbk

*All royalties earned from this book benefit The Sussex Youth Trust, an
organization whose aim is the advancement of the care and education of
young people who are in need. The Trust has a commitment to research and
training, as well as to the provision of special education facilities. Its Registered Address is 23 New Road, Brighton BN1 1WZ.*

Contents

Acknowledgements

The author and publishers would like to thank the following for permission to reproduce copyright material: The American Psychological Association for table 5.3; The American Sociological Association for figure 4.1; Blackwell Scientific Publications for figure 2.5; British Medical Journal for figures 2.1 and 2.6; Cambridge University Press for figures 7.1, 8.2 and 8.3; Daedalus, Journal of the American Academy of Arts and Sciences for figures 3.3a and 3.3b; Family Planning Information Service for tables 7.4 and 7.5; HMSO for figure 8.1; Macmillan Publishing Co., Inc. for figure 7.2; National Children's Bureau for tables 5.1 and 5.2; The National Council on Family Relations for table 7.2; New Society for table 8.2; NFER Publishing Co. for figure 3.1; Open Books for figure 2.7; Pergamon Press, Inc. for table 8.1; Plenum Publishing for figures 2.4, 4.2 and 9.2; Routledge & Kegan Paul for figures 5.1, 5.2, 6.1, 6.2, 6.4, 9.3, tables 7.1, 7.3 and 7.6; Routledge & Kegan Paul and Basic Books for extract on pp. 169–70; Sage Publications for figure 6.5; Scientific American for figures 2.2 and 2.3; Scottish Academic Press for figure 3.2; Social Forces for table 6.1; The Society for Research in Child Development for figure 6.3.

Preface

Adolescence is a complex and contradictory stage of development. There are a number of reasons for this. In the first place research findings do not always match with theory, and there are times when neither research nor theory appear to bear much relation to everyday experience. Another feature of the situation is that adolescent behaviour itself is frequently paradoxical. For example, conformity may go hand-in-hand with rebellion, while spontaneity alternates with sullen reserve. Planning for the future, which is considered essential at one moment, is rejected at the next in favour of the demands of the present. A spirit of fierce independence is transformed in the space of a few minutes into childish dependence, yet the most difficult teenager may become, almost overnight, a delightful and rewarding companion.

Contradictions of this sort, not surprisingly, create in most adults a sense of bewilderment. Equally confusing are the discrepancies which exist between the images of young people as they are presented in newspapers, or on film and television, and the behaviour of the great majority of adolescents in our society. On the one hand it must seem from the media as if there is no escape from the anger, violence and mindless drifting of the younger generation, yet on the other hand, countless hard-working or exam-oriented teenagers are in evidence in every neighbourhood. We have to conclude that it is in the nature of adolescence to encompass such opposites and extremes, and diverse elements of this sort result inevitably in the characterization of this stage of development as a puzzle. Contained within the puzzle, however, is an intellectual challenge, and it is in response to this challenge and as an attempt at finding some solutions to the puzzle that this book has been written.

It is sometimes asked what is meant by the term 'adolescence'.

Because of wide individual differences it is not easy to provide a concrete answer to the question, but here adolescence is treated as that stage in the life cycle which begins at puberty and ends when the individual reaches maturity. Naturally, there are many definitions of maturity, but for the sake of convenience we may take the political definition as being as good as any, namely the age in Great Britain when young people are entitled to the vote. By and large, therefore, the age span treated here ranges from twelve to eighteen, although in some sections the reader will find that the boundaries have become a little blurred.

I should also say a word about the interviews, brief extracts of which feature at the end of most chapters. My aim has simply been to provide the views of a few normal adolescents on the topics discussed. The full interview is set out in an appendix at the end of the book. Although a lot of preliminary work was done to iron out any problems in the interview, it is perhaps inevitable that some questions were more successful than others at eliciting the beliefs and opinions of the young people involved. The interviews were carried out in different parts of the country – primarily in Newcastle, East Sussex, Leicestershire and the London Borough of Redbridge – and in different types of school. Approximately equal numbers of boys and girls were involved, but no serious attempt was made to obtain a cross-section of all young people. Those who took part were simply a random group, selected by teachers as being articulate, willing to participate, and between the ages of fifteen and seventeen. Among this group it was not possible to include working adolescents, nor are there any individuals from special schools or institutions for those with particular difficulties. While I actually interviewed a large number of adolescents, in the final analysis I have only used material from about a dozen individuals. These have been selected with the intention of reflecting as many different views as possible. No attempt has been made to use the interview material as support for a particular argument, and I hope that the only bias discernible on my part is one in favour of the exchange of views between adults and young people.

I am extremely grateful to all those adolescents who generously shared their private thoughts with me. They deserve a special vote of thanks. In addition to them many other people have contributed to this book, and to all of them I wish to express my gratitude. Grant McIntyre's enthusiasm played a large part in getting the project off the ground in the first place. Chris Bacon, Patrick Eavis, Ingrid Lunt and Phillip Rogers allowed me access to their schools, and helped immeasurably with the interviewing. Peter Barnes, Halla Beloff,

Sidney Crown, Ellen Noonan and Stephen Wolkind read the whole or parts of the manuscript, and made many valuable comments. Maria Bowering, Sheila Miles and Sue Wells cheerfully typed successive drafts of various chapters. Finally, I owe a particular debt to Eva, my companion throughout. Her ideas permeate most sections of the book, and her encouragement kept me going when the end appeared to be nowhere in sight.

London
June 1979

JOHN C. COLEMAN

1
Introduction

Adolescence is universally acknowledged to be a critical phase in human development, yet in comparison with other stages of the life cycle it has received relatively little attention from psychologists or other social scientists. This situation badly needs to be remedied, and just such an opportunity has now arisen, for the psychology of adolescence has taken remarkable strides in the last few years. One of the primary reasons for this is that an increasing body of research has become available which relates to the course of normal adolescent development. The results of a number of large-scale studies have begun to appear in the literature, substantially expanding and improving our knowledge of the teenage years. This evidence has, as we shall see, had a profound effect on many widely held assumptions about young people, and has led to an urgent need for new theoretical approaches in this area.

Closely associated with this is a growing awareness that events in the first five years of life are not the only events which have fundamental implications for later development. For many years it has been widely believed that what happens in infancy represents the foundation stone for later personality development, and that many of the effects of the experiences of these early years are irreversible. However, it is increasingly recognized that experiences during other critical phases of development, especially during adolescence, have an equally important bearing on what happens in later life. This realization, that adjustment in adolescence has critical implications for adult development, as well as for the health of society in general, has led to a new surge of interest in the adolescent years.

Another change which has occurred in the last few years concerns a shift of emphasis in the way adolescence is portrayed. Today writers are far less likely to describe this period in static terms as a single stage, or even a series of sub-stages, in the life cycle. Empirical evidence has clearly shown that too much individual variation exists for young people of the same chronological age to be classified together, and there is now a preference for viewing adolescence as a transitional process rather than as a stage or number of stages. To conceptualize the period in this way implies that adolescence needs to be understood as a time during which the individual passes from one state – childhood – to another – maturity, and that the issues and problems faced by individuals during this period are predominantly the result of the transitional process.

This transition, it is believed, results from the operation of a number of pressures. Some of these, in particular the physiological and emotional pressures, are internal, while other pressures which originate from peers, parents, teachers and society at large, are external to the young person. Sometimes these external pressures hurry the individual towards maturity at a faster rate than he or she would prefer, while on other occasions they act as a brake, holding the adolescent back from the freedom and independence which he or she believes to be a legitimate right. It is the interplay of these forces which, in the final analysis, contributes more than anything else to the success or failure of the transition from childhood to maturity.

So far two types of explanation concerning the transitional process have been advanced. The psychoanalytic approach has concentrated on the psycho-sexual development of the individual, and has looked particularly at the psychological factors which underlie the young person's movement away from childhood behaviour and emotional involvements. The second type of explanation, the sociological or social-psychological, represents a very different perspective. While it has never been as coherently expressed as the psychoanalytic view, it is nonetheless of equal importance. In brief, this explanation sees the causes of the adolescent transition as lying primarily in the social setting of the individual, and concentrates on the nature of roles and role conflict, on the pressures of social expectation, and on the relative influence of different agents of socialization. Both these theories will be described in some detail here, for they form an essential background to the main body of the book, one of the major aims of which is to illustrate the contradictions which currently exist between research and theory.

Psychoanalytic theory

The psychoanalytic view of adolescence takes as its starting point the upsurge of instincts which is said to occur as a result of puberty. This increase in instinctual life, it is suggested, upsets the psychic balance which has been achieved by the end of childhood, causing internal emotional upheaval and leading to a greatly increased vulnerability of the personality (Freud, 1937). This state of affairs is associated with two further factors. In the first place, the individual's awakening sexualilty leads him or her to look outside the family setting for appropriate 'love objects', thus severing the emotional ties with the parents which have existed since infancy. Secondly, the vulnerability of the personality results in the employment of psychological defences to cope with the instincts and anxiety which are, to a greater or lesser extent, maladaptive.

Blos (1962, 1967), a prominent psychoanalytic writer, has described adolescence as a 'second individuation process', the first having been completed towards the end of the third year of life. In his view both periods have certain things in common: there is an urgent need for psychological changes which help the individual adapt to maturation; there is an increased vulnerability of personality; and finally, both periods are followed by specific psychopathology should the individual run into difficulties. Furthermore, an analogy can be drawn between the transformation in early childhood from a dependent infant to a self-reliant toddler, and the adolescent transition to adult independence. In the latter the process of disengagement, that is, the finding of a love object outside the family, involves the renunciation of dependency and the loosening of early childhood ties which have, until puberty, been the major source of emotional nurturance. In some senses just the reverse has happened in early childhood. The child, in an attempt to become separate from the loved one, namely the mother, internalizes her. This allows him to become independent while retaining inside himself a representation of the figure he needs. In adolescence, however, the individual has to give up the internalized figure in order to disengage himself and make possible the search for new love objects in the outside world.

If, for the psychoanalysts, disengagement is one key to the adolescent process, another is the significance of regression, which usually means a manifestation of behaviour more appropriate to earlier stages of development. It has been shown how the process of individuation is dependent upon the severance of childhood emotional attachments; however, these attachments can only be surrendered, so it is believed, by a re-animation of infantile involvements and patterns of behaviour. As Blos (1967) explains: 'The adolescent has to come into emotional contact with the passions of his infancy and early childhood in order for them to surrender their original cathexes; only then can the past fade into conscious and unconscious memories . . .' (p. 178). The French have a phrase: 'reculer pour mieux sauter', which roughly means: to retreat first in order to leap further, which seems to describe succintly the psychoanalysts' view of the importance of regression.

Blos provides a number of examples of regressive behaviour. One such example is the adolescent's idolization of famous people, especially pop stars and celebrated sporting personalities. In this phenomenon, he argues, we are reminded of the idealized parent of the younger child. Another example of behaviour in which can be recognized reflections of earlier states is the emotional condition similar to 'merger' – the sensation on the part of the individual of becoming totally submerged by or 'at one with' another. In this condition the adolescent might become almost completely absorbed in abstract ideas such as Nature or Beauty or with political, religious or philosophical ideals.

Ambivalence is another example of behaviour which reflects earlier stages of childhood. According to the psychoanalytic view, ambivalence accounts for many of the phenomena often considered incomprehensible in adolescent behaviour. For example, the emotional instability of relationships, the contradictions in thought and feeling, and the apparently illogical shifts from one reaction to another reflect the fluctuations between loving and hating, acceptance and rejection, involvement and non-involvement which underlie relationships in the early years, and which are reactivated once more in adolescence. Such fluctuations in mood and behaviour are indicative also of the young person's attitudes to growing up. Thus while freedom may at times appear the most exciting of goals, there are also moments when, in the harsh light of reality, independence and the necessity to fight one's own battles becomes a daunting prospect. At these times childlike dependence exercises a powerful attraction, manifested in periods of uncertainty and self-doubt, and in behaviour which is more likely to bring to mind a wilful child than a young adult.

A consideration of ambivalence leads us on to the more general theme of nonconformity and rebellion, believed by psychoanalysts to be an almost universal feature of adolescence. Behaviour of this sort has many causes. Some of it is a direct result of ambivalent modes of relating, the overt reflection of the conflict between loving and hating. In other circumstances, however, it may be interpreted as an aid to the disengagement process. In this context if the parents can be construed as old-fashioned and irrelevant then the task of breaking the emotional ties becomes easier. If everything that originates from home can safely be rejected then there is nothing to be lost by

giving it all up. Nonconformity thus facilitates the process of disengagement, although as many writers point out, there are a number of
intermediate stages along the way. Baittle and Offer (1971) illustrate
particularly well the importance of nonconformity and its close links
with ambivalence:

> When the adolescent rebels, he often expresses his intentions in a
> manner resembling negation. He defines what he does in terms of
> what his parents do not want him to do. If his parents want him to
> turn off the radio and study this is the precise time he keeps the
> radio on and claims he cannot study. If they want him to buy new
> clothes, the old ones are good enough. In periods like this it
> becomes obvious that the adolescent's decisions are in reality
> based on the negative of the parents' wishes, rather than on their
> own positive desires. What they do and the judgements they make
> are in fact dependent on the parents' opinions and suggestions, but
> in a negative way. This may be termed a stage of 'negative depen-
> dence'. Thus while the oppositional behaviour and protest against
> the parents are indeed a manifestation of rebellion and in the
> service of emancipation from the parents, at the same time they
> reveal that the passive dependent longings are still in force. The
> adolescent is in conflict over desires to emancipate, and the rebel-
> lious behaviour is a compromise formation which supports his
> efforts to give up the parental object and, at the same time,
> gratifies his dependent longings on them. (p. 35)

One final matter associated with disengagement needs to be mentioned as an integral feature of the psychoanalytic view of adolescence. This is the emphasis placed on the experience of separation
and loss which occurs as a result of the severance of the emotional
ties. For some writers (for example, Root, 1957) this experience is
close to the adult phenomenon of mourning and grief which follows
the death of a loved one; for others it is sufficient to stress the inner
emptiness with which the adolescent must deal until mature emotional relationships are formed outside the home. To describe this
state Blos has coined the term 'object and affect hunger'. He believes
that the adolescent need for intense emotional states, including
delinquent activities, drug and mystical experiences, and short-lived
but intense relationships, may be seen as a means of coping with the
inner emptiness. Blos includes here the need to do things 'just for
kicks', which he argues simply represents a way of combatting the
emotional flatness, depression and loneliness which are part of the
separation experience. He also indicates his belief that both 'object'
and 'affect' hunger find some relief in the adolescent gang or peer

group. This social group is often, quite literally, the substitute for the adolescent's family, and within it he may experience all the feelings so essential for individual growth such as stimulation, empathy, belongingness, the opportunity for role-playing, identification and the sharing of guilt and anxiety.

To summarize, three particular ideas characterize the psychoanalytic position. In the first place adolescence is seen as being a period during which there is a marked vulnerability of personality, resulting primarily from the upsurge of instincts at puberty. Secondly, emphasis is laid on the likelihood of maladaptive behaviour, stemming from the inadequacy of the psychological defences to cope with inner conflicts and tensions. Examples of such behaviour include extreme fluctuations of mood, inconsistency in relationships, depression and nonconformity. Thirdly, the process of disengagement is given special prominence, for this is perceived as a necessity if mature emotional and sexual relationships are to be established outside the home. In addition, there is one further aspect of psychoanalytic theory, the stress placed on identity formation and the possibility of identity crisis, which has not yet been mentioned. This feature of the theory is most closely associated with the name Erik Erikson, whose views will be described in detail in chapter 4. His theoretical approach, however, fits closely with that of Anna Freud and Peter Blos, and all three represent a view of adolescence which might be expected to result from experience in a clinic or hospital setting. Central to this view are concepts of difficulty and disturbance, and closely allied to it is the theme of adolescent turmoil. The validity of such notions will be considered once the empirical evidence has been reviewed.

Sociological theory

As has been indicated the sociological view of adolescence encompasses a very different perspective from that of psychoanalytic theory. While there is no disagreement between the two approaches concerning the importance of the transitional process, it is on the subject of the causes of this process that the two viewpoints diverge. Thus while the one concentrates on internal factors, the other looks to society and to events outside the individual for a satisfactory explanation. For the sociologist and the social psychologist 'socialization' and 'role' are two key concepts. By socialization is meant the process whereby individuals in a society absorb the values, standards and beliefs current in that society. Some of these standards and values will refer to positions, or roles, in society, so that, for example,

there will be expectations and prescriptions of behaviour appropriate to roles such as son, daughter, citizen, teenager, parent and
so on. Everyone in a society learns through the agents of socialization, such as school, home, the mass media, etc., the expectations
associated with the various roles, although, as we shall see, these
expectations may not necessarily be clear-cut. Furthermore, socialization may be more or less effective, depending on the nature of the
agents to which the individual is exposed, the amount of conflict
between the different agents and so on. During childhood the individual, by and large, has his or her roles ascribed by others, but as he
or she matures through adolescence greater opportunities are available, not only for a choice of roles, but also for a choice of how those
roles should be interpreted. As will become apparent it is implicit in
the social-psychological viewpoint that both socialization and role
assumption are more problematic during adolescence than at any
other time.

Why should this be so? In attempting to answer this question we
may first of all consider roles and role assumption. It is the belief of
most sociologists that a large proportion of an individual's life is
characterized by engagement in a series of roles – the sum total of
which is known as the role repertoire. The years between childhood
and adulthood, as a period of emerging identity, are seen as particularly
relevant to the construction of this role repertoire, for the following
reasons. Firstly, features of adolescence such as growing independence
from authority figures, involvement with peer groups, and an
unusual sensitivity to the evaluations of others, all provoke role
transitions and discontinuity, of varying intensities, as functions of
both social and cultural context. Secondly, any inner change or uncertainty has the effect of increasing the individual's dependence on
others, and this applies particularly to the need for reassurance and
support for one's view of oneself. Thirdly, the effects of major
environmental changes are also relevant in this context. Different
schools, the move from school to university or college, leaving home,
taking a job, all demand involvement in a new set of relationships,
which in turn lead to different and often greater expectations, a
substantial reassessment of the self, and an acceleration of the process of socialization. Role change, it will be apparent, is thus seen as
an integral feature of adolescent development.

Elder (1968) advances this argument by distinguishing two types
of role change. On the one hand the young person experiences
'intra-role change'. In this the individual is exposed to new role
demands, since as he gets older expectations gradually increase. His
role remains the same, but within that role different things are

expected of him – his teacher may expect better performance, his parents more independence, and so on. On the other hand, the individual also acquires entirely new roles. Evidently this discontinuity is more abrupt, and is often more difficult to cope with. The change, for example, from school to full-time work, usually requires very considerable adaptation, and remnants of the dependent student role are often seen in the young worker. The acquisition of new roles is usually coupled with gradual changes of an intra-role nature, and the two facilitate or hinder each other depending on factors such as the part played by the parents or other significant figures, the relevance of past learning skills to new role demands, the range of the adolescent's role repertoire, and so on. In general, it is argued that adolescents experience more or less discontinuity, and that as the degree of role change increases, successful adaptation to the new set of role demands becomes more problematic.

While role change may be one source of difficulty for the adolescent, it is certainly not the only one. Inherent in role behaviour generally are a number of potential stresses, some of which have been elaborated by Thomas (1968), and which would appear to be particularly relevant to young people. In the first place Thomas describes role conflict. Here the individual occupies two roles, let us say son and boyfriend, which have expectations associated with them which are incompatible. The individual is thus caught in the middle between two people or sets of people, who expect different forms of behaviour. Thus in the case of son and boyfriend, the teenage boy's mother might put pressure on him to behave like a dutiful child, while his girlfriend will expect him to be independent of his parents and to care for her rather than for anyone else. Such a situation is one which few young people can avoid at some time or another. Next, Thomas mentions role discontinuity, a phenomenon to which we have already referred. Here there is a lack of order in the transition from one role to another. Many years ago, Ruth Benedict (1938) drew attention to the fact that primitive cultures provided more continuity in training for responsibilities, sexual maturity and so on than Western societies, and the situation has hardly improved today. Role discontinuity is said to occur when there is no bridge or ordered sequence from one stage to the next, or when behaviour in the second stage necessitates the unlearning of some or all of that which was learnt earlier. One only has to think of the inexperience among school leavers of the work situation, or the grossly inadequate preparation for parenthood in our society to appreciate the point. Thirdly, Thomas draws attention to role incongruence. Here the individual is placed in a position for which he or she is unfitted; in other words the role ascribed by others is not the one that the individual would have chosen. Good illustrations from adolescent experience would be parents who hold unrealistically high expectations of their teenage children, or who, alternatively, fight to maintain their adolescent sons and daughters in childlike roles.

Implicit in these theoretical notions is the view that the individual's movement through adolescence will be very much affected by the consistent or inconsistent, adaptive or maladaptive expectations held by significant people in his or her immediate environment. Two other writers may also be mentioned as having contributed to this point of view: Brim (1965) and Baumrind (1975). Brim was particularly interested in the adolescent's views of the prescriptions or expectations that adults hold concerning the behaviour of young people. He argued that the more we know of these perceptions, the more likely we are to understand the roles that adolescents adopt:

> We should attempt to describe personality by reference to the individual's perceptions of himself and his behaviour, and of the social organisation in which he lives. We should be interested in the kinds of people he says are of the greatest significance to him, and interested in what he thinks others expect him to do, and in what they think about his performance. We should also know whether or not he accepts what others prescribe for him as right and legitimate, or whether he thinks their expectations are unfair. . . . (p. 156)

In Brim's view, then, the development of role behaviour will be determined to a large extent by an interaction between the individual's relationships with significant others and his or her perceptions of the expectations of those significant figures. Such an argument accords closely with that of Baumrind. In her discussion of adolescent socialization she introduces the concept of 'reciprocal role assumption', that is, the effects which prior role assumptions by other family members have on the role the individual may assume. An example which she gives is a situation in which both parents are exceptionally competent managers, thus preventing the young person from developing managerial skills since, while readily available for modelling, such skills are not needed within the family setting. Another example might be a mother who assumes a child-like dependent role, thus forcing her daughter into a maternal role because of the void which she, the mother, creates.

Up to this point our discussion has concentrated on the features of role behaviour which lead sociologists and social psychologists to view adolescence not only as a transitional period, but as one which contains many potentially stressful characteristics. However, the process of socialization is also seen by many as being fraught with conflict at this stage. The work of Elder (1975) may be taken as one example of such a belief. In his view socialization processes interact with social change, and he draws particular attention to two changes which have occurred in the last decade or so: the prolonged dependence of young people as a result of increased opportunities for secondary and higher education, and the decline in the role of the family. These phenomena have, in turn, had a number of consequences. In the first place industrialized societies have witnessed increasing age segregation, with a decline in the time adults and teenagers spend together. Secondly, the peer group has assumed an ever more important role, precisely as a result of the abdication of responsibility by parents in the upbringing of their teenage children. Finally, the adolescent is exposed to a large variety of socialization agencies, including secondary school, the peer group, adult-directed youth organizations, the mass media, political organizations and so on, and is thus presented with a wide range of potential conflicts in values and ideals.

All these factors are seen by Elder as making socialization more uncertain, and causing major difficulty for the young person in establishing a bridge towards the assumption of adult roles. Brofenbrenner (1974), in his discussion of the alienation of young people, made very similar points, and it is a common assumption among those writing from the sociological point of view that the social changes of the last twenty years or so have created ever-increasing stresses for young people. In particular it should be noted that most writers see little of value in what they believe to be the decline of adult involvement and the increasing importance of the peer group. Among such writers the adolescent peer group is frequently described as being more likely to encourage anti-social behaviour than to act as a civilizing agent, and though it is accepted that the effects of peer involvement depend on the standards and activities of the peer group, there is undoubtedly a general feeling that when young people spend a considerable amount of time with individuals of their own age more harm than good is likely to come of it. While, on the one hand, there is clearly some logic in the view that the adolescent who is deprived of adult company is at a disadvantage in the transition towards maturity, on the other hand research does not bear out the myth of the all-powerful peer group (see chapters 5 and 6) and it is still very much an open question as to what effect increasing age segregation has on the socialization process.

To summarize, the sociological or social-psychological approach to adolescence is marked by a concern with roles and role change, and with the processes of socialization. There can be little doubt that adolescence, from this point of view, is seen as being dominated by stresses and tensions, not so much because of inner emotional instability, but as a result of conflicting pressures from outside. Thus, by considering both this and the psychoanalytic approach, two mutually complementary but essentially different views of the adolescent transitional process have been reviewed. In spite of their differences, however, the two approaches share one common belief, and that is in the concept of adolescent 'storm and stress'. Both theoretical approaches view the teenage years as a 'problem stage' in human development, and it is important to recognize that there is, as yet, no theoretical approach which embodies as its main tenet the essential normality of the adolescent process. The rest of this book will look individually at various aspects of adolescent growth and change, and will concentrate particularly on the empirical evidence which has recently become available. A close examination of this evidence will make it possible, in the final chapter, to match theory and evidence and to consider to what extent new theoretical approaches are necessary.

2
Physical development

Puberty and the growth spurt

Having considered two theoretical approaches in the previous chapter we may now turn our attention to the different aspects of growth and change which together make up the adolescent experience. The first of these is physical development. In considering the picture as a whole there seems little doubt that some of the most important events to which young people have to adjust are the multitude of physiological and morphological changes which occur during early adolescence, and which are associated with what is generally known as puberty. This term derives from the Latin 'pubertas', meaning age of manhood, and is usually considered to date from the onset of menstruation in girls and the emergence of pubic hair in boys. However, as we shall see, these two easily observable changes are each only a small part of a complex process involving many bodily functions. Puberty is accompanied by changes not only in the reproductive system and in the secondary sexual characteristics of the individual, but in the functioning of the heart and thus of the cardio-vascular system, in the lungs which in turn affect the respiratory system, in the size and the strength of many of the muscles of the body, and so on. Puberty, therefore, must be seen as an event in the physical life of the body with wide-ranging implications, the most important of which will be considered in this chapter.

One of the many physical changes associated with puberty is the 'growth spurt'. This term is usually taken to refer to the accelerated rate of increase in height and weight that occurs during early adolescence. Typical curves for individual rates of growth are illustrated in figure 2.1. It is essential to bear in mind, however, that there are very considerable individual differences in the age of onset and duration of the growth spurt, even among perfectly normal children, as illustrated in figures 2.2 and 2.3. This is a fact which parents and adolescents themselves frequently fail to appreciate, thus causing a great deal of unnecessary anxiety. In boys the growth spurt may begin as early as ten years of age, or as late as sixteen, while in girls the same process can begin at seven or eight, or not until twelve, thirteen or even fourteen. For the average boy, though, rapid growth begins at about thirteen, and reaches a peak somewhere during the fourteenth year. Comparable ages for girls are eleven for the onset of the growth spurt, and twelve for the peak age of increase in height and weight. As we have noted other phenomena associated with the growth spurt are a rapid increase in size and weight of the heart (the weight of the heart nearly doubles at puberty), an accelerated growth of the lungs, and a decline in basal metabolism. Noticeable to children themselves, especially to boys, is a marked increase in physical strength and endurance. Sexual differentiation is also reflected in less obvious internal changes, as Katchadourian (1977) points out.

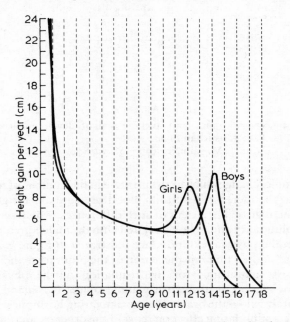

Figure 2.1 Typical velocity curves for supine length or height in boys or girls. These curves represent the velocity of the typical boy or girl at any given instant.
(From J. M. Tanner, R. H. Whitehouse and M. Takaishi (1966) *Archives of Disease in Childhood*, 41.)

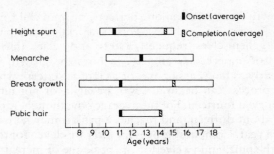

Figure 2.2   Normal range and average age of development of sexual characteristics in females.
(From J. M. Tanner (1973) *Scientific American*, 229.)

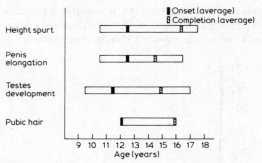

Figure 2.3   Normal range and average age of development of sexual characteristics in males.
(From J. M. Tanner (1973) *Scientific American*, 229.)

For example, changes such as the increase in the number of red blood cells, and the increase in systolic blood pressure are far greater in boys than in girls. The extent of such differences, which seem likely to be evolutionary and to be associated with the male's greater ability to undertake physical exertion, are illustrated in figure 2.4.

It may be noted that it is the action of the pituitary gland which is of greatest significance for the regulation of the physiological changes which occur during early adolescence. This gland, located immediately below the brain, releases activating hormones. These in turn have a stimulating effect on most of the other endocrine glands, which then release their own growth-related hormones. Among the most important of these are the sex-hormones, including testosterone in males and oestrogen in females, which stimulate the growth of mature sperm and ova. However, these hormones also combine

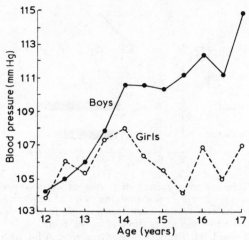

Figure 2.4   Differences in systolic blood pressure between boys and girls at puberty.
(From W. Montagna and W. A. Sadler (eds) (1974) *Reproductive Behavior*, Plenum.)

with others, such as thyroxine from the thyroid gland, and cortisol from the adrenal gland, to activate the growth of bone and muscle which leads to the growth spurt.

Sexual maturation is closely linked with the physical changes described above. Again the sequence of events is approximately eighteen to twenty-four months later for boys than it is for girls. For boys the first sign of the approach of puberty is most commonly an increase in the rate of growth of the testes and scrotum, followed by the growth of pubic hair. Acceleration of growth of the penis and the appearance of facial hair frequently accompany the beginning of the growth spurt in height and weight, and it is usually somewhat later than this that the voice breaks, and the first seminal discharge occurs. In girls, enlargement of the breasts and the growth of pubic hair are early signs of puberty, and are followed by the growth of the uterus and the vagina. The menarche itself occurs relatively late in the developmental sequence, and almost always after the peak velocity of the growth spurt. The sequence of events in boys and girls is illustrated in figures 2.5 and 2.6.

In his recent book Tanner (1978) has drawn attention to an important difference between boys and girls in the relative positions of the height spurt in the whole sequence of events at puberty. It has only recently been realized, as a result of detailed longitudinal studies

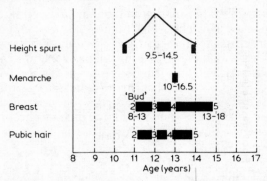

Figure 2.5   Diagram of sequence of events at adolescence in girls. An average girl is represented; the range of ages within which some of the events may occur (and stages in their development) is given by the figures directly below them.
(From J. M. Tanner (1962) *Growth at Adolescence*, Blackwell Scientific.)

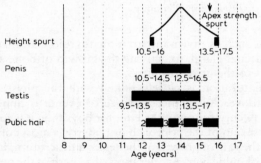

Figure 2.6   Diagram of sequence of events at adolescence in boys. An average boy is represented; the range of ages within which each event charted may begin and end (and stages in their development) is given directly below its start and finish.
(From W. A. Marshal and J. M. Tanner (1970) *Archives of Disease in Childhood*, 45.)

(Eveleth and Tanner, 1977), that girls experience their height spurts considerably earlier than boys. Thus the differences between the sexes in the age of peak velocity is about two years, while the differences in the appearance of pubic hair is about nine months. The first appearance of the breasts in girls precedes the increase in the size of the testes in boys by even less of a time gap. Thus the growth spurt is placed earlier in the sequence in girls than it is in boys. The practical effects of this are that in girls the first event of puberty is often an increase in height, which frequently goes unnoticed. In boys on the other hand, peak height velocity usually occurs late in the sequence, and after pubic hair has appeared and genitalia have started to grow. Thus, as Tanner points out, boys who are late maturers can be reassured that their height spurt is still to come if genital development is not far advanced, while girls who are worried about being too tall can be informed that their height spurt is nearly over if menarche has already occurred.

Psychological effects of puberty

The changes discussed above inevitably exercise a profound effect upon the individual. The body alters radically in size and shape, and it is not surprising that many adolescents experience a period of clumsiness as they attempt to adapt to these changes. The body also alters in function, and new and sometimes worrying physical experiences such as the girl's first period, or the boy's nocturnal emissions, have to be understood. Perhaps most important of all, however, is the effect that such physical changes have upon identity. As many writers have pointed out, the development of the individual's identity requires not only the notion of being separate and different from others, but also a sense of self-consistency, and a firm knowledge of how one appears to the rest of the world (for further consideration of this issue see chapter 4). Needless to say dramatic bodily changes seriously affect these aspects of identity, and represent a considerable challenge in adaptation for even the most well-adjusted young person. It is unfortunate that many adults, having successfully forgotten much of their own adolescent anxiety, retain only a vague awareness of the psychological impact of the physical changes associated with puberty.

Experimental evidence has clearly shown that the average adolescent is not only sensitive to, but often critical of his or her changing physical self (Clausen, 1975). Thus, probably largely as a result of the importance of films and television, teenagers tend to have idealized norms for physical attractiveness, and to feel inadequate if they do not match these unrealistic criteria. Lerner and Karabenick (1974) showed that adolescents who perceived themselves as deviating physically from cultural stereotypes were likely to have impaired self-concepts, and many other studies have pointed out the important role that physical characteristics play in determining self-esteem, especially in the younger adolescent. Thus, for example, both Rosen and Ross (1968), and Simmons and Rosenberg (1975) have reported studies in which adolescents were asked what they did and did not like about themselves. Results showed that those in early adolescence used primarily physical characteristics to describe themselves, and it was these characteristics which were most often disliked. It was not until later adolescence that intellectual or social aspects of personality were widely used in self-descriptions, but these characteristics were much more frequently liked than disliked. It is, therefore, just at the time of most rapid physical change that appearance is of critical importance for the individual, both for his or her self-esteem, as well as for popularity (see chapter 6).

Early and late development

Since individuals mature at very different rates, one girl at the age of fourteen may be small, have no bust and look very much as she did during childhood, while another of the same age may look like a fully-developed adult woman, who could easily be mistaken for someone four or five years in advance of her actual chronological age. The question arises as to whether such marked physical differences have particular consequences for the individual's psychological adjustment. The issue of specially early or late development is one to which considerable attention has been paid in the literature. By and large, evidence from work by Tanner (1962) and others has shown that whether puberty occurs early or late bears little relation to abnormality in physical development. Thus, for example, slowness in beginning the growth spurt does not appear in any way to be indicative of later physical difficulty. However, there is good evidence both from Europe and from North America to show that those who mature earlier physically score higher on most tests of mental ability and perform better in the classroom than their less mature peers. The differences between the groups are not great but are consistent, and one implication of this is that in age-linked examinations physically fast maturers have an advantage over those who develop more slowly (Tanner, 1978).

The age of onset of puberty is also associated with other psychological consequences. Results of work carried out at the University of California (Jones and Bayley, 1950; Mussen and Jones, 1957) have shown that where boys are concerned those who were among the slowest 20 per cent to develop physically were rated by adults as less attractive, less socially mature, and more restless, talkative and bossy. In addition they were seen by their peers as being less popular, and few of them were leaders. On a personality test this group revealed more feelings of inadequacy, negative self-percepts, feelings of rejection and persistent dependency needs. Many of these difficulties appeared to persist over a period of time, for when they were followed up at the age of thirty-three a majority of the group still showed difficulties in personal adjustment (Jones, 1957).

Whereas for boys it is only slow physical development which appears to be associated with poor psychological adjustment, the picture among girls is rather more complicated. Differences between early and late maturing girls are not as great, and furthermore the advantages and disadvantages of early versus late maturation may vary with time. Thus Faust (1960) showed that among twelve-year-old girls early maturation was a definite handicap in relation to social prestige. At this age girls valued more highly the personality traits associated with the pre-pubertal stage of development than those related to sexual maturity. However by fourteen or fifteen the picture had changed, and traits associated with early maturation were, by this time, the most highly valued. Other studies have shown differences in interests between thirteen-year-olds who have reached menarche and those who have not (e.g. Davies, 1977), and a report by Buck and Stavraky (1967) has indicated that early maturing girls have higher feminity scores on a sexual identity test, and furthermore, that these individuals also tend to marry earlier than late maturing girls. Thus there appears to be little doubt that the age of onset of puberty is associated with particular patterns of psychological adjustment. In general, apart from young adolescent girls, early maturation is related to general self-confidence and social maturity. This is hardly surprising given the advantages, both in terms of physique and self-image, which stem from early maturation. In view of this the most important task for adults in this sphere is undoubtedly to work to counteract the psychological disadvantages faced by the late maturer.

The secular trend

The term 'secular trend' has been used to describe the biological fact that over the last hundred years the rate of physical growth of children and adolescents has accelerated, leading to faster and thus earlier maturation. This trend has been particularly noticeable in the growth rates of two- to five-year-olds, but it has also had many implications for adolescent development. Full adult height is now achieved at a much earlier age (i.e. between sixteen and eighteen), final adult stature and body weight have increased, and many investigators have reported that height and weight during adolescence are greater today than they have ever been. Meredith (1963), for example, found that fifteen-year-old American white boys were 5.25

inches taller in 1955 than they were in 1870, and Tanner (1962) reports a study of English boys attending Marlborough College who were measured at an average age of sixteen and a half in 1873, and at that time had a mean height of 65.6 inches. Eighty years later boys of the same age in the same school were 69.1 inches tall, a gain of 4.1 inches, or about 0.5 inches per decade. Muuss (1970) makes it clear, however, that it is not only height and weight that are increasing:

> The knights' armour in medieval European castles serve as powerful illustrations of the secular trend since the armour seems to be made to fit average ten- to twelve-year-old American boys of today. The seats in the famous La Scala opera house in Milan, Italy, which was constructed in 1776 to 1778, were thirteen inches wide. Thirty years ago most states outlawed seats that were less than eighteen inches wide. In 1975 comfortable seats will need to be twenty-four inches wide. The feet of the American male at the present time grow 1/3rd of an inch every generation, which means an upward change of one shoe size per generation. Today the shoes worn by the average male are 9–10B, while his grandfather in all probability wore a size seven shoe. (p. 170)

The maturation of the reproductive system is also affected by the secular trend. Tanner (1978) estimates that in average populations in Western Europe there has been a downward trend in the age of menarche of about four months per decade since 1850. He and his co-workers have collected together much of the available data, which are summarized in figure 2.7. It will be seen that the mean age of menarche has continued to drop in most countries up to 1970, although this decline does seem to have slowed down in Norway and in some parts of Great Britain (Poppleton and Brown, 1966). It remains to be seen whether similar results will be obtained in other countries in the near future or whether the secular trend will re-appear in the 1980s in Great Britain and Norway.

In spite of these two very recent exceptions to the rule, the secular trend is a remarkable phenomenon, and various explanations have been advanced to explain it. Conger (1977) is particularly critical of two of these explanations. In the first place he dismisses the view that girls growing up in the tropics reach puberty earlier than those living in milder climates. Although many writers have put forward such a view, Conger is convinced that the reliable evidence does not show climate to have any direct influence on maturational rate. In this he is supported by recent findings reported by Eveleth and Tanner (1977) concerning the mean age of menarche in the years 1960–75 in a wide range of countries all over the globe. To take but a few at random,

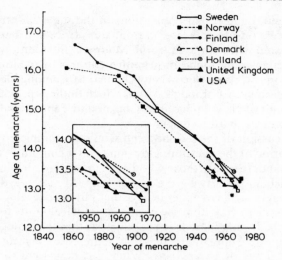

Figure 2.7   Secular trend in age at menarche, 1860–1970.
(From J. M. Tanner (1978) *Foetus into Man*, Open Books.)

the mean age of menarche in Burma is reported as being 13.2, in Mexico 12.8, in London 13.0, in Oslo 13.2, in Uganda 13.4 and in the USA 12.8. From these figures climate certainly does not appear to be a significant factor determining the age at which girls reach puberty. Secondly, Conger has no sympathy for the social scientists who believe that some relentless evolutionary trend is at work. On the contrary, both he and Tanner are firmly of the belief that we must look to the social changes inherent in present day society if we are to find a reasonable explanation for these phenomena. In particular they take the view that improved nutrition, as well as better health care, housing, and social conditions generally are the primary causes underlying the secular trend.

Supporting evidence for this may be drawn from three sources. In the first place it is clear that within individual countries those who have benefitted most from improvements in health care, nutrition and living conditions, namely working-class children, are the ones who have also shown the most accelerated rates of growth. Secondly, there is reliable evidence to indicate that during periods of nutritional deprivation (i.e. during World War II in European countries) rates of growth did not accelerate and the age of menarche was significantly retarded (Tanner, 1962). Finally, the results of the work of Eveleth and Tanner (1977), already discussed above, also cast light on this question. For example, where comparisons are available between rural and urban populations in the same country, age of menarche is considerably later in rural areas (12.8 in urban Madras as compared with 14.2 in rural Madras). In addition delayed menarche was only found in primitive cultures or in situations of deprivation (15.5 and 18.0 in New Guinea, 14.9 among black urban South Africans, 13.8 among Eskimos). Such findings provide a basis for the point of view espoused by Conger and Tanner, and seem, at least at present, hard to dispute.

No discussion of the secular trend would be complete without a consideration of the question: How long will it continue? While, on the one hand, there are those who have fantasies of girls in the year 2240 reaching puberty by the age of four (Muuss, 1970), on the other, writers such as Tanner believe that physical development can only be accelerated within the ultimate biological limits for a given population. Tanner himself (1970) suggests that the biological limit for European populations may be represented by an average menarcheal age of 12.25 years. While this may seem to some an unduly conservative estimate, perhaps the problem should be considered in the same light as that of the breaking of athletic records. While man will undoubtedly continue to reduce the time taken to run a mile, the amount by which the record is broken each time will gradually decrease. Thus it may be that while the twentieth century has seen a reduction in the age of menarche by four months per decade, possibly in the next century the reduction will average one month per decade, or even less. It is surely reasonable to assume that the continuation of the secular trend will be primarily dependent on the degree to which standards of living continue to improve.

Interview

To conclude this chapter we may briefly consider responses to one of the interview questions. Details of this interview, and of the teenagers involved will be found in the preface. Readers should remember that those concerned were in the fifteen to seventeen year age range, were all in school, and represented a very small but random selection of those attending the schools visited by the author. No attempt was made to obtain a cross-section of all young people, nor was the interview designed to illustrate any particular point. The purpose may simply be summarized by saying that the author thought it would be worthwhile to be able to give the reader not only his views on the topics discussed in this book, but the equally important views of some adolescents as well.

The question relevant to this chapter was:

In early adolescence – usually around eleven or twelve – people experience something called the growth spurt, when their bodies change and grow very quickly. Do you remember this? How did you feel about it at the time?

Of all the questions in the interview this was probably the most difficult for teenagers to answer, and their inhibitions are clearly reflected in some of their responses.

Elizabeth (17 years): Yes, well, I felt indifferent really, because I'd been taught about it in school. If it wasn't for school maybe I'd have thought totally differently because my mother, my parents, hadn't given me any inclination of how quickly you do develop at that age. But school did do something for me because they had sex education there from the age of about eight, so you knew it was coming. So when it came it was something you took absolutely naturally.

Sarah (16 years): No, I don't think I really realized when it happened. Well, my behaviour . . . I realized when it changed, you know, but the physical bits – no.

Valerie (17 years): Yes around the second or third year I sort of grew from this high to this high. How did I feel about it? Not very pleased, because I seemed . . . because I tended to be growing a lot more than the others in the class, so I felt a bit out of it. How did I get over it? Well, they all just sort of caught up.

Karen (15 years): No, I can't really remember it. It was very gradual you know. I remember when I came to this school, say in the first year, I remember I was more attracted to boys than when I was in the junior school. I remember that, but I don't remember sort of anything else.

Harriett (16 years): Yes, I remember I went through a stage when none of my clothes were good enough for me. I really hated . . . you know, I made a great fuss especially about my parents, and clothes and things. They all sort of wasn't good enough. As I've got older I've become happier with my appearance or whatever, I've got more confidence in myself. I think when I was younger I disliked myself rather than what I looked like.

Adam (17 years): Well I started to grow very quickly when I was about ten, and it lasted for about three years. I've more or less stopped now, and I think my ways began to change very rapidly then as well. I mean I began to think differently during that time. I think it's stopped now though – well me ways are still changing but physically I've stopped. How did I feel about it at the time? I wasn't really too bothered. I towered above everybody else. I quite enjoyed it actually – I don't think it hindered me in any way.

Paul (17 years): I think in a sort of way you notice it in other people. Really well-developed kids you sort of think 'Will I ever grow like that – or when?' But I think it's a gradual change, or it was with me. You used to notice when you were getting bigger than the younger children, especially towards the fourth year. I think you could tell the change then. How did I feel about it at the time? Well I felt I was progressing. I was quite pleased because you don't like to be left behind by all the rest, you like to keep up with them. You don't like to be different from the rest, like if you're smaller and that, and that could create problems I think.

3

Thinking and reasoning

Cognitive development in adolescence is one of the areas of maturation which is least apparent to observers. It has no external and
visible correlate, as with physical maturation, nor is it manifested in
any tangible alteration in behaviour, and yet changes in this sphere
are occurring all the time. Furthermore, changes in intellectual function have implications for a wide range of behaviours and attitudes.
Such changes render possible the move towards independence of
both thought and action, they enable the young person to develop a
time perspective which includes the future, they facilitate progress
towards maturity in relationships, and finally, they underlie the
individual's ability to participate in society as worker, voter, responsible group member and so on. This chapter will begin by considering the views of Piaget, for it was he who first drew attention to the
importance of the intellectual development which follows puberty.
Some attention will also be paid to modern work in the Piagetian
tradition, and some of the limitations of this approach will be
discussed. The chapter will cover some other examples of work on
adolescent reasoning, and will, in addition, consider the development of both moral and political thought in adolescence.

Formal operations

The work of Jean Piaget, the Swiss psychologist, is the most obvious
starting place for a consideration of cognitive development during
the teenage years. It was he who first pointed out that a qualitative
change in the nature of mental ability, rather than any simple
increase in cognitive skill, is to be expected at or around puberty, and
he argued that it is at this point in development that formal operational thought finally becomes possible (Inhelder and Piaget, 1958).

A full description of Piaget's stages of cognitive growth is beyond the scope of this book, but may be found in any standard text on child development (for example, Mussen, Conger and Kagan, 1974). For our purposes the crucial distinction is that which Piaget draws between concrete and formal operations. During the stage of *concrete operations* (approximately between the ages of seven and eleven) the child's thought may be termed 'relational'. Gradually he or she begins to master notions of classes, relations and quantities. Conservation and seriation become possible, and the development of these skills enables the individual to formulate hypotheses and explanations about concrete events. These cognitive operations are seen by the child simply as mental tools, the products of which are on a par with perceptual phenomena. In other words the child at this stage seems unable to differentiate clearly between what is perceptually given and what is mentally constructed. When the child formulates an hypothesis it originates from the data, not from within the person, and if new contradictory data are presented he or she does not change the hypothesis, but rather prefers to alter the data or to rationalize these in one way or another.

With the appearance of *formal operations* a number of important capabilities become available to the young person. Perhaps the most significant of these is the ability to construct 'contrary-to-fact' propositions. This change has been described as a shift of emphasis in adolescent thought from the 'real' to the 'possible', and it facilitates a hypothetico-deductive approach to problem solving and to the understanding of propositional logic. It also enables the individual to think about mental constructs as objects which can be manipulated, and to come to terms with notions of probability and belief.

This fundamental difference in approach between the young child and the adolescent has been neatly demonstrated in a study by Elkind (1966). Two groups of subjects, children of eight to nine years and adolescents between thirteen and fourteen, were presented with a concept-formation problem, involving pictures of wheeled and non-wheeled tools and wheeled and non-wheeled vehicles. The pictures were presented in pairs with each pair including both a wheeled and non-wheeled object. In each case the child was asked to choose one member of the pair. Choosing a wheeled object always made a light go on whereas choosing a non-wheeled object did not. The problem for the subject was to determine the kind of picture that would make the signal light go on every time. Differences in the manner in which adolescents and younger children handled the task were clearly illustrated. Only half of the younger children were able to arrive at the notion that it was the choice of a wheeled object which made the light go on. Furthermore it took those children who did succeed almost all of the allotted seventy-two trials to arrive at a correct solution. On the other hand, all of the adolescents solved the problem, and many did so in as few as ten trials. The tendency of adolescents to raise alternative hypotheses successively, test each against the facts, and discard those that prove wrong was apparent in their spontaneous verbalizations during the experiment (for example, 'maybe it's transportation . . . no, it must be something else, I'll try. . . .'). In this fashion they quickly solved the problem. The younger children, however, appeared to become fixated on an initial hypothesis that was strongly suggested by the data (for example, tool versus non-tool or vehicle versus non-vehicle). They then clung to this hypothesis even though they continued to fail on most tests. Although the adolescents might also have considered such likely hypotheses initially, they quickly discarded them when they were not substantiated by subsequent evidence. It appeared that an important part of the younger child's greater inflexibility was an inability to differentiate the hypothesis from reality. Having once adopted an hypothesis it became 'true', and the child then felt no need to test it further. Indeed, according to Elkind, he or she seemed unaware of the hypothetical quality of the strategy, and seemed to feel that it was imposed from without rather than constructed from within. This particular piece of research represents an excellent illustration of Piaget's view that it is the adolescent's awareness of possibility that enables him or her to distinguish thought from reality.

Elkind's study is concerned with one aspect of formal operational thought. Inhelder and Piaget (1958) have developed an ingenious set of tests for the investigation of many different aspects of logical thinking, and some of these have been widely used by other research workers. One such test is known as the Pendulum Problem. Here the task involves discovering which factor or combination of factors determines the rate of swing of the pendulum. The task is illustrated in figure 3.1, and depends for its solution once again on the ability of the individual to test alternative hypotheses successively. Another well-known problem is that of the Rings, bearing directly on the concept of proportionality. The experiment is described as follows:

Rings of varying diameters are placed between a light source and a screen. The size of their shadows is directly proportional to the diameters and inversely proportional to the distance between them and the light source. Specifically, we ask the subject to find

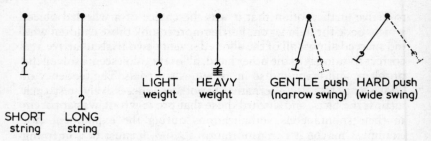

SHORT   LONG
string   string

LIGHT   HEAVY   GENTLE push   HARD push
weight   weight   (narrow swing) (wide swing)

Figure 3.1   The Pendulum Problem. The task is to determine which factor
or combination of factors determines the rate of swing of the
pendulum.
(From original research for M. Shayer (1979) *Science Reasoning Tasks*, NFER.)

Instructions: We are going to make a pendulum, using either a
SHORT or LONG string, and a LIGHT or HEAVY weight, and we will
exert a GENTLE or HARD push.

two shadows which cover each other exactly, using two unequal
sizes of ring. To do so he need only place the larger one further
from the light, in proportion to its size, and there will be compensation between distances and diameters. (Dulit, 1972, p. 290)

Clearly, formal operational thought cannot be tested using a single
problem or task. Any investigator must use a range of tests, and
attempt to construct some overall measure of the individual's ability
to tackle problems of logical thought in a number of areas. In
relation to this it is important to bear in mind that the development
of formal thinking is certainly not an all-or-none affair, with the
individual moving overnight from one stage to another. The change
occurs slowly, and there may even be some shifting back and forth,
as suggested by Turiel (1974), before the new mode of thought is
firmly established. Furthermore, it is almost certain that the adolescent will adopt formal modes of thinking in one area before another.
Thus, for example, someone interested in arts subjects may use
formal operational thinking in the area of verbal reasoning well
before he or she is able to utilize such skills in scientific problem
solving.

In addition to these points recent research indicates that in all
probability Piaget was a little too optimistic when he expressed the
view that the majority of adolescents could be expected to develop
formal operational thought by twelve or thirteen years of age. While
studies do not entirely agree on the exact proportions reaching

various stages at different age levels, there is a general consensus that up to the age of sixteen only a minority reach the most advanced level of formal thought. In Great Britain studies by Shayer *et al.* (1976, 1978), using a number of scientifically oriented tasks – including the Pendulum Problem – in a standardized procedure on over a thousand young people, have shown that slightly less than 30 per cent of sixteen-year-olds reach the stage of early formal thought and only 10 per cent reach the level of advanced formal thinking. These findings are illustrated in figure 3.2. Research carried out in Australia by Connell *et al.* (1975) amplifies these results. In this study a verbal reasoning task was used, and again with a large group of teenagers evidence showed that only 44 per cent had reached the stage of formal thought by sixteen. No distinction was made here between early and late stages of this type of thinking. Studies such as these indicate that intelligence is associated with the development of formal thought, but it is not sufficient to explain the fact that by school-leaving age a good proportion of adolescents are still at the level of concrete operational thought. In her wide-ranging review of the area Niemark (1975) quotes a number of studies which show that even in adulthood substantial minorities are failing to attain formal operational thought. As Piaget himself acknowledges in his

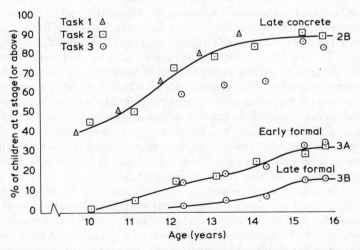

Figure 3.2   Proportion of boys at different Piagetian stages as assessed by three tasks.
(From M. Shayer and H. Wylam (1978) *British Journal of Educational Psychology*, 48.)

most recent article (1972), such findings must inevitably lead to a radical re-formulation of our notions of adult cognitive ability in Western society.

We have already noted that intelligence is likely to play a role in the development of this level of thinking. Yet this variable is not sufficient to explain why formal operations appear in one child at twelve, and in another at sixteen. Inhelder and Piaget (1958) paid remarkably little attention to this problem, contenting themselves simply with some speculation about the relation between intellectual and social development. They appear to suggest that as social pressures operate on the individual, encouraging him or her towards maturity and independence, so intellectual skills develop, enabling the young person to cope with the new demands of a more adult life. This is hardly a very satisfactory explanation, although it may indeed turn out that social and intellectual maturation are correlated. Kohen-Raz (1974) took a rather different approach, carrying out a study in which he attempted to see whether physical or sexual maturity correlated in any way with the appearance of formal operational thought. Unfortunately he ran into a number of methodological problems, but his results showed, at best, only a very weak relation between the occurrence of puberty and the shift from one stage of thinking to another.

Surprisingly there is little else in the literature which sheds much light on such an important topic, as Niemark (1975) indicates. However, some rays of hope have been shed recently by a study carried out by Cloutier and Goldschmid (1976), who were interested in the personality factors which might be associated with formal reasoning. Although unfortunately their sample ranged in age only from ten to twelve, they were able to show that those who were most advanced on Piagetian tests of thinking were likely to be: active and quick to respond; able to generate original ideas; rated by teachers as being difficult to discipline; frequently having doubts about their own capacities; and able to initiate activities when left alone. While these results must be viewed with some caution for the time being, the study does at least point in the right direction.

What other factors might be involved? Intelligence only contributes a small proportion of the total variance. Perhaps attention should be paid to the type of school and the attitudes of teachers. Cloutier and Goldschmid indicate that self-image might be important, but what about achievement motivation, or position in the peer group? Also, the impact of parental attitudes and the home environment should undoubtedly be examined. At this point, it must be accepted that there are no definite answers to the question of what it is which determines the appearance of formal operational thinking. It is already clear that many factors will be involved, and the solution unlikely to be a simple one. However, one thing is certain; this is a question which needs to be answered as soon as possible if the psychology of Piaget is to remain relevant to the education of young people.

Adolescent reasoning

Almost all those interested in the development of adolescent thought have used Piaget's work as a starting point. One writer who provides an especially good example of the way in which it is possible to elaborate on the work of Piaget is David Elkind. In his development of the notion of egocentrism in adolescence Elkind (1967) has extended our notion of the reasoning of young people in an important way. He argues that while the attainment of formal operational thinking frees the individual in many respects from childhood egocentrism, paradoxically at the same time it entangles him or her in a new version of the same thing. This is because the achievement of formal operational thought allows the adolescent to think not only about his own thought, but also about the thought of other people. It is this capacity to take account of other people's thinking, argues Elkind, which is the basis of adolescent egocentrism. Essentially the individual finds it extremely difficult to differentiate between what others are thinking about and his own preoccupations. He assumes that if he is obsessed by a thought or a problem then other people must also be obsessed by the same thing. The example given by Elkind is that of the adolescent's appearance. To a large extent teenagers are preoccupied with the way they look to others, and they make the assumption that others must be as involved as they are with the same subject. Elkind ties this type of egocentrism in with a concept of what he calls 'the imaginary audience'. Because of his egocentrism the adolescent is, either in actual or fantasized social situations, anticipating the reactions of others. However, these reactions are based on a premise that others are as admiring or critical of him as he is of himself. Thus he is continually constructing and reacting to his 'imaginary audience', a fact which, according to Elkind, explains a lot of adolescent behaviour – the self-consciousness, the wish for privacy, the long hours spent in front of a mirror. All these and many other aspects of teenage behaviour, it is argued, may be related to the 'imaginary audience'.

There is one other significant aspect of adolescent egocentrism, seen as an example of over-differentiation of feelings, which Elkind calls the 'personal fable'. Possibly because the adolescent believes he is of importance to so many people (his imaginary audience) he comes to see himself and his feelings as very special, even unique. A belief in the unique nature of the individual's misery and suffering is, of course, a familiar theme in literature, and Elkind suggests that it underlies the young person's construction of his 'personal fable'. In essence this is the individual's story about himself, the story he tells himself, and it may well include fantasies of omnipotence and immortality. It is not a true story, but it serves a valuable purpose, and is exemplified in some of the most famous adolescent diaries. In this sort of material one can get closest to a belief in the universal significance of the adolescent experience, and it is out of this belief that the 'personal fable' is created. Elkind argues that these two foundations of adolescent egocentrism – the imaginary audience and the personal fable – are useful explanations for some aspects of adolescent cognitive behaviour, and may be helpful in the treatment of disturbed teenagers. One example he gives is that of adolescent offenders. Here it is often of central importance to help the individual differentiate between the real and the imagined audience which, as Elkind points out, often boils down to discrimination between real and imaginary parents.

Another aspect of reasoning, highlighted by the work of Peel in Britain, is the nature of adolescent judgement. In order to investigate this Peel (1971) designed a number of stories describing realistic situations, and asked young people to comment upon them. One example was:

> All large cities have art galleries and Italy is exceptionally rich in art treasures. Many people travel to Italy, especially to enjoy these old paintings, books and sculptures. Floods in the Florence area recently damaged many of these great works. Old paintings are rare, valuable and beautiful, and should be kept safely stored.
> Question: Are the Italians to blame for the loss of paintings and art treasures?

The reponses to this question and to others of a similar sort may be classified on the basis of the judgement employed. Peel distinguished three levels: Level 1, where the reasoning is inadequate and based on irrelevant information; Level 2, where the individual's judgement is adequate but highly specific, and Level 3, where reasoning goes beyond the specific content and considers a range of possibilities. Different levels of reasoning are exemplified in the following answers:

> No, because they've got lots of treasures. (Level 1)

Well I shouldn't think so, not really, because of the floods, I mean they didn't let it come, did they? (Level 2)

Well, not entirely, but they were partly to blame because they could have put them somewhere where they weren't damaged by the floods. But if there was nowhere to put them they were not to blame. (Level 3)

Peel showed that a marked change took place between thirteen and fifteen years of age. By fifteen the large majority of pupils involved in this study had reached Level 3 – a level at which abstract thought is possible, and where circumstances can be taken into account when making judgements. Peel's work has also extended into the realm of concept-formation during adolescence. In this context, seen as being directly relevant to the classroom situation, studies have explored the way in which young people make sense of a new concept which is introduced in their work. For instance, teenagers come across a term in a history or geography textbook that they do not understand. How do they determine its meaning? In order to explore this problem Peel and de Silva (1972) constructed passages typical of any standard textbook, but they inserted a nonsense word instead of the actual concept. The following example will illustrate the procedure:

> The East India Company was the first and the greatest of companies which was to play a leading part in the development of the British Empire. Financed chiefly by the city merchants, it held a virtual KOHILAK of trade with India, and was frequently accused of having too restrictive an outlook. Yet for many years it was the only source of capital for English enterprises in India, owned or chartered ships which carried goods to and fro, and made arrangements to market them at their own destination. (p. 129)

Pupils were then asked what the term KOHILAK meant, and once again responses were classified according to the level of thought involved. Substantial changes were shown with age, and in this way Peel and de Silva were able not only to chart developmental progress, but also to throw light on the level and type of thought which teachers might expect at different age levels.

Moral thought

In recent years considerable interest has been expressed in one particular aspect of cognitive development, namely, moral thought.

Once again Piaget's notions have formed the springboard for later thinking on this subject, and although there have been a number of different theories put forward to explain the development of concepts of morality in young people (see Weinreich-Haste, 1979, for review) the 'cognitive-developmental' approach of Piaget and Kohlberg is undoubtedly more relevant to adolescence than any other. In his work on the moral judgement of the child Piaget (1932) described two major stages of moral thinking. The first, which he called *moral realism*, refers to a period during which young children make judgements on an objective basis, for example by estimating the amount of damage which has been caused. Thus a child who breaks twelve cups is considered more blameworthy than one who only breaks one cup, regardless of the circumstances. The second stage, applying usually to those between the ages of eight and twelve, has been described as that of the *Morality of co-operation*, or the *morality of reciprocity*. During this stage, Piaget believed, decisions concerning morality were usually made on a subjective basis, and often depended on an estimate of intention rather than consequence.

Kohlberg (1964, 1969) has elaborated Piaget's scheme into one which has six different stages. His method has been to present hypothetical situations containing moral dilemmas to young people of different ages, and to classify their responses according to a stage theory of moral development. A typical situation, now well-known as a result of extensive use by many research workers, is the following:

In Europe a woman was very near death from a very bad disease, a special kind of cancer. There was one drug that doctors thought might save her. It was a form of radium that a druggist in the same town had recently discovered. The drug was expensive to make, but the druggist was charging ten times what the drug cost him to make. He paid 200 dollars for the radium, and charged 2,000 dollars for a small dose of the drug. The sick woman's husband, Heinz, went to everyone he knew to borrow the money, but he could only get together a thousand dollars, which is half of what it cost. He told the druggist that his wife was dying, and asked him to sell it cheaper, or let him pay later. But the druggist said 'No, I discovered the drug, and I'm going to make money from it'. So Heinz got desparate and broke into the man's store to steal the drug for his wife.

Question: Should the husband have done that?

Based on responses to questions of this sort Kohlberg has described the following stages of moral development:

Pre-conventional

Stage 1 'Punishment-obedience orientation.' Behaviours that are punished are perceived as bad.

Stage 2 'Instrumental hedonism.' Here the child conforms in order to obtain rewards, have favours returned, etc.

Conventional

Stage 3 'Orientation to interpersonal relationships.' Good behaviour is that which pleases or helps others and is approved by them.

Stage 4 'Maintenance of social order.' Good behaviour consists of doing one's duty, having respect for authority, and maintaining the social order for its own sake.

Post-conventional

Stage 5 'Social contract and/or conscience orientation.' At the beginning of this stage moral behaviour tends to be thought of in terms of general rights and standards agreed upon by society as a whole, but at later moments there is an increasing orientation towards internal decisions of conscience.

Stage 6 'The universal ethical principle orientation.' At this stage there is an attempt to formulate and be guided by abstract ethical principles (for example, The Golden Rule, Kant's Categorical Imperative).

Some of Kohlberg's most interesting work has involved the study of moral development in different cultures. As may be seen in figures 3.3a and 3.3b, an almost identical sequence appears to occur in three widely different cultures, the variation between the cultures being found in the rate of development, and the fact that in the more primitive societies post-conventional stages of thinking are very rarely used.

Kohlberg's findings raise a number of questions. In the first place it may be asked whether there is any relation between Kohlberg's stages and those of Piaget. Kohlberg himself (Kohlberg and Gilligan, 1971) has proposed that while the pre-conventional stages are equivalent to concrete operations, both conventional and post-conventional modes occur once the individual has reached the stage of formal operational thought. More recent studies (Tomlinson-Keasey and Keasey, 1974; Langford and George, 1975) have cast some doubt on this, however, and it now seems most likely that the attainment of formal operational thought is necessary only for post-conventional reasoning. In fact, as Conger (1977) notes, the attain-

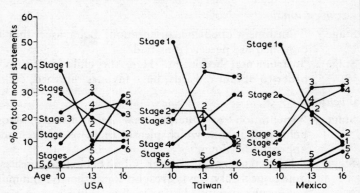

Figure 3.3a Middle-class urban boys in the USA, Taiwan and Mexico. At age 10 the stages are used according to difficulty. At age 13, stage 3 is most used by all three groups. At age 16, US boys have reversed the order of age 10 stages (with the exception of 6). In Taiwan and Mexico, conventional (3–4) stages prevail at age 16, with stage 5 little used.
(From L. Kohlberg and T. F. Gilligan (1971) *Daedalus*, Fall.)

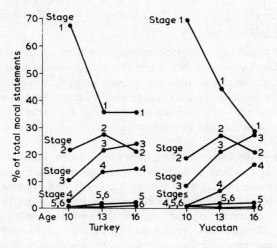

Figure 3.3b Two isolated villages, one in Turkey, the other in Yucatan, show similar patterns in moral thinking. There is no reversal of order, and pre-conventional (1–2) does not gain a clear ascendancy over conventional stages at age 16.
(From L. Kohlberg and T. F. Gilligan (1971) *Daedalus*, Fall.)

ment of an appropriate cognitive stage is probably a necessary but not sufficient condition for the attainment of the corresponding moral stage.

A second question raised by this approach relates to the amount of shifting which is possible from stage to stage. Thus one of the most powerful criticisms of Kohlberg's work (for example, McGeorge, 1974) is that individuals are unlikely to remain at the same level, but may be expected to express different levels of thinking according to the hypothetical situation presented. Another related issue is that which has concerned Elliot Turiel, namely the extent to which the level of moral thought as measured by Kohlberg may be considered a stable attribute. Turiel has investigated this by attempting to alter the young person's moral opinion. Thus in one study (Turiel, 1969), after first determining the adolescent's present stage of moral development, he exposed the teenager to argument in favour of other stages of thinking. His conclusions were broadly that individuals find it easier to accept one stage in advance of their present level of thinking, moderately difficult to agree with an earlier mode of thinking, and almost impossible to move forward by two stages. A further study indicated that while all subjects preferred moral judgements which were in advance of their own, they were also less able to explain or defend such judgements (Rest et al. 1969). Finally, results have also shown that subjects are more likely to shift in their judgements at a later date as a result of the experimental procedure if they have already reached stage 4, but that subjects at stages 3 and below exhibit relatively little long-term effect (Turiel and Rothman, 1972).

Finally, one may ask whether moral judgement as defined by Kohlberg has any relation to actual behaviour. Hogan (1975), in an important paper, has argued that moral judgement alone is only one of a number of factors which will determine the individual's actions in situations where morality is involved. Hogan believes that in addition to moral judgement, moral knowledge, socialization, empathy and autonomy are all relevant variables, and that there is unlikely to be any direct relation between Kohlberg's stages and overt behaviour. One research worker who has attempted to tackle this issue is Fodor (1972). In this study he compared delinquent teenagers with a non-delinquent sample, and showed that those in the delinquent group were, by and large, at a substantially lower level on Kohlberg's test than were the non-delinquents. In addition it was reported that those delinquents who could be persuaded to alter their moral judgements had lower scores than those delinquents who resisted persuasion to change. In a further study Fodor (1973) was able to show that within a delinquent group over 75 per cent of those who were classified as psychopathic (i.e. lacking a sense of guilt) were still at stages 1 or 2, while over 50 per cent of those not classified as psychopathic had reached stages 3 and 4. Thus there appears to be limited evidence to show at least some relation between Kohlberg's stages and behaviour. However, in a more recent study Emler *et al.* (1978) have questioned this conclusion, arguing that the groups chosen for comparison were too dissimilar in the first place. In their research, carried out in Scotland, they asked a group of delinquents to give details of their anti-social activities, and showed that there was no relation at all between level of moral reasoning and the degree and seriousness of self-reported delinquency. Clearly, therefore, this is an area in which more work is needed.

The growth of political ideas

As in the case of moral judgement the young person's political ideas are likely to be significantly influenced by his or her level of cognitive development. In recent years a number of writers have become interested in the shift, which takes place during the adolescent years, from a lack of political thought to, in many cases, an intense involvement in this area of life. How does this occur, and what are the processes involved? At what age do adolescents begin to show an increasing grasp of political concepts, and what stages do they go through before they achieve maturity of political judgement? One of the most important early studies was that undertaken by Adelson and O'Neill (1966). They approached the problem of the growth of political ideas in an imaginative way by posing for young people of different ages the following problem:

> Imagine that a thousand men and women, dissatisfied with the way things are going in their own country, decide to purchase and move to an island in the Pacific; once there they must devise laws and modes of government.

They then explored the adolescent's approach to a variety of relevant issues. They asked questions about how a government would be formed, what would its purpose be, would there be a need for laws and political parties, how would you protect minorities, and so on. The investigators proposed different laws, and explored typical problems of public policy. The major results may be discussed under two headings – the change in modes of thinking, and the decline of authoritarianism with age. As far as the first is concerned, there was a marked shift in thinking from the concrete to the abstract, a finding which ties in well with the work discussed earlier in this chapter.

Thus, for example, when asked: 'What is the purpose of laws?', one twelve-year-old replied: 'If we had no laws people could go around killing people.' In contrast, a sixteen-year-old replied: 'To ensure safety, and to enforce the government.' Another commented: 'They are basically guide-lines for people. I mean like, this is wrong and this is right, and to help them understand' (Adelson, 1971).

The second major shift observed was a decline in authoritarian solutions to political questions. The typical young adolescent (twelve or thirteen years old) appeared unable to appreciate that problems can have more than one solution, and that individual behaviour or political acts are not necessarily absolutely right or wrong, good or bad. The concept of moral relativism was not yet available for the making of political judgements. When confronted with law-breaking, or even mild forms of social deviance, the young person's solution was characteristically:

> . . . simply to raise the ante: more police, stiffer fines, longer gaol sentences, and if need be, executions. To a large and varied set of questions on crime and punishment, they consistently proposed one form of solution: punish, and if that does not suffice, punish harder. . . . At this age the child will not ordinarily concede that wrongdoing may be a symptom of something deeper, or that it may be inhibited by indirect means. The idea of reform and rehabilitation through humane methods is mentioned by only a small minority at the outset of adolescence. (Adelson, 1971, p. 1023)

In contrast the fourteen- or fifteen-year-old is much more aware of the different sides of any argument, and is usually able to take a relativistic point of view. Thinking begins to be more tentative, more critical and more pragmatic.

> Confronting a proposal for a law or for a change in social policy, he scrutinizes it to determine whether there is more to it than meets the eye. Whose interests are served, and whose are damaged? He now understands that law and policy must accommodate competing interests and value, that ends must be balanced against means, that the short-term good must be appraised against latent or long-term or indirect outcome. (Adelson, 1971, p. 1026)

Adelson and his colleagues have extended their work to look at national differences. As part of the study mentioned above they compared American, British and German young people and found that German adolescents were more likely than their American or British counterparts to stress a need for 'order, clarity and direction', and this led them to look towards a single strong benevolent leader who could be relied upon to provide guidance and prevent anarchy and chaos. American adolescents were the most concerned of the three groups with the necessity to achieve a proper balance between the rights of the individual and those of the community as a whole. Like British teenagers, but unlike those living in Germany, American adolescents displayed some ambivalence towards authority; while they admired success, an underlying resentment that all was not equal in a society which claimed to be egalitarian could be detected in their views. According to the results of this study the British adolescents appeared most complex of all. Conger has summarized the findings which relate to young people in Great Britain as follows:

> Part of the British adolescents' ambivalence about authority appeared to stem from the suspicion that the government leaders themselves may not be above trying to obtain an overly large 'slice of the pie'. In sum, British adolescents emerge on the one hand as the most devoted to 'rugged individualism', the most tolerant of eccentricities and individual differences, and the most dedicated to the preservation of personal liberty. On the other hand, they also emerged as the most self-oriented and least concerned, despite support of welfare concepts, with the community as a whole – a tendency characterized by Britishers themselves in the familiar slogan 'I'm alright Jack', indicating that as long as one's own interests are being served, there is little motivation for broader social concern. (1977, p. 535)

Amusing (or irritating) as it may be for readers in Great Britain to see how young people in this country are perceived from across the Atlantic, it would be more reassuring if there was evidence of a greater concern on the part of social scientists to investigate political thought in adolescence. While some other work has been carried out (for example, Crain and Crain, 1974), the field is still almost totally neglected, especially in Europe, and Schaffer and Hargreaves (1978), in their statement on research priorities in the UK, point to the topic of political socialization in adolescence as being in urgent need of further consideration. It is a field of particular interest, not only because of its obvious implications for education and government, but also because of the manner in which intellectual change can be seen to interact with social behaviour.

This chapter began by stating that cognitive growth is less apparent to observers than most aspects of maturation. Yet fundamental changes do occur in young people's cognitive ability between the ages of eleven and eighteen, changes which are no less significant than those which take place during earlier stages of childhood. In this chapter we have examined the nature of formal operational thought, and have noted that this is achieved by considerably fewer teenagers than Piaget at first believed. However, one or two of the more interesting examples of studies of adolescent reasoning have also been reviewed, and these highlight in a more obvious way changes from concrete to abstract thinking which occur in the majority. Finally, we have seen how the development of both moral and political concepts link up with other intellectual changes which are taking place during adolescence. For the young person's view of this process let us now turn to the interview material.

Interview

As part of the interview the following question was asked concerning thought processes:

> It is said that during adolescence there is a change in the way people think, that they are able to think in more abstract terms. An example might be that it becomes easier to see both sides of an argument. Have you noticed this?

Sarah (16 years): Yeah. Well it's just that now if anyone said anything to me that I didn't agree with I'd never let it get away. You know, I like to get right to the bottom of it and see who's right and who's wrong, and if necessary to ask anyone, like an older person available, you know, but I just won't let things slip away.

Elizabeth (17 years): Yes, actually I have. I think it really started off in school – up until the 4th year I hadn't taken a great interest in school. I didn't see the point, I didn't see the absolute point, and the end result seemed so far away – it didn't seem close to you – so that you didn't seem to realize why you had to work. I think really when it was almost nearly at the time that I had to take my O levels that something sort of clicked inside me – you've got to get these O levels because they're important. You see it on television, I mean, but it doesn't register with you. You think, 'Oh all my friends have got jobs – I'll get a job', you know, and then you think to yourself, 'Well, I want to get a good job.' You know, it does click, I think it's a steady process, but in the end something clicks within you, and you know. I think it does with everybody, it's just that some people don't take any notice of it, but I think it's there.

Valerie (17 years): I would say that people were more one-sided actually. At this age if they get something in their minds, like an idea they'll stick to it, whatever they think. I mean, there's always exceptions, but I think that's more true than people seeing both sides really.

Kevin (15 years): Yeah, definitely. When I was at junior school I was always one-sided, you know, this that and the other. I was always just on one side, but now that I've got a bit older, you know, I realize that other people have got an argument as well. You know, their point of view, and my point of view, compare them, you know? Another thing, I've been told a lot of times that me thinking's a lot more mature than what it was, you know that I've got a more mature outlook on life. I've realized I've changed myself, you know, because I've started to do things which I wouldn't have thought I'd done when I was younger.

Richard (15 years): Well, I do find that I form my own opinions now about lots of different things, whereas before I would just say, agree with my Dad in, like, is that a good man on television, or something like this, but now I am forming my own opinions about things, and I do see both sides of things and think before I do things.

Adam (17 years): Well, you think more of a certain thing than you would, you just don't let it pass by. You think more deeply about it, and you take into consideration all the possibilities. I'd say it's definitely changed. You think of more complicated things as well – whereas when you're younger you just put them aside, and now you really think about them.

Stephen (16 years): Oh, that's quite difficult. I think you can express yourself more clearly as a teenager. You are sort of feeling your feet as to how to express yourself, and you're more willing to speak up. When you're a child people say, 'Oh don't listen to him, he's a child', and that sort of thing, whereas as a teenager you get political and moral ideas, which form your whole life. I suppose you speak a lot. Nearly all teenagers have very extreme views, I find. How do moral ideas change? Well I suppose there's a much larger area of grey. When you're a child everything is either right or wrong – like stealing. But as you become a teenager you say, become much more inclined to, say, take someone else's pencil or rubber – things like that. That doesn't matter, because they'll take yours next lesson, that sort of thing. It becomes much less clear where the boundary lies. I suppose that's why you get quite a lot of people who just go too far.

4

Self-concept development

As far as the self-concept is concerned adolescence is usually thought to be a time of both change and consolidation. There are a number of reasons for this. In the first place the major physical changes which occur carry with them, as was noted in chapter 2, a change in body image, and thus in the sense of self. Secondly, intellectual growth during adolescence makes possible a more complex and sophisticated self-concept, involving a greater number of dimensions, and encompassing potential as well as reality. Thirdly, some development of the self-concept seems probable as a result of increasing emotional independence, and the approach of fundamental decisions relating to occupation, values, sexual behaviour, friendship choices and so on. Finally, the transitional nature of the adolescent period, and in particular the role changes experienced at this time would seem likely to be associated with some modification of the self-concept.

In addition to considerations such as these it may be noted that both theoretical approaches mentioned earlier have something to say on the subject of self-concept development. In their emphasis on the stressful nature of adolescence both draw attention to the likelihood that the individual's vulnerability during this period will be reflected in a disturbance of the self-concept. As far as the psychoanalytic approach is concerned reference has already been made to Erikson's contribution, and to his notion of identity crisis. From the sociological viewpoint the young person is seen as having to cope not only with role conflict, but also with what is known as status ambiguity. Society, it is contended by writers such as Rosenberg (1965), has no clearly defined expectations of the individual during his or her adolescent years. Adults respond in a fashion which must appear to the teenager to be highly ambiguous – at times demanding child-like obedience, and at others expecting the self-confidence and independence of an adult. Such uncertainty or ambiguity in status, as well as the various role conflicts mentioned in chapter 1, may be expected to call into question many aspects of the young person's self-concept.

In this chapter we will briefly review the evidence available concerning the adolescent self-concept, in order to see to what extent theoretical notions hold good. In particular we will look at the topic of self-concept development and at the factors which may be expected to affect this, consider Erikson's views and the validity of the notion of identity crisis, and finally we will pay some attention to the important issue of sex-role identity. Firstly, however, a word about terminology. In this area there are especial problems of definition and usage, and so for the purposes of this chapter the term *self-concept* has been chosen to refer to all aspects of the individual's view of his or her self. The term *self-concept* subsumes within it the notion of *self-image* (the individual's description of the self), as well as that of *self-esteem* (the individual's evaluation of the self). The term *identity* is taken here to have essentially the same meaning as *self-concept*, but it will be utilized only in areas where it is in common usage, i.e. in discussion of the works of Erikson and his followers, and in the consideration of sex-role identity.

The development of the self-concept

In considering the development of the self-concept during adolescence we are primarily concerned with two questions, the one relating to stability, and the other to disturbance. In the first place it may be asked whether there is any greater degree of change in the self-concept during this period than there is at any other stage. Theories would lead us to expect alteration in this aspect of the personality; are these expectations borne out by research? Secondly, theories also imply that, quite apart from change in the self-concept, some form of disturbance is to be expected as well. This is an issue which will be considered in detail in the section on identity, but, as we shall see, it is also relevant in the context of self-concept development.

As far as the issue of stability is concerned, the study carried out by Engel (1959) represents a good starting point. She used a well-known approach (the Q-sort technique) for the assessment of self-image, and administered the test to boys and girls at thirteen and fifteen and then again when the subjects were fifteen and seventeen. The results showed a relative stability of the self-image between thirteen and fifteen, as well as between fifteen and seventeen, which was demonstrated by highly significant overall correlations between first and second testing. However, Engel also showed that the 20 per cent of the sample who manifested a negative self-image were significantly less stable in their view of themselves than the majority who expressed a positive self-image. This is a point to which we shall return in a moment. Other longitudinal studies of this nature are, sadly, virtually unknown in the literature. However, evidence from both Tomé (1972) and Monge (1973) do provide support for Engel's conclusions. Both studies, although cross-sectional, investigated the structure of the self-concept at different stages during adolescence, and in the light of their results both writers argue against any major change or re-organization of the self-concept during the years twelve to eighteen.

Katz and Zigler (1967), on the other hand, provide contradictory evidence. The point of their investigation was somewhat different, in that they were interested in the discrepancy between real and ideal self-concept. These dimensions were assessed both by questionnaire and on an adjective check list, and subjects included 120 boys and girls at ages ten, thirteen and sixteen. Results showed that, contrary to expectations, the disparity between the two dimensions of the self-concept increased with age, the highest level of disparity being in the sixteen-year-old group. These results at least lend no support to the view that the relation between two aspects of the self-image remains stable during these years. Another more recent study, which looked particularly at the instability of the self-concept between the ages of eight and eighteen, lends further weight to this view. Simmons *et al.* (1973), in their large-scale study of over 2,500 young people, included a dimension which they labelled 'stability of self'. This was assessed using a five-item questionnaire, which included such examples as : 'A kid told me: "Some days I like the way I am. Some days I do not like the way I am." Do your feelings change like this?' Results showed a marked increase in instability between the ages of eleven and thirteen, but as is clear from figure 4.1, this instability did not diminish until after the age of sixteen.

Studies which have looked specifically at self-esteem do little to clear up the confusion. Thus Piers and Harris (1964), who investigated the level of self-esteem in nine-, twelve- and sixteen-year-olds, showed that, while nine- and sixteen-year-olds had similar levels of self-esteem, in the twelve-year-old group there was a significantly lower level of self-esteem than in the other two age groups. On the other hand, Carlson (1965) who, in a longitudinal design, looked at self-esteem levels at twelve and then again at eighteen, showed no

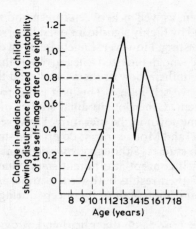

Figure 4.1   Increase in instability of the self-image by age.
(From R. Simmons, F. Rosenberg and M. Rosenberg (1973)
American Sociological Review, 38.)

difference at all between the two age levels. Simmons *et al.* also looked at self-esteem. Their results, although a little difficult to interpret because they included a number of different measures of self-esteem, seem to indicate a major change between the years of twelve and fourteen. In their view:

... the early adolescent has become distinctly more self-conscious; his picture of himself has become more shaky and unstable, his global self-esteem has declined slightly, his attitudes towards several specific characteristics which he values highly have become less positive; and he has increasingly come to believe that parents, teachers and peers of the same sex view him less favourably. (p. 558)

The research reviewed so far illustrates a number of problems inherent in this area. Firstly, age groups and the methods used in the various studies are rarely comparable. Closely related to this is the fact that few investigators concern themselves with the same aspect of the self-concept. In addition it is sometimes unclear as to whether research workers are exploring questions of stability or questions of disturbance. In fact, as we shall see, the two prove to be interrelated, but there is far too much ambiguity on this issue. Thus, for example, research which reports a drop in self-esteem at a particular stage may be providing evidence of a change in the self-concept, but it may also be substantiating a notion of disturbance. The biggest limitation of all, however, concerns the failure of most of these studies to recognize that not all young people will develop in the same way. Individual differences are bound to play their part in determining the extent of both stability and disturbance, and we may, therefore, now turn to a consideration of the factors which might be expected to affect the development of the self-concept.

Factors associated with self-concept development

It would seem reasonable to assume that the self-concept development of young people will vary in relation to a number of background factors. Yet of the studies mentioned in the previous section only one was concerned directly with individual differences. In Engel's (1959) research, as has been mentioned, some 20 per cent of the sample were shown to have a negative self-image on first testing, and it was this group which had the greatest level of instability of the self-image over the two year period of the project. In addition, those with a negative self-image also had higher maladjustment scores on various personality tests. This is an important study for a number of reasons. In the first place it indicates that a relatively small proportion of the total population are likely to show a disturbance of the self-concept. Secondly, it demonstrates that a negative self-image is related to other aspects of personality difficulty. Thirdly, it underlines the fact that questions of change and disturbance are linked, and that very probably a lack of disturbance goes hand-in-hand with a relatively stable self-concept. Finally, it serves to draw attention to the necessity of considering other variables which may be associated with self-concept development.

Rosenberg's (1965) classic study represents one important contribution in this respect. He was able to show that low self-esteem, characteristic of 20–30 per cent of the sample studied, was associated with a variety of factors. The research was concerned with older adolescents, the sample including approximately 5,000 seventeen- and eighteen-year-olds in randomly selected schools in New York. Self-esteem was measured by a ten-item self-report scale (i.e. the degree to which the subjects agreed or disagreed with statements such as 'I feel I am a person of worth, at least on an equal plane with others'). Low self-esteem was shown to be related to depression, anxiety, and poor school performance. Both low and high self-esteem adolescents were similar in wishing for success on leaving school, but the low self-esteem group were more likely to feel they would never attain such success, to prefer a job which they knew was beyond their grasp, and to feel that they did not have the resources necessary for success. The adolescents who were high in self-esteem were significantly more likely than those with low self-esteem to consider the following qualities as personal assets: self-confidence, hard work, leadership potential, and the ability to make a good impression. Low self-esteem adolescents were characterized by a sense of incompetence in social relationships, they felt socially isolated, and believed that other people neither understood nor respected them, and were not able to trust them. Finally, the feeling that their parents took an interest in their affairs was significantly more apparent in those with high self-esteem.

Two other factors which have been shown to be closely related to self-concept are body image and what Rosenberg has called 'the dissonant context'. As far as the former is concerned Secord and Jourard (1953) were the first to show that satisfaction with one's body correlated with positive attitudes to the self. Gunderson (1956), in a study of older adolescent males, showed that deviation from preferred height and weight had a pervasive negative influence on self-esteem, and similar findings in seventeen to twenty-one-year-old women were reported by Jourard and Secord (1955). In relation to the second point, while it has often been supposed that simply belonging to a minority group would have a detrimental effect on self-esteem, recent evidence shows that this is certainly not true today. Conger's (1977) review of research on this topic indicates that, particularly in America, the greatly increased acceptance of blacks and other minority groups in the last decade, in conjunction with the rise of black power and black consciousness, has undoubtedly had a beneficial effect on the self-esteem of adolescents belonging to minority groups. However, Rosenberg (1975) makes an important point when he distinguishes between those belonging to minority groups who are well integrated and who function in a supportive environment, and those who exist in a 'dissonant' or hostile context. To support the argument he reports a study of self-esteem among black students attending integrated and segregated schools in the USA. The results illustrate his point. At all ages – in elementary school, junior high school and senior high school – those black children who attended segregated schools had higher self-esteem than those attending schools which were racially mixed.

Thus it is clear, not only that body image, personality and family background are all variables which affect the adolescent self-concept, but also that the wider social environment exercises an additional influence. Furthermore, we have seen that self-esteem is closely related both to general social adjustment and to stability of the self-concept. On the whole the higher the individual's self-esteem the better adjusted and the more stable in self-concept he or she is likely to be. Before concluding this section one further point needs to be made. The self-concept is a complex phenomenon, and although a number of its aspects have already been discussed, there may yet be further dimensions which have not so far been considered. One example which falls into this category is the distinction between present and future self. Douvan and Adelson (1966) first drew attention to this distinction when they wrote: 'The normal adolescent holds, we think, two conceptions of himself – what he is and what he will be – and the way in which he integrates the future image into his current life will indicate a good deal about his current adolescent integration' (p. 23). In an attempt to test out whether there might be differences between these two aspects of the self, the author, with the help of colleagues, devised a sentence-completion test specifically aimed at differentiating between present and future self image (Coleman *et al.*, 1977). The subjects were working-class boys in an urban area, and results showed that, while the proportions of each age group expressing a negative present self-image remained the same, the numbers expressing negative sentiments concerning their future self-image increased markedly with age. Fears and anxieties about themselves as they grew older appeared to be very much more common in those about to leave school, and phrases such as 'dreary', 'dead', 'depressing' and 'a dreaded age' were in common usage among sixteen-year-olds to describe their future.

More recent research (Miller and Coleman, 1980) has established that concepts of the self in the future are likely to be affected by a number of variables. Boys were shown to express greater anxiety about the future than girls, and social class as well as the imminence of leaving school also appear to play their part. This is a research project which is still in progress, and so firm conclusions should be avoided. For present purposes the important point to note is that the self-concept has a number of dimensions, one of which is a notion of the self in the future. It may well be that for adolescents in particular this component is associated with more stress than it would be for those in other age groups. In view of this it is surprising that although writers such as Elder and Erikson have placed considerable emphasis on the importance of the future for teenagers, such a concept has played virtually no part in empirical research until now.

To summarize to this point, it must first of all be acknowledged that we are hampered by the limited nature of the research evidence, and by the many seemingly contradictory findings. If we return to the

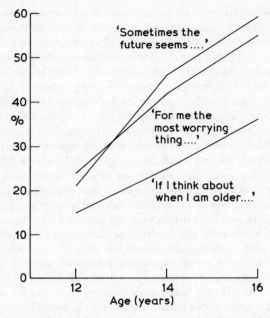

Figure 4.2   Proportions of each age group expressing negative responses
to sentence-stems related to *the self in the future*.
(From J. C. Coleman, J. Herzberg and M. Morris (1977)
Journal of Youth and Adolescence, 6.)

issues mentioned earlier in the chapter, it seems probable that
answers to the questions concerning stability of the self-concept
depend on which aspect of the self-concept one is referring to. Thus,
for example, self-image is probably more stable than self-esteem.
However, it must also be remembered that adolescents do not all
develop in the same way, and we can assume that those with a
negative self-image are less likely to have stable self-concepts than
those whose self-images are generally positive. Furthermore, there
are obviously many variables, such as family background and cultural context, which play their part in determining at least some
aspects of the self-concept. It is not at all clear whether the alterations
in self-concept which do occur in adolescence are any different from
those taking place during other transitional stages in the life cycle,
though further investigation of concepts of the self in the future may
well prove fruitful in this respect. Finally, although the evidence is far
from clear-cut, we have gained a few hints concerning disturbance of
the self-concept. Thus the studies which have been reviewed indicate

that only a relatively small proportion of the total population are likely to have a negative self-image or to have very low self-esteem, and that if such disturbance increases at any stage during the teenage years it is more probable that it will do so in early rather than late adolescence. With these thoughts in mind let us turn to a consideration of the notion of identity crisis.

Identity and identity crisis

In many respects it would be true to say that Erikson towers above all other writers in this particular area. Although a psychoanalyst he is able to take account of social and cultural circumstances, and his writings constitute a great deal more than standard textbooks. *Childhood and Society* (1963) and *Identity: Youth and Crisis* (1968) are viewed as works of literary merit as well as classics in psychology. Perhaps most important, Erikson has, in some subtle way, come to be seen as one of the great commentators on youth. The phrase 'identity crisis' has passed into our everyday vocabulary, and as he himself points out (1968), it can now equally well be used in journalism, as for example in: 'African state faces identity crisis after independence', or among students, as in an announcement he noticed at Harvard: 'Identity crisis. 6.00 p.m. Friday, Room B128. All welcome.' Erikson's contribution is thus far more than that simply of a psychoanalytic theorist, a fact which causes some headaches for anyone attempting to summarize his views.

Let us start by noting that he sees life as a series of stages, each having a particular developmental task of a psychosocial nature associated with it. In infancy, for example, the task is to establish a sense of *basic trust*, and to combat *mistrust*. The maternal relationship is here considered to be crucial in creating a foundation upon which the infant may build later trusting relationships. As far as adolescence is concerned the task involves the establishment of a *coherent identity*, and the defeat of a sense of *identity diffusion*. Erikson believes that the search for identity becomes especially acute at this stage as a result of a number of factors, most of which were mentioned at the beginning of the chapter. Thus Erikson lays some stress on the phenomenon of rapid biological and social change during adolescence, and points especially to the importance for the individual of having to take major decisions at this time in almost all areas of life. In many of his writings Erikson either states or implies that some form of crisis is necessary for the young person to resolve the identity issue and to defeat identity diffusion. Here is how he puts it in one passage:

The final assembly of all the converging identity elements at the end of childhood appears to be a formidable task; how can a stage as 'abnormal' as adolescence be trusted to accomplish it? Here it is not unnecessary to call to mind again that in spite of the similarity of adolescent 'symptoms' and episodes to neurotic and psychotic symptoms and episodes, adolescence is not an affliction but a *normative crisis*, i.e. a normal phase of increased conflict characterized by a seeming fluctuation in ego strength, and yet also by a high growth potential. . . . What under prejudiced scrutiny may appear to be the onset of a neurosis is often but an aggravated crisis which might prove to be self-liquidating and, in fact, contributive to the process of identity formation. (1969, p. 22)

Identity diffusion, according to Erikson, has four major components. In the first place there is the problem of *intimacy*. Here the individual may fear commitment or involvement in close interpersonal relationships because of the possible loss of his or her own identity. This fear can lead to stereotyped, formalized relationships, to isolation, or the young person may, as Erikson puts it, '. . . in repeated hectic attempts and dismal failures, seek intimacy with the most improbable partners' (1968, p. 167). Secondly, there is the possibility of a *diffusion of time perspective*. Here the adolescent finds it impossible to plan for the future, or to retain any sense of time. This problem is thought to be associated with anxieties about change and becoming adult, and often: '. . . consists of a decided disbelief in the possibility that time may bring change and yet also of a violent fear that it might' (1968, p. 169).

Next there is a *diffusion of industry*, in which the young person finds it difficult to harness his or her resources in a realistic way in work or study. Both of these activities represent commitment, and as a defence against this the individual may either find it impossible to concentrate, or may frenetically engage in one single activity to the exclusion of all others. Finally, Erikson discusses the choice of a *negative identity*. By this is meant the young person's selection of an identity exactly the opposite to that preferred by parents or other important adults. 'The loss of a sense of identity is often expressed in a scornful and snobbish hostility towards the role offered as proper and desirable in one's family or immediate community. Any aspect of the required role or all of it − be it masculinity or femininity, nationality or class membership − can become the main focus of the young person's acid disdain' (1968, p. 173).

These four elements, then, constitute the main features of identity diffusion, although clearly not all will be present in any one individual who experiences an identity crisis. In addition to concepts such as these one other notion needs to be mentioned as an integral feature of Erikson's theory, that of *psychosocial moratorium*. By this is meant a period during which decisions are left in abeyance. It is argued that society allows, even encourages, a time of life when the young person may delay major identity choices, and experiment with roles in order to discover the sort of person he or she wishes to be; while such a stage may lead to disorientation or disturbance it has, according to Erikson, a healthy function. As he says: 'Much of this apparent confusion thus must be considered social play – the true genetic successor to childhood play.' (1968, p. 164)

Before concluding this review of Erikson's theory it should be stressed that at no point does he suggest that identity is an issue pertinent only to adolescence. In his view it is a dimension of personality development which runs through the life cycle, presenting itself in an especially acute form during the teenage years. The real problem with Erikson's theory lies in the fact that he has never been specific about the extent of the adolescent identity crisis. His use of terms such as 'normative crisis' and 'the psycho-pathology of everyday adolescence' implies that all young people may be expected to experience some such crisis, yet nowhere does Erikson tackle quantitative issues. He prefers to deal in the qualitative aspects of identity development, and it has been left to others to translate his ideas into a form in which they can be tested empirically.

Among this group James Marcia is the foremost example. Marcia has attempted to identify four major stages in identity development. His method has been to design a semi-structured interview and an incomplete sentences test and to use these with groups of older adolescents, most of whom have been college students in the USA. The four stages, or identity statuses, as they are called, are as follows:

1 *Identity diffusion.* Here the individual has not yet experienced an identity crisis, nor has he made any commitment to a vocation or set of beliefs. There is also no indication that he or she is actively trying to make a commitment.
2 *Identity foreclosure.* In this status the individual has not experienced a crisis but nevertheless is committed in his or her goals and beliefs, largely as a result of choices made by others.
3 *Moratorium.* An individual in this category is in a state of crisis, and is actively searching among alternatives in an attempt to arrive at a choice of identity.
4 *Identity achievement.* At this stage the individual is considered to have experienced a crisis, but to have resolved it on

his or her own terms, and now to be firmly committed to an occupation and ideology.

In Marcia's view these four identity statuses may be seen as a developmental sequence, but not necessarily in the sense that one is the pre-requisite of the others. Only moratorium appears to be essential for identity achievement, since the searching and exploring which characterizes it must precede a resolution of the identity problem. In Marcia's original research (1966) he found that as students moved through the four years of college the proportion of those in the identity diffusion category declined, while the number of identity achievement subjects steadily increased.

Much additional evidence has accumulated concerning these notions of identity status. For example in the 1966 study Marcia also showed that those young people who had reached identity achievement were more resistant to stress on a concept attainment task, and were less vulnerable in their self-esteem when provided with negative information about themselves. Results of a further study (Marcia, 1967) indicated that this group had higher self-esteem in general than those in the other three categories. Toder and Marcia (1973), in an investigation of college women, reported that those who had reached identity achievement were least likely to conform to social pressure, while those in the identity diffusion group were most likely to conform when in a group situation. In a series of studies Waterman and colleagues (Waterman and Waterman, 1971, 1972; Waterman et al. 1974) looked more closely at the changes in identity status during the four college years. They found that in the first six months of the first year about half the population studied changed their identity status in some fashion, and this was true even of a substantial number who initially appeared in the identity achievement category. Such a result seems to cast doubt on the whole process of categorization, but when the students were tested again at the end of the four year college period more stability was apparent. Results from this study showed that by and large those who had reached identity achievement at the end of the first year maintained that status throughout college, being joined on the way by others, so that by the end of the fourth year approximately 45 per cent were in the identity achievement category. Furthermore very few students remained in the moratorium category, although about one third remained in the identity diffusion group, much the same number as at the very beginning of the study.

Work of this type has come in for criticism on a number of counts. Matteson (1977), for example, believes that the four categories are conceptually different, moratorium referring to a process, and the other three representing outcomes. Matteson raises a number of other methodological queries, and argues in addition that it is wrong to treat an identity crisis as a single event. As he says: 'There is considerable evidence that adolescents undergo a series of crises and that at one particular time, one content area may be stable while another area of life decisions is very much in crisis. A separate analysis of each content area of the interview is needed' (1977, pp. 354–5). Such a view is almost identical to the one which will be proposed in the final chapter of this book, when we come to discuss the 'focal' theory of adolescence, and so is worth keeping in mind until that point.

To return to Marcia, it would seem reasonable to conclude that, in spite of valid criticism, a number of findings are likely to hold up. One example would be that those in the identity achievement category are more likely to be better adjusted in a range of social situations. We may also assume that the number of young people falling into this category increases between the ages of seventeen and twenty-one, although we certainly cannot infer that individuals can be assigned to these statuses with any confidence during their first year in college. It is disappointing to note, however, that on the whole this work has provided relatively little insight into the extent of the adolescent identity crisis. In the first place this is because the approach has been used almost exclusively with American college students, and hardly at all with other groups or with younger teenagers. The second reason for this unsatisfying result is that, as Matteson has indicated, the categories themselves are in many ways inadequate for the resolution of a large number of issues relating to adolescent identity.

The studies of Marcia and others we have mentioned do not represent the only examples of attempts to test out Erikson's theory. Some years ago Bronson (1959) investigated identity diffusion in late adolescence by exploring four dimensions of identity – continuity between past and present, level of anxiety, level of uncertainty, and fluctuation of self-evaluation. Howard (1960) studied what she called 'the diffusion of identity consciousness' in adolescent girls, investigating the degree of dissatisfaction experienced by her subjects in their view of themselves. Both these studies were inconclusive, and suffered from being limited to only one age group. More recently Matteson (1975, 1977) has attempted to develop a means of assessing exploration and commitment in four major areas – occupation, values, politics and sex roles – which is not dependent on assigning subjects to identity status categories. The results reflect the value of investigating different areas of life independently, as well as distinguishing between exploration and commitment. Matteson argues that this approach is more satisfactory than that of Marcia, in that it links more closely with other personality variables. In the UK Weinreich (1979) has attempted to study identity diffusion among adolescents coming from immigrant communities. His method involved the use of the repertory grid technique and results showed immigrant girls, especially those from Pakistani families, to have the highest levels of identity diffusion. This is obviously an important study, and it is to be hoped that it will encourage others to pursue similar lines of enquiry.

It will be clear from this discussion that Erikson's notions have stimulated a wide range of research investigations, not only among those concerned with identity diffusion and identity crisis, but also by those such as Rosenberg and his colleagues who preferred to study self-image disturbance. It has to be stated, however, that while there can be no doubt that identity problems do exist among a proportion of teenagers, not one single study has provided support for Erikson's view of the 'normative crisis'. There is simply no evidence to suggest that the great majority of adolescents experience a serious crisis of identity, and most studies seem to conclude that only 25–35 per cent of the total population of teenagers at any age level could be said to have a disturbance in this area. Furthermore what limited evidence there is available would suggest that, contrary to Erikson's belief that late adolescence is the most likely time for young people to experience identity problems, it is around the time of puberty that there is the greatest likelihood of some form of disturbance in the self-concept. Writers such as Erikson and Marcia have suggested that without a crisis of some sort no real resolution of the identity issue is possible. We can be fairly confident in arguing for the contrary view. This is not to deny the fact that a minority of young people do have serious identity problems, the significance of which should not in any way be minimized. It seems probable, however, that for the majority of adolescents the most viable course will be to avoid any sudden identity crisis, adapting very gradually over a period of years to the changes in identity experienced by them.

Sex-role identity

Sex-role identity is one aspect of the self-concept which has hardly been touched on so far. Until recently this has been an issue of relatively little concern to those writing about adolescence, yet in the last year or so a sudden upsurge of interest has been noticeable (for example,

Fransella and Frost, 1977; Cockram and Beloff, 1978; Hutt, 1979; Weinreich, 1978; Douvan, 1979). It is to be hoped that this increase in attention to the topic of sex-role development will go some way towards rectifying the situation noted by Cockram and Beloff when they wrote: 'It might be mentioned . . . that none of the theories [of adolescence] devote very much attention to the development of girls specifically. Development either seems to be assumed to parallel that of boys, or it constitutes an embarrassment to the theory.' (p. 21)

The term 'sex role' is commonly used to refer to a set of standards or prescriptions which describe appropriate masculine and feminine behaviour in a particular culture. Thus from very early childhood individuals learn what is and what is not acceptable behaviour for each of the sexes. This learning may not necessarily take place in an explicit fashion, but will more often be absorbed by the child as one aspect of the general guidelines which exist in his or her environment. As a result of socialization he or she will come to appreciate that such standards exercise both subtle and not so subtle influences on how men and women act in society, and recently considerable interest has been expressed in the way these socialization processes operate. Attention has been focused on the role of the mass media, on children's books, on school teachers' behaviour, expectations for the two sexes, and so on. This is likely to become a growing field of research, and already women's groups have effected some modifications in the stereotypes presented in, for example, introductory reading books.

As far as sex-role identity is concerned, this may be taken to represent the degree to which the individual believes he or she has matched the prescribed sex role. In other words sex-role identity concerns the extent to which a person feels that his or her behaviour is consistent with the standards which operate in the culture to determine male or female behaviour in general. Such concepts may usefully be distinguished from notions of 'gender' and 'gender identity,' which are usually taken to refer more directly to body image and awareness of male and female sexuality (Douvan, 1979). It has been pointed out by some writers (for example, Bee, 1975) that while gender identity is likely to be learnt very early, usually before the age of five, the development of sex-role identity occurs later in childhood, and will probably only become an issue of real significance as the individual enters adolescence.

The fact that sex-role identity becomes problematic during the teenage years appears to be generally accepted by all who have commented on this topic. Why should this be so? In the first place it is argued that before puberty a considerable amount of leeway is permitted in our society as far as sex-appropriate behaviour is concerned. Thus girls can, if they wish, act as 'tomboys' without inviting too much disapproval, while even boys can get away with quiet, reflective activities and a lack of interest in sport up to the age of about ten or eleven. Following puberty, however, two pressures are brought to bear on the individual. First parents, teachers and others see future adulthood approaching, and wish to ensure successful adjustment for the young person as he or she grows up. Secondly, the peer group comes to exercise increasing influence in determining the behaviours which are acceptable. Both groups underline sex-role standards, and indicate in no uncertain manner the penalties which will follow if the adolescent deviates too radically from the norm.

Where comparisons are drawn between adolescent boys and girls it is often noted that sex-linked interests and attitudes come to dominate the behaviour of young people at this stage. Boys can be seen to be preparing themselves for the world of work, often planning ahead for a career and finding ways of acquiring appropriate educational qualifications. In this they are given considerable support and assistance by schools and other social agencies. Girls, on the other hand, are given much less help in this sphere. Partly as a result of this, most have more limited and vaguer career aspirations, frequently assuming that marriage will sooner or later relieve them of the necessity to work. The problem of ensuring that girls do have equal career opportunities is an extremely complex one, but we can agree with Hutt when she says: 'What is to be deplored . . . is the value-system which depreciates the attributes and work of women, so that women underestimate their ability. Such a value system leads inexorably to a discriminating end.' (1979, p. 193.)

This distinction between the sexes leads us to consider a further aspect of sex-role identity, namely the possibility that the development of this type of identity will be more problematic for girls than for boys. The reason which is usually advanced in support of this notion concerns discontinuity of socialization. It will be recalled that discontinuity in this context refers to the lack of an ordered sequence in role expectations from one stage to the next. Thus, for example, Elizabeth Douvan (1979) points out that for boys the major discontinuity occurs in the pre-school years where a discrepancy exists between passive, dependent babyhood, and the independence and self-assertiveness that is expected of the male in his early contacts with peers and the school situation. For girls, however, this discontinuity is seen in its most extreme form during adolescence. During these years females face, according to Douvan, the following situation:

Socialized through childhood in a double system – in which the girl is allowed dependency but is also encouraged and supported through school to be independent, individualistic, competitive and achieving – she now finds that at adolescence she must abandon or disguise these individual competitive traits if she is to be acceptably feminine. Adults, and especially her peer group expect her to shift from direct achievement to vicarious achievement, and to take as her major goals becoming a wife and mother. . . . She is asked to give up established ways of being and behaving, ways practised throughout the primary school years. Abandoning established patterns represents her critical discontinuity. . . . (1979, p. 90.)

Some interesting examples of problems of this sort faced by girls in Britain are provided by Sharpe in her book *Just like a Girl* (1974). Not all writers, however, accept this view of the situation. John Conger (1977), for example, believes that even in adolescence there are more ways in our society for a girl than a boy to establish a successful identity, although as he notes this will not necessarily be with any less difficulty. He suggests two reasons why this should be so. On the one hand he argues that there is more freedom for girls than for boys to engage in cross-sex behaviours. In other words he is suggesting that the masculine sex-role stereotype is more rigid in our society than is the feminine stereotype, thus limiting boys more than girls in their range of behaviours. On the other hand Conger also points out that the traditional female role is at the moment very much in transition, and while this may mean that the girl will be exposed to conflicting social pressures, it will also mean that she has greater freedom to seek alternative solutions to identity problems.

It will be apparent that the different sexes of the writers themselves may be playing a part in this debate. While Elizabeth Douvan points up the difficulties that women face, John Conger stresses the limitations of the male role, and clearly further non-partisan research is required where this issue is concerned. Incidentally, it may be noted that almost all the contributions on sex-role identity mentioned here are the responsibility of women writers. It is about time that men turned their attention to this important topic.

This section may be concluded by briefly considering some of the similarities and differences between adolescent boys and girls in identity development which have been reported in the literature. Studies which have provided such information are disappointingly few and far between, some of the well-known investigations in this area failing even to mention the sex of the subjects involved. One or two findings may, however, be mentioned. As far as self-esteem is concerned Maccoby and Jacklin (1975), who have provided a valuable and exhaustive review of a wide range of studies, are of the opinion that there is no difference at all between the sexes with respect to this dimension of the self-concept. Contrary to common belief there appears to be no evidence at all suggesting that girls have lower levels of self-esteem than boys. Support for this conclusion may be derived from the author's own work (Coleman, 1974), one aspect of which was an investigation of the proportion of boys and girls at eleven, thirteen, fifteen and seventeen having a negative self-image. Results showed no differences between the two sexes at any of the four age levels.

Some writers (for example, Fransella and Frost, 1977; Weinreich, 1978) have drawn attention to the possibility that, while levels of self-esteem may be similar for the two sexes, the basis of such esteem will differ between men and women. A study which is often quoted in support of this view is that of Carlson (1965), already mentioned in a previous section. In this research a distinction was drawn between social and personal orientation in identity development, and the results indicated that while boys became more involved with personal goals as they progressed through adolescence, girls developed in the opposite direction, becoming more socially oriented as they got older. Studies by Marcia and colleagues have also provided hints of differences between the sexes, although it is important to bear in mind that none of these studies actually involved direct comparisons between similar groups of males and females. To take one example Marcia and Friedman (1970) showed that college women in the identity foreclosure group had the highest levels of self-esteem and the lowest levels of anxiety. In other studies Marcia had shown, as noted previously, that men in the identity achievement category had the highest levels of self-esteem. Thus there may be differences here, but further research is needed.

One final example may be drawn from the author's own study (Coleman, 1974) which will be discussed in greater detail in the subsequent chapters. As part of this research a sentence-completion test was given to large numbers of teenagers at four age levels. Some of the sentence stems concerned relationships with parents, as for example: 'When a boy is with his parents . . .' or, for a girl 'When a girl is with her parents . . .' Results showed that in the fifteen-year-old group a similar proportion of boys and girls completed this sentence with a theme reflecting conflict between themselves and their parents. However, when these responses were analysed for content a remarkable difference between the sexes emerged. Whereas boys expressed conflict with their parents in behavioural terms, drawing attention to restrictions and limitations which they felt their parents imposed on them, the girls hardly referred to this problem at all. For them it was their sense of self which was at stake, and difficulties with their parents reflected issues of identity rather than of behaviour. Some examples of responses by teenagers given in the study may clarify the point.

Boys

When a boy is with his parents he feels like hitting them.
When a boy is with his parents he is usually chained up.
When a boy is with his parents he must escape, break out.

Girls

When a girl is with her parents she is not really herself. They think they know her but they don't.
When a girl is with her parents she becomes like them and cannot find her own identity.
When a girl is with her parents she is not often her real self.

Naturally not all individuals expressed their views with such clarity. However, similar concerns on the part of females appear in the interview material considered below, and from examples such as these it would appear that in adolescence girls may have more difficulties than boys in accepting or coming to terms with their own identity, especially in the context of parental relationships. This is a subject which has hardly been touched on in the literature so far, and could represent a useful lead for further investigations of sex-role identity development.

In summary this chapter has covered a wide range of issues. We have looked at self-concept development, and at some of the factors which influence it. We have considered Erikson's theories of identity and identity crisis, and discussed studies which have attempted to place these ideas in a more empirical framework. Lastly, we have paid attention to sex-role identity, and indicated a number of topics and issues which are in need of further investigation. Let us now turn to the interviews, through which run many of the themes which have cropped up in the course of this discussion. In particular a sense of instability of identity, a feeling of self-consciousness, and a pre-occupation with the future will all be apparent in the material.

Interview

The question which was asked in the interview which provided information relevant to this chapter was as follows:

> Another thing that's said to change at adolescence is the way young people think about themselves. It's said that adolescence can be a time of worries and identity problems, with young people asking themselves the question: 'Who am I?' Does this ring any bells for you?

Elizabeth (17 years): Yes, I ask it all the time. I do. You sit there and think 'Who am I?' and 'What am I looking for in life?' And you change your mind so many times, you know you think to yourself: 'When am I actually going to find out what I'm doing is right? I hope I'm not going to change my mind tomorrow.' I think this constantly goes through your mind until you're settled, until you are in the occupation that is right for you. Also that's why I think in some cases that when parents have their own idea about a child and they want them to go into a certain occupation in life, it can really confuse you even more because you're being pushed from one side, and maybe that is right for you, but because you're being pushed into it it's very confusing.

Jill (16 years): Yeah, definitely. I change my mind so often you know, and that annoys us, and I think 'Well, why do I have to change my mind, why do I?' And that's only one small bit, there's sort of 'Why do I have to be here, you know, when I could be somewhere else, you know in a different time?' I went through a phase of you know, my body was here but my mind wasn't and I felt very distant from everybody, but now I'm sort of back on the ground slightly, you know. I still wander off now and again, but you know, about thirteen or fourteen, fifteen, it was really, for about three months, I just wasn't really here. What do I mean? Well I just felt as though I wasn't meself, or I wasn't what I should have been, or I was what other people thought I was. You know, people say: 'Jill knows where she is, she's O.K.', but I felt as though I wasn't myself. I was wondering who I was.

Harriett (16 years): Yes, very much I think. I don't know as I get older I am able to express myself, I've got more confidence, but I still don't know what I am going to do in the future, it's just sort of held in the balance really, you're never quite sure what is going to happen. I don't know, sometimes I feel as if I'm the most important person in the world and sometimes I feel as though I'm just sort of another person. It is very difficult to achieve a balance.

Karen (15 years): Not really, I sometimes think 'Where am I going to?', but I don't think 'Who am I?' I'm sort of . . . actually just now I've been going through a phase where I just wear jeans and plimsoles the whole time with a really sloppy jumper, and I wore it to school yesterday and one of the blokes comes up to me and goes 'Oh God you look scruffy', and I sort of said 'Well I dress to please myself, not society.' And I sort of realized why do these people . . . I mean why do people bother just to impress people – it must be awful to have to do that. I'm myself, and that's all I care about you know. . . . Also I've been thinking there are all these people that are sort of so false. I mean sort of 'Oh hi there! How are you? How's so and so?', and then when they go past you they go 'Oh hello'. I think the last thing I want to do is do that, and so I walk past them and just go 'Hello' you know, because you have to, and then they all start having a go at me because I'm unsociable. I think you know you have to put on an act – it's really painful to sort of smile and say 'Yes, well I'm fine, and how are you?' It's really painful sometimes – all these people are so false and really shallow – they've got nothing to say and they just talk about actually nothing.

Adam (17 years): Not really. I don't think I've really thought or I've really looked at it that way. I don't think that problem's arisen yet.

Kevin (15 years): No – I know who I am – that's flat you know. I know who I am, I know what I want to do with me life, and I know what I intend to do with me life.

Henry (16 years): Yeah, it means that you think you're the only one person in society. I was only thinking that the other day, come to think about it, in a lesson. I was bored with the lesson and I thought 'O.K., I'll grow up, do this and do that.' You only grow up to get married and pay the bills – that's all it is, you know, and I don't see no point in it myself. Obviously I'm not going to kill myself or anything, you know, but I just don't see no point in growing up just to pay bills and that. I mean I obviously don't want to be just fit for nothing – don't get me wrong – but its just that I don't think that's the way to do it.

Paul (17 years): Quite often, yeah. You think what are you going to do, and how are you going to get there, and what will you be in the future, and things like that. You can't really answer those type of questions, but you actually think a lot about yourself, and tend to be more conscious of yourself than you did before you became a teenager. You sort of think a bit more about yourself, and how you go on in school, and what people think of you – and just hope its good.

5
The role of parents and other adults

One of the central themes of adolescent development is the attainment of independence, often represented symbolically in art and literature by the moment of 'departure' from home. However, for most young people today independence is not gained at one specific moment by the grand gesture of saying goodbye to one's parents and setting off to seek one's fortune in the wide world. Independence is much more likely to mean freedom within the family to make day-to-day decisions, emotional freedom to make new relationships, and personal freedom to take responsibility for one's self in such things as education, political beliefs and future career. There are many forces which interact in propelling an individual towards this state of maturity. Naturally both physical and intellectual maturation encourage the adolescent toward greater autonomy. In addition to these factors there are, undoubtedly, psychological forces within the individual as well as social forces in the environment which have the same goal. In the psychoanalytic view, considered in chapter 1, the process of seeking independence represents the need to break off the infantile ties with the parents, thus making new mature sexual relationships possible. From the perspective of the sociologist, however, more emphasis will be placed on the changes in role and status which lead to a re-definition of the individual's place in the social structure. Whatever the explanation it is certainly true that the achievement of independence is an integral feature of adolescent development, and that the role of the adults involved is an especially important one.

In understanding this process it is necessary to appreciate that the young person's movement toward adulthood is far from straightforward. As has been mentioned earlier, while independence at times appears to be a rewarding goal, there are also moments when it is a worrying, even frightening prospect. Childlike dependence can be safe and comforting at no matter what age, if, for example, one is facing problems or difficulties alone, and it is essential to realize that no individual achieves adult independence without a number of backward glances. It is this ambivalence which underlies the typically contradictory behaviour of adolescents, behaviour which is so often the despair of adults. Thus there is nothing adults find more frustrating than having to deal with a teenager who is at one moment complaining of having parents who are always interfering (for example, giving advice) and the next bitterly protesting that no-one takes any interest in him (for example, not giving advice). However, it is equally important to acknowledge that parents themselves usually hold conflicting attitudes towards their teenage children. On the one hand they may wish young people to be independent, to make their own decisions, and to cease making childish demands, whilst on the other, they may at the same time be frightened of the consequences of independence (especially the sexual consequences), and sometimes jealous of the opportunities and idealism of youth. In addition it should not be forgotten that the adolescent years often coincide with the difficulties of middle age for parents. Adjusting to unfulfilled hopes, preparation for retirement, declining physical health, marital difficulties and so on, may all increase family stress, and add further to the problems faced by young people in finding a route to independence which is not too fraught with conflict.

The question 'how much conflict?' is one which has intrigued and puzzled almost all who have attempted to understand the adolescent process, and it will be considered in this chapter as part of the more general issue of the so-called 'generation gap'. In addition a number of other common themes run through the literature, and in this chapter some attention will be paid to the topics of the exercise of power and decision-making within the family, to the part played by parents as role models, and finally to the adolescent's gradually changing attitudes to authority. It should be noted that the so-called 'parent-peer' issue, that is, the question of the relative influence of parents and peers upon young people, will be dealt with in chapter 6.

The 'generation gap'

The concept of a generation gap has a long history in psychology. It is also continuously popular with television, the press and other media for it has a certain sensational quality about it. In this respect it has strong affinities with other concepts such as 'storm and stress' and 'identity crisis'. There is no clear consensus as to the exact meaning of the phrase. For Bengtson (1970), for example, it simply refers to some form of conflict between the generations. A more fundamental divergence is portrayed by J. S. Coleman (1961), for whom the adolescent world represents a quite separate culture, isolated to a large extent from adults and possessing its own norms and values. Yet again a somewhat different emphasis is given by Adelson (1970) who, in an article entitled 'What generation gap?', put forward the view that those who believe in such a concept see the young as being in rebellion against parental authority, espousing left-wing and often revolutionary political views, and being at the opposite end of the spectrum from their parents where issues such as sexual behaviour and drug use are concerned. Whatever its definition, however, there are many who, for good reason, have serious doubts about the validity of the concept.

An article by Bandura (1972) may be taken as one example of this sceptical view. He argues that the whole notion of rebellion against parental authority is simply without any basis in reality. By drawing upon some evidence published a decade earlier (Bandura and Walters, 1959), he shows that the evidence from ordinary middle-class adolescents and their families reflects stability and co-operative mutually satisfying relationships rather than embattled hostility and disturbance. Bandura takes a number of propositions which stem from the concept of a generation gap and compares them with his own research findings. First, it might be supposed that during adolescence parents become more controlling and restrictive. However, exactly the opposite picture emerged from the interview data, with both parents and youngsters describing how, as they moved through adolescence, their relationships became easier as they became more able to trust each other. A second supposition concerns independence; it is suggested that adolescents are involved in a fundamental struggle to emancipate themselves from parental ties. Again Bandura and Walters found no support for this point of view. Bandura writes that in his estimation the establishment of independence from parents, rather than just beginning, has been more or less completed by the time the young person becomes adolescent. He goes on to say that in his sample the autonomy of the adolescent seemed to pose more of a problem for the parent than for the teenager; many fathers, for example, regretting the companionship they had lost. Finally Bandura considers conformity to peer group values, and here again finds little evidence to support the traditional view. The adolescents whom he interviewed appeared to be discriminating and selective in their choice of reference groups, and there were few signs of 'slavish conformity'. In general, peer group values did not appear to be in direct opposition to family values, nor did it appear that membership of a peer group generated family conflict.

Douvan and Adelson, in their book *The Adolescent Experience* (1966), provide further support for this view. They reported the results of interviews with over 3,000 teenagers across the USA. The results indicated a general picture of minor conflicts between parent and adolescent, focusing especially on issues such as make-up, dating, leisure activities, music and so on. As far as major values were concerned, however, very little difference emerged. On issues of morality, political or religious beliefs and sexual attitudes, the divergence of opinion was minimal. In fact the vast majority of teenagers, far from despising or rejecting their parents, actually looked up to them and valued their advice.

Studies carried out in the UK and Europe portray a very similar picture. In Fogelman's (1976) report of the work carried out by the National Children's Bureau, entitled *Britain's Sixteen-Year-Olds*, findings on relationships within the family corroborate all that has been said so far. In this study the parents were given a list of issues on which it is commonly thought adults and young people of this age might disagree. The results indicated a situation which was, from the parents' point of view, a harmonious one. The two most commonly reported areas of disagreement – dress or hairstyle, and the time of coming in at night – are what might be expected, but even here only 10 per cent of parents said that they often disagreed about these things. The views of the parents are illustrated in table 5.1.

The young people confirmed the attitudes of their mothers and fathers. They agreed that appearance and evening activities were sometimes an issue of disagreement in the home, but otherwise they reported an atmosphere free from major conflict. It is of interest to note that about two thirds of those with brothers and sisters said they quarrelled between themselves, yet 'many wrote a qualifying note to the effect that although they might often quarrel with a brother or sister, or disagree with their parents, this did not mean there was anything wrong with the underlying relationship' (1976, p. 36). Family relationships as seen by the teenagers in this very large sample of over eleven thousand individuals are illustrated in table 5.2.

The work of Rutter and colleagues (1976) – work we shall have occasion to refer to in more detail in chapter 8 – should also be mentioned in this context. In this wide-ranging survey of all fourteen-year-olds on the Isle of Wight, parents, teachers and young people themselves were extensively interviewed. As one aspect of the

Table 5.1   Disagreement between parents and study child (parent's report)
(N = 11,531)

	Often	Sometimes	Never or hardly ever
	%	%	%
Choice of friends of the same sex	3	16	81
Choice of friends of the opposite sex	2	9	89
Dress or hairstyle	11	35	54
Time of coming in at night or going to bed	8	26	66
Places gone to in own time	2	9	89
Doing homework	6	18	76
Smoking	6	9	85
Drinking	1	5	94

(From K. Fogelman (1976) *Britain's Sixteen-Year-Olds*, National Children's Bureau.)

study Rutter examined the degree of alienation between the generations as experienced either by the adolescents or by their parents. The results showed that in only 4 per cent of the total group did the parents feel an increase in alienation at this stage of adolescence, while amongst the young people themselves only 5 per cent reported actual rejection of their parents. A further 25 per cent expressed some degree of criticism.

The general picture is thus emerging of a relatively harmonious situation at home for the majority of young people today. However, adolescents do 'seek to be independent', of that there is no dispute, and so the question arises as to how common sense and research evidence can be fitted together. In the first place, it is clear that some adolescents do, temporarily at least, come into conflict with or become critical of their parents. In addition, there is no doubt that some parents do become restrictive, attempting to slow down the pace of change. Research has shown that there are a number of factors which affect the extent of the conflict occurring in the home. Thus, for example, Lesser and Kandel (1969), in their study of parent and adolescent relationships in Denmark and the USA, demonstrated that while there was no evidence to support the existence of a

Table 5.2   Family relationships (children's report) (N = 11,045)

	Very true %	True %	Uncertain %	Untrue %	Very untrue %
I get on well with my mother	41	45	8	4	1
I get on well with my father	35	45	13	5	2
I often quarrel with a brother or sister	23	43	10	19	5
My parents have strong views about my appearance (e.g. dress, hairstyle, etc.)	15	33	19	27	6
My parents want to know where I go in the evening	27	51	8	11	3
My parents disapprove of some of my male friends	9	19	18	37	16
My parents disapprove of some of my female friends	5	15	18	40	22

(From K. Fogelman (1976) *Britain's Sixteen-Year-Olds*, National Children's Bureau.)

generation gap in either country, there were big differences in the way the issue of independence was handled in the two countries. Adolescents in the USA appeared to be given less independence by their parents, and to feel that where disagreements existed they had less room to act independently than their Danish counterparts. Naturally, such feelings bear directly on the amount of conflict experienced by parents and young people.

A further important variable is age. Here the author's own work is relevant, for in the large-scale study of adolescents between the ages of eleven and seventeen already referred to in the previous chapter (Coleman, 1974), the results make it apparent that young people's feelings of conflict increase as a function of age, but reach a peak at different stages for boys and girls. As was pointed out earlier it is also important to recognize that the focus of conflict is likely to be different for the two sexes. The results pertaining to age differences are illustrated in figure 5.1.

A recent study by Smith (1978) draws attention to a further

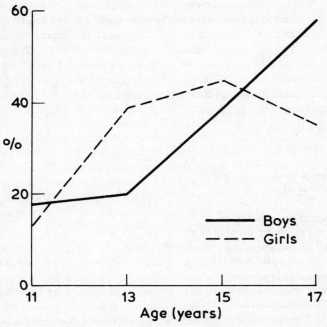

Figure 5.1   Proportions of each age group expressing themes of conflict with parents on one item of a sentence-completion test.
(From J. C. Coleman (1974) *Relationships in Adolescence*, Routledge & Kegan Paul.)

relevant variable, that of social class. He interviewed parents of sixteen-year-olds in Britain, and asked for their views of this age group. He found that middle-class parents expressed much more favourable views than working-class parents. For example, while 31 per cent of working-class parents were unfavourably inclined towards this age group only 18 per cent of middle-class parents responded in this way. The adults in the study were also asked whether a number of statements could, in their opinion, be applied to all, most, some, a few, or none of the teenagers they knew. The working-class group contained a much higher proportion of people who related highly deviant items to most or all teenagers. Thus drink was mentioned by 14 per cent, sex by 14 per cent, drugs by 5 per cent, political demonstrations by 3.5 per cent and violence by 4 per cent. The middle-class respondents, on the other hand, contained a much higher proportion who saw most or all teenagers as considerate to others (43 per cent) and bright and interesting (60 per cent). As Smith says: 'Whilst I am not suggesting that more than a small proportion of working-class respondents see teenagers as being typified by grossly deviant activities, the pattern which emerges does seem to show a distinctly more negative response on behalf of the working class' (1978, p. 149).

Findings such as these serve to remind us that attitudes between the generations involve a two-way process, and there have been some suggestions in the literature that adults are more negative towards young people than the other way around. Musgrove (1964), for example, found in his study of inter-generation attitudes in England that adolescents showed themselves to be better disposed towards adults than adults were disposed towards them. He reported that it was more common for adults to express disapproval of young people than for the opposite to occur. Eppel and Eppel, in their study of adolescent morality (1966), drew attention to a similar possibility. In summarizing their work they write:

> The picture that has emerged of this group of young working people (15–17 years of age) is that most of them regard themselves as belonging to a generation handicapped by distorted stereotypes about their behaviour and moral standards. Many feel this so acutely that they believe whatever goodwill they manifest is at best not likely to be much appreciated and at worst may be misinterpreted to their disadvantage. The view was repeatedly expressed or implied that the behaviour of a delinquent or anti-social fringe had unfortunately been extended to characterize their whole generation. (p. 213)

The interview material at the end of this chapter indicates that such feelings are very much part of today's social climate, but it is important not to lay too much stress on this issue. As we have seen the results of Fogelman's (1976) study show that adults are generally positive in their attitudes, certainly towards their own teenage children, and many other studies have corroborated this. To take one further example, the author and colleagues (Coleman et al. 1977), in a study of the attitudes of working-class parents and teenagers to each other, showed that while both generations agreed that young people were more noisy and untidy than adults, both generations also agreed that there was relatively little difference between them where more fundamental personality attributes such as honesty and perseverance were concerned. If anything, these results showed that young people evaluated adults more highly than adults evaluated themselves, but that both generations perceived young people in much the same way.

How, it may be asked, can all these findings be fitted into a coherent picture? Perhaps the first thing to say is that while on the one hand the notion of a full-scale generation gap is obviously not sustained by the research evidence, on the other hand it cannot simply be dismissed as a complete fiction. One important reason for the confusion which exists lies in the difference between attitudes towards close family members, and attitudes to more general social groupings, such as 'the younger generation'. Thus, for example, teenagers may very well approve and look up to their own parents while expressing criticism of adults in general. Similarly, parents may deride 'hippies', 'drop-outs' or 'soccer hooligans' while holding a favourable view of their own adolescent sons and daughters. Another fact that needs to be stressed is that there is a difference between feeling and behaviour. Adolescents may be irritated or angry with their parents as a result of day-to-day conflicts, but issues can be worked out in the home, and do not necessarily lead to outright rejection or rebellion. Furthermore, as Conger (1977) points out, too little credit is given to the possibility that adults and young people, although disagreeing with each other about certain things, may still respect each other's views, and live in relative harmony together under the same roof. Thus there seems to be little doubt that the extreme view of the generation gap, involving the notion of a war between the generations, or the idea of a separate adolescent subculture, is dependent on a myth. It is the result of a stereotype which is useful to the mass media, and given currency by a small minority of disaffected young people and resentful adults. However, to deny any sort of conflict between teenagers and older members of society is equally false. Adolescents could not grow into adults unless they were able to test out the boundaries of authority, nor could they discover what they believed unless given the opportunity to push hard against the beliefs of others. The adolescent transition from dependence to independence is almost certain to involve some conflict, but its extent should not be exaggerated.

The exercise of power and decision making within the family

The decline of adult authority over the last twenty years or so has been a recurrent theme among writers concerned with adolescent development. In discussing this phenomenon and in searching for causes most point to the complex and far reaching changes which have occurred within our society as a result of political and social transition. Changes in the political scene may be related to specific events, such as the effect of the Vietnam war on American youth, or they may be connected with more general issues, such as the increasing awareness of corruption among elected politicians, the inability of the welfare state to combat poverty, and the failure of governments to cope with the diminishing resources of the world. Social changes include the decline of organized religion, increasing automation at work, poor employment prospects for many young people, and so on. In 1960 President J. F. Kennedy spoke of a 'new age' and a 'new frontier', for at that time there was a spirit of optimism running through industrial societies. Now, twenty years later, young people sense that their parents do not have the answers; they are aware that there are no ready solutions to the major problems which their elders face – over-population, the nuclear arms race, pollution and so on – and they therefore cannot accord an older generation the respect which it once held. Diana Baumrind puts it well when she says: 'The major challenge to authority today is not that the young have no respect for authority, but that they have little reason to have respect for authority' (1968, p. 269).

One danger in the expression of this view, that adult authority has declined markedly over the last two decades, is the related assumption that therefore adults have a relatively limited role to play in their dealings with young people. Such a belief could not, of course, be further from the truth, for in a situation where the values of society are in flux adolescents will be more rather than less in need of guidance and direction. As John Conger says: 'The real question is not whether parental models are any longer important; rather it is what kind of parental models are necessary and appropriate in preparing contemporary adolescents to deal with the largely unpredictable world of tomorrow' (1977, p. 221).

It is towards this question – which sorts of parental models will be most adaptive in the present situation – that the research of Elder (1963), Baumrind (1968) and Bowerman and Bahr (1973) has been directed. In the first study Elder differentiated three types of parental control – autocratic control, in which parents generally told adolescents what to do, democratic control, in which the adolescent participated in decision making but did not have the final word, and permissive control, where the young person could make up his own mind. These levels of control were then correlated with items indicating confidence in ability to make wise decisions, and the tendency to make decisions with or without prior consideration of advice from others. Among both boys and girls the level of parental control was directly related to a tendency to let others make decisions; a feeling of confidence in self-direction was most prevalent amongst youngsters with democratic parents, and least common amongst those who had no voice in making their own decisions. Further results of the study demonstrated that within each model parents who tried to make the exercise of parental power 'legitimate' in their children's eyes through the use of frequent explanations of their conduct were more likely to facilitate optimal development. However, frequency of explanation undoubtedly had its greatest effect among families where parents were either permissive or autocratic. Among democratic families, where communication and relationships were already good, explanations had relatively less effect. Thus the study indicates that adolescents who are provided with experience in decision making under parental supervision, and who receive explanations from parents, are most likely to be independent, to want to be like their parents, and to mix with friends who are approved by their parents. As Elder says, in a later article: 'By maximizing parent-adolescent interaction, increasing trust and the legitimacy of rules, and providing experience in self-reliance, this type of relationship provides a facilitative environment for acquiring autonomy and learning adult standards of behaviour' (1968, p. 286).

In Baumrind's (1968) study much the same distinction is made between types of parental control. However, instead of using the word 'democratic' Baumrind prefers the term 'authoritative', for this allows her to contrast such a model with that of the 'authoritarian' parent. She argues that while the authoritarian parent 'attempts to shape, control and evaluate the behaviour of the child in accordance with a set standard of conduct', the authoritative one values and encourages the development of autonomous self-will. However, unlike the permissive or neglectful parent he or she also values the assumption of responsibility and the internalization of personal discipline. The key, therefore, in Baumrind's view is the simultaneous encouragement of autonomy and responsibility – characteristics of behaviour which in other models of parenting are valued singly, but not in combination. Thus, for example, the permissive parent would undoubtedly encourage autonomy, but would not at the same time value the taking of responsibility within the family.

Finally, the work of Bowerman and Bahr (1973) may be mentioned. In their study they concentrated on the nature of conjugal power, that is the way in which parents of teenage children shared power between them, and they differentiated three possible family structures – patriarchal, matriarchal and equalitarian. They then examined the degree of identification between adolescents and their parents in these three situations, and showed clearly that, as might be expected, young people were most likely to look up to their parents and to want to be like them in families where power was shared equally between mother and father. Furthermore, the results showed that when one parent was perceived as having less influence within the family than the other, irrespective of whether the pattern was matriarchal or patriarchal, the adolescents identified less with both parents. Finally, while identification with mother appeared to differ little if she was more or less influential, identification with father was significantly lower when he was perceived as the less powerful of the two. These findings apply to both sexes, but are most marked among girls.

It will be apparent that all three studies provide much the same answer to the question: 'What is the most appropriate model for parents to follow in interaction with their teenage children?' In spite of today's rapidly changing fashions and uncertain values adolescents do not respond well to a permissive family environment, in which they are left to get on with their own lives and make their own decisions. On the other hand, it is clear that an authoritarian use of power in the family is equally inappropriate. Adolescents need direction, but most of all they need to have the opportunity of observing and living with parents who share power and influence, as well as the possibility of learning to play a part as a responsible member in the family decision making process.

Parents as role models

Parents fulfil many different functions for the developing adolescent, and one of these functions relates to the provision of what are known as role models. Here the parents represent examples of the ways in which such things as sex roles and work roles may be interpreted, providing prototypes against which the young person will evaluate other interpretations of these roles. It is of course true that children throughout their early lives depend on their parents for primary knowledge of such role behaviour, but obviously these models become crucial during adolescence, since it is at this time that the young person begins to make his or her own role choices. Thus, for example, while both parents' attitudes to work will be pertinent all through childhood, these will become relevant in a somewhat different and more immediate way when the teenager is facing questions about what he or she is going to do after leaving school. As we have seen in chapter 1, role change is likely to be a major feature of adolescent development, and it will be evident, therefore, that the role models available to the young person at this stage in life will be of great significance.

It is important to be clear, however, that the likelihood of role

decisions or choices being influenced by the parents will be determined not only by the nature of the role model, but also by the degree
of identification between parent and child. The topic of identification is a large one, and will not be dealt with in any depth here.
Interested readers may refer to Conger (1977). Suffice it to say that
the degree of identification, that is, the extent to which the young
person incorporates as his or her own the attitudes and characteristics belonging to another person, will depend on a number of factors.
Among these the degree of warmth and affection experienced by the
child in the relationship with the parents will undoubtedly be of
central importance. An additional factor, as we have seen in the
previous section, will be the structure of the family, and the child's
involvement in decision making processes. Thus it will be apparent
that in considering parents as role models we cannot ignore the
question of identification. It is this characteristic of the relationship
which determines the final impact of parents as models, as will
become clear when examining some of the evidence which has
accumulated on this topic. Before we do so, however, it should be
noted that virtually all the studies to be mentioned have been carried
out in the USA. There is, unfortunately, a dearth of European evidence in this area, and thus caution should be exercised in drawing
general conclusions from the research findings.

Let us first of all turn our attention to the development of sex roles,
a topic already considered in some detail in the previous chapter. As
far as boys are concerned research has indicated that adolescents
whose fathers provide a moderately masculine role model, but who
are also involved in the feminine caring side of family life, adjust
better as adults and experience fewer conflicts between their social
values and their actual behaviour. Boys whose fathers provide role
models which are at either extreme – excessively masculine or predominantly feminine – appear to adjust less well. To take one
example from the experimental literature, the studies by Mussen and
others (Mussen, 1962; Mussen et al., 1963, 1974) have shown that
although during adolescence those boys with strong masculine role
models and stereotyped masculine behaviour seem to be the best
adjusted – to be the most popular, to have high self-esteem and so on
– when followed up ten years later they appeared to do less well in
adulthood than men who during adolescence had more ambivalent
role models and more 'feminine' interests. Thus it would seem that
for boys at least a rigid adherence to stereotyped sex-role behaviour
may be adaptive in adolescence but not so helpful in adjustment to
the demands of adult life.

If sex-role development is complicated for boys, it is certainly just as problematic for girls. There are at least three reasons for this. First, sex roles are usually less clear for girls than they are for boys; second, in many circumstances higher status is accorded to masculine roles, so that girls may face confusion as to which is more preferable; and third, women's position in society is at present passing through a period of rapid change, making it even more difficult for adolescent girls to make personal choices in line with what is or is not expected of them. In Conger's (1977) view, based on research findings, it is perfectly possible for girls, no matter whether they are identified with a mother who is 'traditional' and 'feminine' or with one who is more liberal, independent and socially assertive, to adjust well as women themselves. The important point is that they do have someone positive with whom to identify, someone who has resolved her own problems of sexual identification. It appears to be those whose sex-role behaviour is based on rejection of a not very loving mother, or on identification with a mother who has herself failed to resolve her own identity problem, who have difficulties in adjustment.

Such a formulation is supported by the research of Douvan and Adelson (1966). In their large-scale investigation of 3,000 girls across the USA they described three patterns of sex-role development. Girls with a strong and straightforward feminine sex-role identification identified strongly with their mothers, with whom, by and large, they had close relationships. Of all the groups analysed this group most often chose their mothers or some other female relative as an ideal adult. These girls were compliant in the home, and clearly obtained considerable satisfaction from the feminine role. At the opposite extreme girls with strong anti-feminine identifications were least likely to choose women at all as ideal adults. Girls in this group described poor relations at home, restrictive attitudes on the part of their parents, and strong feelings of resentment towards their mothers. Falling between these two groups was a third category, those girls who, although strongly feminine, could and did recognize attractions in the traditional masculine role. As in the case of the first group, girls of this type appeared to be modelling themselves after parents with whom they had close positive relationships. Mothers of girls in this group, however, were likely to be ambitious, highly educated and working outside the home. They encouraged their daughters towards independence, more so than the traditional feminine group, and allowed them a much greater share in decision making within the family. As Conger points out, these studies, along with many others, underline the advantages of growing up in a caring family where the same sex parent represents a workable and rewarding role model. Within the framework of a relatively healthy family both boys and girls whose parents are moderately flexible in their own sex roles appear to be more secure and relaxed in the development of their personal identity.

As far as parents as work role models are concerned very much less evidence is available. In general many of the same things must apply. Close positive relationships are most likely to facilitate the use of the parent as a work role model, although this does not necessarily mean taking the same type of job as the mother or father. Much more important here are the transmission of attitudes to work, and the general area of work interest. Thus the boy whose father is a doctor does not himself need to go into medicine to have seen in his father a positive role model. More important will be a job which requires further education, which has a high professional standing, and which may in some way involve caring for others. In one interesting study by Bell (1969), the effects of father as role model at the ages of seventeen and twenty-seven were investigated. Results showed that those adolescent boys whose fathers acted as the most positive (i.e. highly evaluated) role models at seventeen were likely to adjust best in their future careers. However, interestingly those who, at twenty-seven, still saw fathers as the most positive role models were not likely to be functioning as well in their jobs as those who had, by this time in their careers, sought other non-family role models. In a slightly different study by Baruch (1972), women's attitudes to work were assessed as a function of their own mother's attitudes and experiences. Here results showed that women between the ages of nineteen and twenty-two held attitudes towards work, towards feminine competence (i.e. the ability to hold down a job), and towards the dual career pattern (the combination of motherhood and a career) which resulted directly from their mother's experiences and beliefs. Women whose mothers had not worked devalued feminine competence, and whether a woman was favourable towards the dual career pattern depended directly on whether her mother supported it or not, and if she worked, whether she believed she had suffered as a result of so doing. Thus in different ways both Bell and Baruch indicate how parents play a critical part as role models where work adjustment is concerned. More studies of this sort are badly needed, but the significance of those already carried out cannot be ignored.

Lastly in this section we can learn something of the function of parents by glancing briefly at the studies of the effects of parental absence. In this area once again research is more readily available in the case of boys. Thus there is an accumulation of evidence to show that boys from father-absent homes are more likely than those who have fathers living at home to encounter difficulties in a wide variety of areas (Conger, 1977). They are, for example, more likely to score lower on traditional intelligence tests, perform less well at school, and to be less popular in their social group. Interestingly, their intellectual performance differs significantly from that of other boys, in that they are more likely to obtain higher scores in tests measuring verbal ability than in those concerned with mathematics. Such a picture is in direct contrast to the usual male pattern of better performance in mathematics, and closely resembles the typical female pattern of intellectual functioning (Carlsmith, 1964). Furthermore, as is probably well known, boys from father-absent homes are more likely to drop out of school, to be impulsive in their behaviour, and to become involved in activities such as delinquency, which carries with it an aura of exaggerated toughness and masculinity. It should be noted, however, that the incidence of these difficulties, especially delinquency, is closely related to a number of other factors, such as the reason for father's absence (i.e. death or divorce), the nature of the relationship between father and son where divorce or separation has occurred, as well as more general variables such as social class. In spite of this, however, it will be clear that almost all of these differences between boys with and without fathers in the home may be seen to be directly related to the absence of an appropriate role model.

While there have been many fewer studies with girls, much the same conclusions may also be drawn here. The work of Hetherington (1972) provides an excellent example. In an elaborate study, which included observations of teenage girls between the ages of thirteen and seventeen in a community recreation centre, interviews with the girls, and their mothers, as well as the administration of various personality tests, she was able to show only too clearly the effects of paternal absence on the behaviour of these girls. According to Hetherington, these were, 'manifested mainly in an inability to interact appropriately with males'. In particular the daughters of divorcees spent a large proportion of their time seeking out male company and engaging in sex-related behaviour. While on interview these girls showed no lack of preference for the female role, they were rarely observed in typical female activities. This was explained by the fact that they simply spent so much of their time hanging around the areas where male activities were carried out, such as the carpentry shop, basketball court and so on. In contrast to this group, daughters of widowed women appeared much more likely to avoid contact with male peers. These girls tended to be inhibited and lacking in confidence, and thus to manifest behaviour which was exactly the opposite of that observed in daughters of divorced parents. As Hetherington says: 'it is argued that both groups of girls were manifesting deviant behaviours in attempting to cope with their anxiety and lack of skills in relating to males' (p. 324). Some of these findings are illustrated in table 5.3.

Table 5.3   Means for daughter interview measures

Interview variable	Father absent		Father present	F	P
	Divorced	Death			
Security around male peers	2.71	2.62	3.79	4.79	.010
Security around male adults	2.12	2.12	3.66	11.25	.001
Heterosexual activity	4.83	2.62	3.83	12.96	.001
Conflict with mothers	5.08	3.63	4.08	5.64	.005
Positive attitude toward father	3.08	4.66	4.21	7.57	.001
Father's warmth	3.33	4.50	3.87	2.82	.060
Father's competence	3.16	4.75	4.12	6.65	.002
Conflict with father	4.43	2.25	3.46	7.03	.002
Relations with other adult males	3.29	3.12	4.54	5.08	.009
Self-esteem	2.87	3.58	4.04	3.34	.040

(From E. M. Hetherington (1972) *Developmental Psychology*, 7.)

In summary we have seen that, at least based on American evidence, the function of parents as role models during adolescence is a surprisingly significant one. It is undoubtedly a popular assumption that, all things being equal, parents have a more important part to play during childhood than during adolescence. Our brief review indicates that this is far from the truth. At a time when role models are necessary to a far greater extent than ever before, it is upon parents above all that adolescents depend for knowledge and example. On their interpretation of such things as work and sex roles will be based the adolescent's adjustment to the choices with which he or she will be faced.

Attitudes to authority

Changing attitudes to authority are an integral feature of the achievement of independence, and must inevitably form one part of the process of adolescent development. While in the literature this is a topic which has received scant attention, it would seem obvious that the transition within an individual from a stage in which authority is accepted to one in which it can be questioned, challenged, and if necessary rejected, must be both a fascinating and important one, especially in view of the decline in adult authority which has been discussed earlier. Clearly, a number of factors will play their part in such a process. Adults will exercise their authority in different ways, so for example, as we have seen, some will attempt to make it legitimate by providing explanations and some will not. Some will wish to share their power with young people at an early stage, while others will keep it to themselves for as long as possible. In addition, adolescents will inevitably meet with a wide range of authority figures, and will experience many different uses of power and influence. They will perceive some as more justifiable than others, and will have different expectations and make different demands on the varying authority figures with whom they will come into contact. None the less a major change will occur at some period between early and late adolescence, a change involving a fundamental reorientation of attitudes towards authority, and it is at this change that we shall now look.

In one of the earlier studies on the subject Tuma and Livson (1960) developed a 'conformity scale', making it possible for them to rank individual adolescents on the degree to which they accepted authority. The five-point scale was as follows:

5   Hectic drive to conform.

4   Real urge to conform, to be accepted, to avoid friction, etc.

3   Occasional assertions of individuality but for the most part accepts regulations, rules, social standards without much wear and tear.

2   Individual tries to sidestep rules and regulations and to avoid conformity. Passive resistance or avoidance of situations where rules or regulations would have to be met.

1   Extremely resistive to rules, regulations and authority. Extreme individualism and non-conformity.

The study itself was a very small one, involving only forty-seven subjects, but it had the advantage of being longitudinal, rating the adolescents for conformity at three ages (fourteen, fifteen and six-teen) in situations at home, at school, and with their peers. Findings showed that conformity was lowest in the home, and greatest in peer group situations, and that, for boys at least, there was a close association between conformity and social class, conformity being greatest among middle-class teenagers. In addition, conformity scores for this group changed very little between the ages of fourteen and sixteen. There was also great similarity between boys and girls, the only significant difference being that at sixteen girls were more conforming than boys in peer group situations.

At first sight these results appear to be in direct contradiction to the contention that attitudes to authority undergo a marked change as a function of age during adolescence. However, let us now look at a rather different piece of evidence. In the author's own work (Cole-man, 1974), a sentence-completion test was given at four age levels – eleven, thirteen, fifteen and seventeen. One sentence stem in this test read as follows: 'If someone gives orders to a group. . . .' Responses were classified according to whether the individual expressed a desire to conform (for example, 'If someone gives orders to a group everyone thinks he will obey') or whether some challenge to authority was implied (for example, 'If someone gives orders to a group he is a very conceited and selfish person'). Results are illustrated in figure 5.2, and indicate that a change in attitude does occur within this age range, but that this applies primarily to the younger age groups. Thus it may be that the results of the Tuma and Livson study are not inconsistent, but simply reflect attitudes to authority in an age span where the major re-orientation has already occurred. However, it should be noted that these studies have major limitations, the first because of the small numbers involved, and the second because we have extrapolated results from only one item of a wide-ranging set of tests. Findings such as these should be treated as pointers, but pointers in an important direction none the less.

The study by Douvan and Adelson (1966), also mentioned pre-viously, is another which includes at least some reference to author-ity. In this case a distinction was drawn between three types of discipline used in the home: physical, psychological (based primarily on verbal admonition) and deprivation (involving the loss of free-dom, mobility, finance, etc.) – and these were related to the adoles-cent's attitude to authority. Girls were shown to be most compliant where physical punishment was in use, and least conforming with psychological types of punishment. Boys, however, while manifest-ing a similar pattern, showed two further important characteristics which did not apply in the case of the girls. Boys who were physically

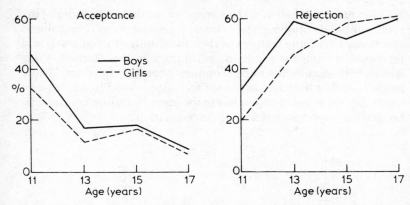

Figure 5.2   Proportions of each age group expressing acceptance and rejection of authority on one item of a sentence-completion test.
(From J. C. Coleman (1974) *Relationships in Adolescence*, Routledge & Kegan Paul.)

punished showed a striking resentment of their parents at the same time as being dependent and submissive, and, in addition, appeared under-developed in regard to social behaviour and the internalization of controls. Douvan and Adelson constructed an index indicating the degree of internalized morality. One of the items composing the index was: 'When might a boy break a rule?' Results showed interesting differences between the groups, for those who had been physically punished were most likely to give as examples situations when for some reason authority was not present, while those in the deprivation and psychological punishment groups gave examples of emergencies, accidents and outright rebellion. Clearly, in considering attitudes to authority in adolescence, age and social class are not the only factors to be taken into account, but, as other research reviewed has also shown, the family context is crucial.

Finally, reference may be made to a study carried out by the author in collaboration with Eva Zajicek (1980). This study involved working-class teenagers in an urban environment, and addressed itself to a number of questions, among which were the issues of what young people expected of ideal authority figures, and how these young people felt conflicts between themselves and adults ought to be resolved. In relation to the first question we were keen to look specifically at the issue of how much autonomy adolescents seek in their relationships with adults. The teenagers who took part in the study were between the ages of fourteen and sixteen and the results are illustrated in figure 5.3. Data are given for the proportions of the total sample mentioning three dimensions – support, control and autonomy – as being features of their ideal authority figures. It will be apparent from the results that, contrary to expectations, these adolescents seem hardly to be clamouring for their freedom. Where mothers and fathers are concerned teenagers would like at least as much control as autonomy, while in the school situation control is of far greater importance than self-determination.

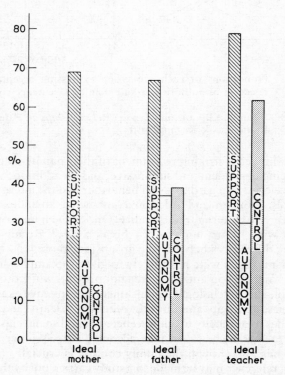

Figure 5.3   Proportions of young people mentioning three dimensions as aspects of their ideal authority figures.
(From J. C. Coleman and E. Zajicek (1980) *Adolescence*, in press.)

This finding is amplified somewhat by the other results of the study – those relating to the adolescent's preferred solution to conflict. In line with Elder's (1963) work we differentiated three types of resolution – democratic, authoritarian and permissive – and asked the adolescents which type they thought most appropriate in conflicts they experienced at home and in school. The results are illustrated in figure 5.4, and show that while young people appear to feel that they can and would like to be involved in the resolution of conflicts in the home, in the school situation there are many more issues requiring adult intervention.

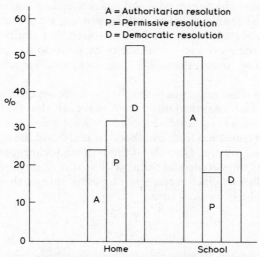

A = Authoritarian resolution
P = Permissive resolution
D = Democratic resolution

Figure 5.4   A comparison of preferred resolutions to conflicts at home and at school.
(From J. C. Coleman and E. Zajicek (1980) *Adolescence*, in press.)

One of the obvious reasons for this difference is the context in which power is exercised. In school it is, by and large, control over others which is at issue, since the conflicts mentioned in this study were almost all to do with delinquent and disruptive behaviour. While the adolescents in this sample wished to have a say in their own activities, they were concerned about the disruptive behaviour of their peers and saw a need for effective authority to control this. In the much smaller family group, however, young people saw them-selves as participants in the exercise of power, and here they had a much greater sense of their own ability to contribute in a responsible way to the decision-making process.

To summarize, it will be apparent that there is still much to be learnt about changing concepts of authority in adolescence. No-one doubts that fundamental changes do occur, but what little evidence there is hints that the most radical of these shifts in attitude may take place at an earlier stage than has previously been assumed. Yet, if this is so, adolescent behaviour still appears to reflect a process of change as late as seventeen, eighteen or nineteen, so that a more thorough understanding of the whole issue of authority in adolescence is urgently needed. That the issue is of importance is amply demonstrated by the evidence reviewed in this chapter. In particular it has been noted that sharing power and influence, and learning to be involved in the family decision making process are essential ingredients for social maturation; we have also seen that adults who seek to legitimize their exercise of authority by providing explanations are more likely to be effective in their relationships with young people.

Apart from these results perhaps the most important findings are those which show that the family context is critical not only for the provision of work- and sex-role models, but for the whole course of the adolescent transition from childhood to adulthood. Thus, contrary to popular assumption, the role of the parents for teenagers seems likely to be as important and influential as it is during early childhood, a conclusion which receives strong support from the interview material to which we now turn.

Interview

Two questions were asked in the interview which are relevant to the topics we have been considering in this chapter. Firstly:

> Obviously parents are very important for adolescents – what do you think are the most important things parents ought to provide?

Elizabeth (17 years): I think it's a liberal attitude really. I think that's one of the most important things. I think parents should bring the children up the way that they're used to, but also show them the choices that there are. I think in the most simple cases where a child is doing wrong the parent will say 'Don't do that', but I think what should be said more is 'Don't do that because this and this will happen.' I think this is sometimes forgotten when bringing up kids.

Jill (16 years): Advice, good home background, and to know that you can go and talk to your Mum and Dad, which I can. I don't tell them everything you know, but any problems at school I go and discuss with them. I mean they don't say: 'You've got to do this and you've got to do that.' They just say, especially my dad, 'Well, you know, we can do this, or we can do that, it's up to you.' So you know, it's advice really, because I mean they are older, and have probably been through what you're going through at that minute.

Karen (15 years): Knowledge of fellers and sex and problems. Just to sort of equip you for the big bad world outside. Also, you know comfort, because its a cruel world at the moment, isn't it, especially at the moment? Understanding really, they've got to try to understand you.

Richard (15 years): They should provide obviously food and board, but I don't think they should say to you all the time – well, my parents don't – but they say to you 'I'm looking after you and I give you clothes and all that.' because its their bound (*sic*) duty as parents that they should look after you, and they should really respect you a bit more. They should bear with you a bit if you like, and they should accept a bit more the things you like when you are young. They should accept it a bit more and put themselves in your place when, you know, they were your age.

Henry (16 years): Thoughtfulness really. My parents are not at all like that, that's one thing. For instance they're forever shouting and things like that, you know what I mean, and my Dad hasn't sort of helped me out for ages. My Dad will help me so long as its just sitting in a chair and not moving out. He'll occasionally take me to the pictures, but you don't want to keep going to the pictures. Like I want to go the the Custom Car Show, but he won't take me, you know what I mean. Perhaps when I was younger, about eight or nine, he used to take me out, but he don't now, not for about the past six years.

It's taking an interest – yeah. Like for instance when it comes to education. I don't like asking me Mum for money, I like to try and get me own, but I need a folder – since Monday I been having a go at her about a folder, and I said 'Give me the money to get it.' But she says 'No, I'll get it.' You know I don't think she realizes, you know, that I really need it. I think it's because they were never at school much, you know what I mean?

Adam (17 years): Security I would say. It's good for somebody to feel secure, and loved by their parents, and to have someone to fall back on if they've got troubles. Its always good to have someone to talk to if you've got something on your mind.

The second question concerned the generation gap, and ran as follows:

A phrase that is often used when talking about teenagers is the 'generation gap'. Do you know what is meant by that? Do you think there is any truth in it?

Karen (15 years): Well I'm all for equal rights. I don't know exactly what you're asking, but I'll say what I think. I'm always sort of going on at my parents, sort of saying that we've got equal rights to them, and they have really got no right to tell us what to do. O.K., we are under sixteen etc., etc., but. . . . We get a lot of say in our house, and, you know, it is really sort of democratic. We are sort of really a democratic family and I really hate it when my parents say 'Do this' and you've got to do it and you've got no say in the matter. You're like a robot doing things that other people tell you and you've got no choice. We've often talked about it and its definitely wrong – but then there's got to be a limit.

Elizabeth (17 years): Yes, to a certain extent I do because at adolescence, there's a stage where even if the children know that what the parents are saying is right, I think that there's something rebellious inside them that makes them sort of want to go astray from that. I think that's where it all sort of stems, and both are very strongminded – the parents in bringing the children up the way they think is right, and the children rebelling against that absolutely.

Sarah (16 years): Yes, I think so, because the old people they seem to have a backward opinion of what we think. You know, like they always say 'I didn't do that in my days', but they just don't realize that they did do such things. You know, maybe it wasn't exactly the same, but they did step out of line you know, some time or another, and they just don't think that we should do it today. You know, so they've had their time, and they don't wish us to have ours.

Jill (16 years): Oh, I don't know, because I can never really decide what the 'generation gap' is. I know it's, you know, me and me parents, but I don't find there's any gap there. You know, I get on well with me Mum and Dad. But then could you say me aunty who is twenty-four is a generation gap away from me? I find that it's hard to define a generation – I seem to get on with everybody O.K.

Valerie (17 years): Yes, well, you sort of get on a bus and there's all these parents sitting there and going 'Tut! tut! tut!' just because you're wearing a pair of jeans and got long hair and things. You can hear them all just sort of think . . . 'Oh, just because she's like that. . . .' You know they've seen somebody like that doing something wrong and they think everybody's like that.

Henry (16 years): Oh yeah, there is a lot. I mean, I don't know, just silly things like I can remember a kid, he was walking along the road singing, not loud, just like me mates and I am I suppose, imitating the pop stars, and this woman comes along and goes 'Disgusting'. It wasn't loud, or anything like that – just singing. I don't know, perhaps because she was old and that, but she wasn't exactly some old woman of eighty, you know, she was sixty perhaps. You find a lot of people like that really.

Kevin (15 years): Well people are always saying all these things about all these young long-haired layabouts, always getting into fights and things like that, gangs of them going around. But it just hasn't happened at the time you know, it's been going on for years. But people always emphasize, you know, it's the youngsters of today – the youth of today.

6
Friendship and
the peer group

Friends, companions and peers are generally considered to play an especially important role in the development of the young person during adolescence. There are a number of reasons underlying this assumption, some of which we have already touched on in our review of theory in chapter 1. In the first place, the process of disengagement from parents and from the family setting, a process which is considered to be an integral feature of adolescence, leaves an emotional gap in the lives of young people. This gap has to be filled, and in the large majority of cases it is to the peer group that the young person will turn for support during the transitional period. A second reason for the importance of the peer group is that common experiences create bonds between people. Thus teenage reliance on friends and peers is strengthened by the fact that conflicts, anxieties and difficulties at home can be shared with others, and often thereby resolved, as a result of mutual sympathy and understanding.

A third reason sometimes given for the close bonds which develop between adolescents and other young people is the vulnerability experienced by many during this stage of their lives. Where individuals are lacking in self-confidence, uncertain of their own capabilities, and having to adjust to major changes, there is likely to be an especially strong need for support. Since it is precisely at this point in time that young people feel least able to turn to their parents, it is hardly surprising to find peers occupying a position of central importance. Finally, as many recent writers have pointed out (for example, Bronfenbrenner, 1974; Elder, 1975; Salmon, 1979), we live today in a world of increasing age segregation. Parents, it is argued, are spending less and less time with their teenage children, in a sense almost abdicating responsibility for their upbringing. Understandably this trend is seen as increasing the importance of the peer group.

The assumptions outlined above relate primarily to the supportive role of the peer group. It is perhaps inevitable, however, that assumptions such as these have led many to the conclusion that the peer group, by providing support, also exercises a powerful influence upon both the attitudes and behaviour of young people. This issue was briefly referred to in chapter 1 when mention was made of the belief that when adolescents spend most of their time with others of their own age more harm than good is likely to come of it. While it is understandable that adults should make assumptions about the power of the peer group, two points need to be borne in mind. Firstly, a distinction must be drawn between the supportive function of the peer group, and the extent of its influence, for the two are not necessarily synonymous; and secondly, even if the peer group is influential in some respects, great care must be taken before concluding that such influence is harmful. In this chapter we shall have the opportunity of examining questions such as these in some detail, but before considering the role of peers in the wider social setting some attention will be paid to questions concerning friendship in adolescence.

Friendship

Age

Friendship may be taken to refer specifically to close relationships between two or perhaps more individuals, involving more self-disclosure and being of a more intimate nature than relationships among peer group members generally. The first question which is of interest in this context concerns age. If friends have an important role to play in providing support during the transitional process of adolescence, then it might be expected that the meaning of friendship will change as the individual moves through various stages of his or her development. Writers who have been concerned with adolescent friendship have, by and large, been of this opinion. Anderson (1939), for example, illustrated the ways in which friendships became both more organized and more differentiated as the individual involved grew older. In addition his observations led him to conclude that the peer group becomes more effective in motivating behaviour, as well as more influential in determining attitudes and values, as a function of age. A series of studies carried out by Horrocks and his colleagues (Horrocks and Thompson, 1946; Thompson and Horrocks, 1947; Horrocks and Buker, 1951) concerning the stability of friendship at different ages represents another illustration of early work in the field. These studies showed that friendship becomes increasingly more stable from the age of five to eighteen, with only minor fluctuations in a trend which is almost linear. The method used here involved asking subjects to name their three best friends, and repeating the same question two weeks later. From this the authors derived a measure of 'friendship fluctuation' based on the number of changes made during the two week period. Horrocks made it clear that there was considerable fluctuation even at seventeen and eighteen, in spite of the steadily increasing stability with age. He explained this by arguing that most adolescents will have more than three good friends, and thus to a certain extent chance factors will influence which of the three are chosen on any particular day. Douvan and Gold (1966), reviewing this work, were critical of the method used, arguing that a two week time span is narrowly restricted. They point out that the method gives no information at all on the nature of the relationships being studied, and provides only a limited perspective on the concept of stability.

To date the most thorough analysis of changes in friendship as a result of age is probably that of Douvan and Adelson (1966), although it is important to note that they have only been able to make age comparisons for girls. They distinguish between three phases of adolescence – early, middle and late – and report quite distinct patterns associated with each of these stages. In the earliest phase (eleven, twelve and thirteen years) friendship appears to 'centre on the activity rather than on the interaction itself'. Friends are people with whom things can be done, but there is as yet no notion of depth or mutuality, or even of much feeling, in the friendship relationship. In middle adolescence (fourteen, fifteen and sixteen years) the stress is almost entirely on security. What is needed in a friend at this stage is that she should be loyal and trustworthy – someone who will not betray you behind your back. Douvan and Adelson reasonably ask the question: 'Why such an emphasis on loyalty?' Their answer is twofold. First, that the girl is seeking in the other some response to or mirroring of herself, that she is in need of someone who is going through the same problems at the same time. In some senses it could be argued that the middle adolescent girl is dealing with her problems by identification, and therefore the friend who leaves her, leaves her to cope with her impulses on her own. The authors explain it by saying that: 'With so much invested in the friendship, it is no wonder that the girl is so dependent on it' (p. 189). Second, the authors point out that middle adolescence is the time when a girl is likely to first begin to date. Therefore she will need a friend as a source of guidance and support, as a person with whom she can share confidences, and as someone who will not abandon her in favour of boys.

In contrast to all this, by late adolescence (seventeen years and over) friendship, according to Douvan and Adelson, is a more relaxed, shared experience. 'Needing friendship less, they are less haunted by fears of being abandoned and betrayed' (p. 192). Although being able to share confidences is still important, by this time there is a greater emphasis on the friend's personality and interests – on what she can offer to the relationship – and a greater degree of appreciation of individual differences. Furthermore, by this time, more important heterosexual relationships are likely to have developed, which do of course have the effect of lessening the investment in same sex friendships. In this outline of Douvan and Adelson's findings the emphasis has been entirely on girls. This is because their interview was used on large samples of girls between the ages of eleven and eighteen, but only.included a smaller sample of boys in the fourteen to sixteen year age range. Where comparisons were possible, however, they did point up some important sex differences, and these will be outlined in the next section.

More recent work has also supported Douvan and Adelson's account of the developmental process associated with friendship. In the study of relationships in adolescence referred to in previous chapters (Coleman, 1974), the author was able to show a very similar age pattern to that described by other workers where friendship was concerned. The study involved a comparison of eleven-, thirteen-, fifteen- and seventeen-year-olds, and illustrated that the greatest insecurity in friendship and fear of rejection occurred at fifteen years of age. These results will be outlined in more detail below. In addition, Bigelow and La Gaipa (1975) carried out some research in which they asked children and adolescents to describe their expectations of their best friends. The results indicated the way in which different dimensions of friendship emerged as a function of age, and emphasized the late appearance of concepts such as loyalty, intimacy, the opportunity of giving help, and so on. Such dimensions appeared for the first time between the ages of thirteen and fifteen, thus corroborating Douvan and Adelson's view of friendship in middle adolescence.

In conclusion, there is little doubt that age is a factor which needs to be taken into account where adolescent friendship is concerned. Empirical findings are consistent with the expectation that young people will have different needs at different stages, needs which are reflected in the nature of the friendship relationship. In particular the results of research are cumulative in the impression they give that the middle adolescent years are the ones of greatest stress in this respect, especially for girls. For both sexes, however, this middle period represents a stage during which friendships play a particularly important role, and no doubt resulting from this, are unusually vulnerable to jealousy, insecurity and fears of disloyalty.

Sex differences

Surprisingly few writers have paid much attention to the variable of sex differences in considering friendship in adolescence. Horrocks and his colleagues did discriminate between boys and girls, but showed minimal differences between the sexes where friendship fluctuations were concerned. The work of Powell (1955) indicated that anxiety over friendship followed much the same age course for males and females, but that the anxiety level of girls remained higher than that of boys for two or three years. This finding is consistent with the conclusions drawn by Douvan and Adelson who, because of the design of their study, were able to make comparisons between the sexes during middle adolescence. Here they found that boys differed quite considerably from girls in the expectations they had of friendship. Themes such as sensitivity and empathy were hardly mentioned by boys, while common pursuits, gang activities, and the need for help when in trouble all featured prominently amongst male responses. As the authors point out, such differences are hardly surprising. For girls in our society a stronger interpersonal orientation is expected, the capacity for intimacy and dependency are not only acceptable but highly valued, and there is little doubt that the processes of socialization all tend in this direction. For boys, however, the stress is placed on skills, achievement and self-sufficiency. Such an orientation toward activity and autonomy clearly does not facilitate close intimate friendships in adolescence.

Evidence obtained by the author (Coleman, 1974) provides further support for this view. One of the relationships investigated in this study was that of friendship in the small group. A sentence-completion test was used to assess the responses to this situation. The results indicated, first, that girls undoubtedly express more anxiety about this sort of relationship at all age levels. Tensions, jealousies and conflicts between close friends were very much more common in the girls' descriptions of friendship than in those of the boys. This difference is illustrated in figure 6.1. Secondly, where a further analysis was carried out of responses classified as Negative (i.e. those where problems or difficulties were manifested) girls were shown to express a significantly greater proportion of responses in which

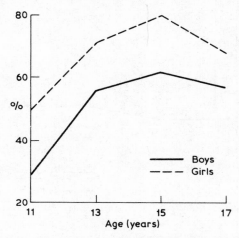

Figure 6.1   Proportions of each age group expressing themes of anxiety on sentence-completion test items concerning friendship.
(From J. C. Coleman (1974) *Relationships in Adolescence*, Routledge & Kegan Paul.)

themes of rejection or exclusion from a friendship appeared. This was particularly striking in the fifteen-year-old age group, and is illustrated in figure 6.2. A finding which ties in well with the work of Douvan and Adelson was that where boys expressed difficulties over friendship these tended to focus on quarrels, outright disputes over property, leisure-time activities and girlfriends. A further interesting corroboration of these results is reported by Feshbach and Sones (1971). They studied the reactions of fourteen- and fifteen-year-olds to the presence of a newcomer amongst a small group of friends, and showed that girls were less welcoming, and were more likely than boys to express negative or rejecting attitudes.

In summary we cannot say that friendship is more or less important for one or other of the sexes. What is clear, however, is that girls express more anxiety about this relationship, particularly in middle adolescence, and it seems probable that Douvan and Adelson are correct in pointing to the differing socialization processes, as well as to the high value which is placed on intimacy and dependency for girls, as the causes of this discrepancy. In addition, and closely interconnected, we have seen that friendship is likely to have a somewhat different meaning for boys and girls. While the former lay stress on relationships which are action-oriented, for girls the satisfaction of emotional needs tends to predominate. In general, however, the evidence of sex differences is comparatively sparse, especially during

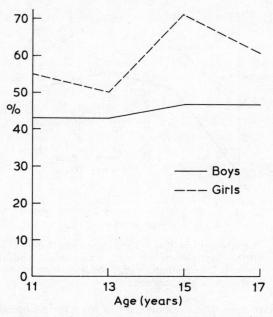

Figure 6.2 The proportions of boys and girls responding with items indicative of fear or rejection amongst the total expressing negative themes regarding friendship.
(From J. C. Coleman (1974) *Relationships in Adolescence*, Routledge & Kegan Paul.)

early and late adolescence, and it seems likely that this is a topic which would repay further investigation.

Family background

Although there have been few direct studies of the effects of family background on adolescent friendship, quite a considerable amount of evidence has accumulated on this topic, mainly in research projects primarily concerned with other issues. In the first place it is clear that the structure of the family (presence or absence of parents, as well as sex and number of siblings) has an important part to play. Numerous studies (for example, Lynn and Sawrey, 1959; Hetherington, 1966; Biller and Bahm, 1971) have shown that paternal absence for prolonged periods of time seriously affects the sex-role development of boys, and thus, in turn, their adjustment in the peer group. The sorts of people chosen as friends, the nature of the friendship, and the types of demands made upon this relationship are all affected. One important point to bear in mind, however, is the particular reason for paternal absence. Thus studies have indicated that the effects on children and adolescents are different according to whether the father has died or the parents have separated because of conflict between them. To take one example, McCord *et al.* (1962) showed that delinquent activity was very common among teenage boys whose families had been disrupted because of divorce, but boys whose fathers had died did not have any higher rates of delinquency than those with intact families. Similarly, Hetherington (1972), in a study mentioned in the previous chapter, demonstrated that in girls, although relationships with peers were affected by paternal absence no matter what the cause, significant differences existed between those who were daughters of divorced women and those who were daughters of widows.

In addition to the structural characteristics of the family deriving from presence or absence of parents, the structure of sibling relationships also needs to be considered, for there are some indications, primarily from work with younger children, that this variable may affect both the individual's interest in peers, as well as the way he or she relates to others. It was the work of Schachter (1959) which first drew attention to the role of birth order; his work appeared to show that first born children were more likely than those born later to seek the company of others, especially when placed in a stressful setting. Subsequent studies have failed to replicate many of Schachter's findings, and the question of the effects of birth order has become a somewhat contentious one. However, it is probably safe to say that sibling position is one variable affecting sociability, but that it should not be considered in isolation from other factors such as the number and sex of other siblings. Although there are a number of studies which have investigated the role of these variables in friendship patterns in young children (for example, Koch, 1957; Lewis and Rosenblum, 1975) there appear, unfortunately, to be very few studies of this sort with adolescents.

One exception to this rule is the study of Douvan and Adelson (1966). In their careful analysis of family structure they looked at a number of dimensions in order to see what effects these would have on adolescent adjustment. Thus family size, death, divorce, sibling position and maternal employment were all considered in relation to a range of behaviours, including involvement with peers. In the first place, findings showed that divorce has a differential effect on boys and girls. According to Douvan and Adelson while girls, as a result of this experience, are more involved in same sex friendships, and are more mature in their friendship relationships, boys, on the other hand, appear to have less self-control, to be less mature, and more easily driven to non-conforming behaviour. In contrast to this Douvan and Adelson reported that teenagers who have lost a parent through death appear in most respects to be very similar to those with intact families. As far as family size is concerned they reported that children from large families are more oriented towards peer values, are more independent, and are more involved in peer activity. Position in the family also appears important since the youngest children in this study were more likely to express a strong sense of loyalty to their friends, were more likely to share leisure activities with friends rather than with family members, and were more influenced by peer pressures. Finally, maternal employment seemed to have a much greater effect on girls than on boys, for where the mother was in full-time employment girls were more likely to spend time alone or with friends rather than with family members.

In addition to structural variables attention also needs to be paid to processes in the family. On intuitive grounds it seems probable that attitudes and values in the home, the quality of interaction between parents and children, and parental personality may all affect the adolescent's relationships with friends in one way or another. Although, as has been mentioned, there are few studies which have looked directly at this issue, some hints concerning these issues may be gained from the literature. To take one example, Peck (1958), in his study of 'Prairie City' adolescents, analysed ten family variables and twenty-nine personality variables in an attempt to get at the factors in the family background which determined adolescent personality. The main finding concerned a dimension Peck characterized as 'ego strength' (defined by a cluster of intercorrelated items measuring the individual's capacity to react to events), a dimension which was shown to be closely related to stable consistency and mutual trust and approval between parents and children. In addition to this finding, however, he also showed that general friendliness and spontaneity in social relationships was associated with a lenient and democratic family atmosphere. Another study of a similar nature is the Berkeley Growth Study. A report by Bayley and Schaefer (1960) on this study indicated that early maternal patterns of autonomy and control relate most closely to extroversion in adolescent boys, whereas in girls there is little relation between early maternal behaviour and adolescent personality. On the other hand, concurrent maternal behaviour did appear to correlate with both extroversion and popularity in adolescent girls. Mothers who were themselves socially outgoing and autonomy-generating tended to have daughters who exhibited similar traits.

Both these studies have important limitations, which are typical of early longitudinal studies in developmental psychology. Both have designs which are dependent on correlational analyses, and both involve very small samples. Today such designs appear to be unduly simplistic. Findings of this sort must, therefore, be treated with caution, especially in view of the many intervening variables which have not been considered. A rather different example may be gleaned from the study carried out by Glen Elder (1963). In this research, it will be recalled, a distinction was drawn between three types of parent-child interaction – permissive, democratic and autocratic – and a note was also made of the frequency of explanations given by parents when questioned about family rules. One of the issues studied was the reaction of adolescents when their parents developed a strong objection to their friends. Of particular interest was the finding that there were two conditions under which young people were unlikely to take much notice of parental strictures, and these were the permissive and autocratic types of control where explanations were infrequent. Thus Elder showed that the effect of particular types of parental power assertion combined with a lack of explanation had very specific implications for the way in which adolescents handled potential clashes over friendship. Clearly these patterns of family communication are of relevance to a wide range of adolescent behaviours, but this study is one of the few to have shown directly how attitudes to friendship will be affected by family variables.

From these few examples, therefore, it is evident that not only the structure but also the processes at work within the family will have a marked effect upon the way in which adolescents relate to their friends. Paternal absence, especially if it is a result of separation or divorce, is likely to lead to increased demands upon friends of both sexes, demands which will not always be of an appropriate nature. However, further research is needed on this topic, especially in view of the contradictory findings of Hetherington and Douvan and Adelson. Family size and sibling position are also variables which are likely to play their part in determining behaviour in this domain. Finally, the relationship between parents and adolescents is certain to be a critical factor, and here again there is obviously scope for further worthwhile research. If friendship plays an important role in adolescent development, there can be little doubt that family background determines to a large extent the use which individuals are able to make of such relationships.

The peer group

Popularity

Up till this point we have been considering issues relating to friendship in a personal sense. Let us now turn to topics concerning the wider peer group, and to some of the issues raised in the introduction to this chapter. A question of some importance in this respect and one which provides an obvious link between the topics of friendship and the peer group is that of popularity. What factors lead to popularity, and what are the effects, both on popular and unpopular individuals, of peer group criteria for social acceptability? The study of popularity has a long history, and in the literature there are a number of studies which have been designed to investigate this issue. On the whole there has been relatively little disagreement amongst them. Arbitrarily the studies may be divided into those carried out pre- and post-1960, with the work of J. S. Coleman (1960, 1961) representing the dividing line between the two groups. A hallmark of all the early studies was a concern to discover the personality characteristics associated with popularity. Thus Kuhlen and Lee (1943) studied six groups of children from villages and rural areas in New York State, including over 100 boys and girls at ages twelve, fifteen and eighteen. These researchers compared the personality characteristics of the most popular 25 per cent with the least popular 25 per cent in each of these six groups. For young people of both sexes and all ages the traits that made for popularity were cheerfulness, friendliness, enthusiasm, enjoying jokes and initiating games and activities.

Gronlund and Anderson (1957) carried out a similar study, using a sociometric test and asking pupils to indicate five individuals preferred as work companions, play companions and seating companions. The subjects were thirteen and fourteen years of age, from schools in a small city in Illinois. These researchers distinguished between the most socially acceptable, the most socially neglected and the most socially rejected pupils. They showed that, on the whole, similar personality traits to those mentioned by Kuhlen and Lee characterized the most accepted pupils. However, in addition to these dimensions good looks were mentioned by both girls and boys as being important, with the description 'active in games' also being of great significance for boys. It was also noted that a trait defined as 'talkative' was frequently mentioned as belonging to rejected individuals. As the authors point out: 'The results of this study clearly indicate that strong positive personality characteristics are associated with social acceptability among junior school pupils' (p. 337).

A third study, by Wheeler (1961), may be mentioned which,

although falling technically into the post-1960 era, belongs with the work of the earlier period. Wheeler carried out almost exactly the same type of study in Australia as his predecessors had in the USA. He found once again that there were relatively few differences between the sexes, or between age groups, and that cheerfulness, good looks, physique and sociability were the most important determinants of popularity, with the additional dimension of sporting ability being frequently mentioned by boys. One important sidelight on the pre-1960 work arose from the California studies of early and late pubertal development, already referred to in chapter 2. Jones and Bayley (1950) reported that peers described late maturers as more restless, less reserved, less grown-up and more bossy. In a later report by Jones (1958) it was stated that the late maturers were chosen much less frequently than early maturers for positions of leadership in their school, and were much less prominent in extra-curricular activities. It is not unreasonable to assume, therefore, that the dimensions already considered, such as good looks, sporting ability and so on, are connected with the individual's general rate of maturation.

The work of J. S. Coleman (1960, 1961) marked a watershed in studies of popularity primarily because of his shift of emphasis. The early work discussed above concentrated on attributes of popularity, but did not attempt in any way to consider the implications of popularity in the wider social setting. By concentrating on the concept of status and the notion of an élite Coleman introduced a new dimension into the study of popularity, and turned attention to the impact of peer group values upon the school system as a whole. He studied the attributes of the leading crowds in ten different schools, and argued as a result of this work that, by and large, sporting ability for boys and success in social relationships for girls were the factors which determined membership of the élite. As one part of the study boys were asked in a questionnaire to name the best athlete, the best student and the boy most popular with the girls. As Coleman says: 'In every school, without exception, the boys named as the best athletes were named more often – on average over twice as often – as members of the leading crowd than were those named as the best students' (1960, p. 339). Other findings showed how boys responded to the question 'How would you most like to be remembered in school: as an athletic star, a brilliant student, or most popular?' Once again athletic success was shown as being by far the most highly valued achievement. A third question in the study was 'What does it take to get into the leading crowd?' For boys sporting ability, personality and good looks were most frequently mentioned, while for girls good looks, personality and good clothes came at the top of the list. In all cases school performance came relatively low down, although this was mentioned more frequently by boys than girls.

Writers who have followed Coleman have tended to criticize him for the fact that he has over-generalized from his findings, and placed far too heavy an emphasis on the anti-intellectual bias of the peer group. Many commentators (for example, Campbell, 1964; Douvan and Gold, 1966; Rutter et al., 1976) have pointed out that he found very considerable differences between schools, that his statistics were dubious in the extreme, and that he reported evidence which showed that a positive evaluation of academic achievement varied directly as a function of social class. In addition, although athletes were chosen as being more popular than scholars in all schools, in most cases the unusual 'athlete-scholars' were the most popular of all, thus illustrating an interaction effect of these two attributes. It is essential, therefore, to bear in mind that although sporting ability in boys and social success for girls are undoubtedly critical factors in determining popularity and membership of the leading crowd, that fact alone does not lead to the conclusion that achievement in school work is necessarily undervalued, or that adolescent peer groups are always anti-intellectual.

In assessing Coleman's work it is important to distinguish between his reputation and the actual results of his study. The very title of his book – The Adolescent Society – has placed him firmly in the camp of those who see adolescents as members of a distinct and separate subculture within society, having essentially different norms and values from those of the adult world. In fact it is probable that Coleman's book has done more to give impetus to this view than almost any other single work, and he must certainly bear some responsibility for this stereotype which has close associations with the notion of a 'generation gap', and which, as we have seen, raises rather contentious issues. As far as the actual results of his study are concerned, however, it should be noted that at least some of his findings do tie in with earlier studies, and are also corroborated to some extent by subsequent research. To take one example, Horowitz (1967) collected sociometric data from eight schools across the USA, each school representing one of the eight regional areas defined by the US Office of Education. He concluded that the best predictors of popularity in both sexes were scores on an English test, an involvement in sporting activities, and self-rating personality scales of sociability and leadership. He noted that a particularly important additional variable for predicting boys' popularity was their knowledge of sports. As Horowitz puts it:

The present data delineate a pattern of interpersonal values in the adolescent world of American high schools which is similar to the one described by Coleman in his extensive study, *The Adolescent Society*. The present results support . . . [the findings] . . . in showing strong relationships between interest and achievement predictors from both the intellectual and athletic domains. (p. 174)

Finally we may turn our attention to a study which has served to highlight a limitation, not only of Coleman's work, but of other studies of popularity as well. Cavior and Dokecki (1973) were interested in the relation between popularity, physical attractiveness, and attitude similarity. They concluded that physical attractiveness and attitude similarity were positively correlated both at eleven and seventeen years of age and, as we would expect, that both these factors were strongly related to popularity. However, the importance of this study lies in the fact that the authors, rather than looking only at the extremes of variables such as popularity and physical attractiveness, analysed their data by taking into account the full range of scores. Thus they were able to show, for example, that physical attractiveness determines popularity for the most and least attractive subjects, but has little effect on the large number of subjects in the averagely attractive category. In this way Cavior and Dokecki indicate that it is perfectly possible to be popular without being in the highly physically attractive group, and thereby draw attention to the fact that, by and large, studies of popularity have concentrated on the extremes of personality or achievement without paying sufficient attention to those in the middle range.

In summary we may, with little hesitation, conclude that attractive personality characteristics, good looks, and sporting ability for boys, as well as academic success in some circumstances, are all associated with popularity. However, it is important to bear in mind that possession of any one of these traits or attributes is neither a necessary nor a sufficient cause for popularity. Furthermore, far too little attention has been paid to the teenagers who do not fall at the extremes of attributes such as sporting ability or good looks. The whole field is one which badly needs further exploration, and in particular it is to be lamented that there have been virtually no European studies at all in this area. As the work of J. S. Coleman has shown, the values and attitudes current in adolescent peer groups have implications not only for young people themselves, but for all the social institutions with which they are in contact. In addition, if the peer group is as powerful an agent of socialization as many believe, then a greater understanding is urgently needed of the nature of the influences which stem from it. Are these constructive or destructive, and to what extent are individual teenagers affected by such influences? It is to this issue that we now turn.

Conformity

It is not difficult to see why the notion of conformity ranks high among popular conceptions of adolescence. The peer group, as has been noted, assumes especial importance during this stage of development. Young people need to distinguish themselves from adults and, therefore, adopt styles of dress, language, musical tastes and so on which set them apart from their elders. In addition, security is to be found in being like the crowd, a feeling clearly expressed in some of the interview material at the end of the chapter. At times when self-confidence is lacking, and questions of identity seem complex and worrying it is undoubtedly difficult to stand out as an individual, and comforting to be able to merge with a larger group. Needless to say, however, the urge to conform is not uniformly high during adolescence; age is an important factor, and there are wide individual differences. Especially important is the fact that, although conformity may be evident in superficial areas such as dress, this does not mean that young people can be pressured into behaving in a manner which they consider to be wrong. This point is particularly relevant where anti-social behaviour is concerned. It is all too frequently assumed that because adolescents conform to peer group standards in some respects, they will conform to pressures to engage in delinquent activities. As will become apparent this assumption is far from the truth, and what limited evidence there is on this subject leads to the conclusion that peer group influence is only one among many factors which draw teenagers into anti-social behaviour. Let us first of all look briefly at the experimental studies of conformity.

Among the most well-known of these is the work of Costanzo and Shaw (1966), who used a classic method derived from social psychology (Asch's paradigm) to look at the effects of group pressure on teenage behaviour. They asked subjects, in a laboratory setting, to make a decision about the length of a line where the illusion was given that all members of the group differed from the subject. The sample included twenty-four subjects at each of four age levels, each age group being equally divided between boys and girls. The authors showed that susceptibility to group pressure was significantly related to age, though not in a straightforward linear fashion. Results, as illustrated in figure 6.3, indicated a relatively low degree of conformity in the seven to nine age range, the highest level of conformity between eleven and thirteen, and a gradual decrease in susceptibility to group pressure from then onwards. Interestingly the level of conformity in the nineteen to twenty-one year age range appeared to be approximately the same as it had been between seven and nine years of age, and it is noteworthy that this developmental pattern is identical for boys and girls, although the latter are somewhat more conforming.

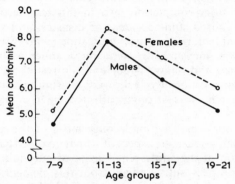

Figure 6.3   Mean conformity as a function of age.
(From P. R. Costanzo and M. E. Shaw (1966) *Child Development*, 37.)

Further studies which have provided similar evidence are those of Iscoe *et al.* (1963) and Landsbaum and Willis (1971). In the latter study a slightly different design was used to that employed by Costanzo and Shaw, in that subjects worked in pairs rather than in a group. This experiment demonstrated that neither intelligence nor extended contact between partners had any effect, but that conformity was significantly greater between the ages of thirteen and fourteen than it was between eighteen and twenty-one. Although the younger adolescents did not report less self-confidence, they actually performed as if they were more uncertain since they changed their original decisions to fit with their partners opposing judgements more often than did those in the older group. Harvey and Rutherford (1960) were also interested in the same problem, but in their case they investigated the effect of high and low group status upon conformity behaviour. In their design, subjects first made a decision involving a preference for one of two pictures in an art judgement test; they then received a communication indicating the choice of a high status member of the group. In a subsequent task, it was then noted what proportions of each group altered their choice in line with that of a high status member. The results showed that low status members were more susceptible to influence than those of high status, that girls were more susceptible to status than boys up to the age of fifteen, and that in general the status of the individual in the group was related to the amount of influence he or she had upon others. Costanzo (1970) added a further dimension to studies of conformity by investigating the effects of self-blame. In this study subjects ranged in age from seven to twenty-one, and self-blame was assessed by a story-completion test. In this test heroes of stories inadvertently caused some accident or disaster, and subjects were asked to complete the stories, indicating who was to blame. Conformity was measured in the same manner as in the earlier study (Costanzo and Shaw, 1966) and the results showed clearly that, although conformity followed a similar developmental pattern, its extent was strongly affected by the degree of self-blame.

Finally, mention may be made once more of the author's own study (Coleman, 1974), one aspect of which involved a developmental investigation of the adolescent's sense of autonomy in relation to the peer group. Results derived from this element in the study might be expected therefore to cast some light both on conformity and on the opposite side of the coin. In particular the focus here was on the interaction between increasing independence and declining conformity as a function of age. One sentence stem in the sentence-completion test which was used in the study read as follows: '*If someone is not part of the group. . . .*' Responses were scored as being either Constructive or Negative, where a Negative reponse indicated conformity and implied that to be outside the group was in some way harmful or damaging. A Constructive response indicated that there were definite advantages in being independent from the group. Some examples of Constructive responses are: '*If someone is not part of the group* he enjoys it because he is not following the sheep' or '*If someone is not part of the group* they are much respected and admired.' Two examples of Negative themes are: '*If someone is not part of the group* he is looked upon as an outcast' or '*If someone is not part of the group* he feels inferior to them.' The results showed that independence (Constructive responses) remained at a very low level in the eleven-, thirteen- and fifteen-year-old groups, but increased significantly at seventeen. Correspondingly, conformity (Negative responses) declined sharply from the age of fifteen onwards although this decline was less marked for girls than it was for boys. These results are illustrated in figure 6.4,

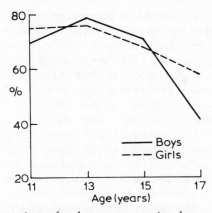

Figure 6.4 Proportions of each group expressing themes of conformity on a sentence-completion test item concerning relationships within the peer group.
(From J. C. Coleman (1974) *Relationships in Adolescence*, Routledge & Kegan Paul.)

and are consistent with those of Costanzo and Shaw (1966) and Landsbaum and Willis (1971).

To summarize to this point, we have seen that conformity is at its height among the early adolescent group, but that it diminishes significantly from about fourteen or fifteen onwards. These experimental results are corroborated by some of the opinions expressed in the interview material at the end of the chapter. The studies also show that conformity is affected by status in the peer group, by the degree of self-blame, and very probably by many other personality factors as well. While to some extent girls may be more conforming than boys, the differences between the sexes are generally small. On the whole it appears that by middle adolescence some individuals are able to see that there are advantages to be gained from independence, and the number taking such a view increases rapidly from this stage onwards. It is a great pity that no attempts have been made to link experimental studies of conformity with an understanding of the genesis of anti-social behaviour. However, the conclusions outlined above provide a useful background to the next topic to be considered, namely the influence of the peer group upon anti-social behaviour.

The peer group and anti-social behaviour

In considering conformity we have, in effect, been discussing the general issue of the power of the peer group, and we have noted that this will vary depending on age, personality, family background and so on. However, this general question must be distinguished from the rather more specific issue of whether the influence of the peer group is in an anti-social direction. To what extent, it may be asked, is anti-social behaviour caused as a result of peer group pressure? As has already been pointed out, we can accept the proposition that teenagers are influenced by their contemporaries, without necessarily concluding that this influence is harmful. Thus the peer group may determine hairstyle and dress, taste in music and so on, without being a nursery for crime. The question of the extent of the effect of the peer group on anti-social behaviour is an extremely important one, with direct social and practical relevance. None the less, it must be recognized that the issue is complex, and lacks any simple answer.

In the literature there is no difficulty in discovering diametrically opposed viewpoints. To take an example, Akers (1970), writing on alcoholism and its associated problems, comes down firmly on the side of those who believe that the peer group should, by and large, be seen simply as an extension of the values and behaviours which operate in the home setting. As he says:

Drinking *may* be used as a test of loyalty to peer groups precisely because it is discouraged by adults. The contrary evidence, however, is compelling. The probability of alcohol use increases with age, i.e. as assumption of adult roles is approached. There is a demonstrated relationship between the drinking behaviour of parents and their offspring. A majority of adolescents in our society would in all probability come to use alcohol eventually even if there were no peer group experience at all since young people tend to perceive some drinking as an integral part of normal adult behaviour. The emphasis of this evidence overwhelmingly favours adolescent identification with adulthood, rather than hostility to adult goals or authority. (p. 386)

The opposite point of view is expressed by Plant (1975) in his work on drugtakers. According to his account the influence of friends is paramount as a determining factor in the development of this behaviour. He writes:

Virtually all respondents attributed their first drug experiences to the direct influence and encouragement of friends and peers whom they knew well. It was clear that drugtaking developed as a group activity, and was part of the leisure behaviour of those interviewed and observed. Furthermore, within the group drugtaking was a much discussed and conspicuous form of behaviour. Several individuals spoke of the tremendous peer group pressure to use drugs. . . . These reports, together with my own field experience, confirmed the view that there was an emphatic process of socialization amongst certain groups of young people which instilled the image of drugtaking as a prestigious and beneficial activity. (p. 76)

These two quotations illustrate not only opposing viewpoints, but also the fact that numerous features of the picture have to be taken into account if any sense is to be made of this somewhat puzzling issue. For example, we need to recognize that social influence operates in various ways, and that a distinction must be drawn between different forms of anti-social activity. We also have to acknowledge that some young people will be more vulnerable to peer group pressure than others, and finally we must bear in mind that there may be a difference between the influences that lead to initiation into anti-social behaviour, and those that operate to maintain that behaviour once it has already started. Let us deal with each of these points in turn.

In the first place, there are clearly many types of social influence. At one extreme, influence can be entirely indirect with an individual – perhaps a respected adult – acting as a model for a young person. Under such circumstances the adult may increase the likelihood that the teenager will imitate certain forms of behaviour simply as a result of the relationship between them, and not because of the exercise of any pressure or coercion. The effect of such modelling may not be evident until a considerable period of time has elapsed. On the other hand, influence may be immediate and direct, where, for example, an individual or group attempts to control the behaviour of others by threatening unpleasant consequences unless the person concerned conforms. In relation to the influence of the peer group it is usually considered to be the fear of rejection or ridicule which acts as a sanction, powerful enough in adolescence to ensure that members of the group toe the line.

This distinction between different types of influence assumes considerable importance in the context of the teenage peer group, for the reason that, if a number of young people spend time together, and together become involved in some form of anti-social behaviour, then it is not unnaturally assumed that the direct influence of members of the group was at work. However, far less attention is paid to the indirect influences which may have been operating, and which may, in some circumstances, be even more powerful than direct peer group pressure. The research carried out by Martin Plant (1975) among drugtakers in Cheltenham illustrates this well. As was indicated above, he is quite clear that it was the peer group itself which was the predominant influence on this form of behaviour. Yet he reports that the great majority of the parents of the addicts he studied were also substantial drug users, only the drugs they used were socially acceptable. While the parents of these young people were vehemently opposed to the use of marihuana, they themselves were heavy drinkers or smokers, or were individuals who made considerable use of barbiturates, tranquillizers or other prescribed drugs. Thus it is impossible to say that the influences at work in the home did not play their part, and while undoubtedly many types of influence lead to any one type of behaviour, the direct influence of the peer group must be viewed in the context of all other known factors.

A second point to be considered is that different forces may be at work in the genesis of the various types of anti-social behaviour. This was clearly illustrated in a recent study carried out in the USA by Denise Kandel *et al.* (1978), in which they distinguished between parent influence, peer influence, the adolescent's attitudes, and his or her involvement in other deviant activities as factors which could predict drug or alcohol use. They were able to show that although other variables played their part, it was parental behaviour which was the most critical factor in leading the young person into early experiments with alcohol. Where drug use was concerned, however, no one factor stood out; the teenager's attitudes, poor parent-child relationships, the influence of one best friend, and involvement in other deviant activities all contributed to the total picture. Thus it is essential to distinguish between types of anti-social behaviour and not to assume that similar factors will operate in all situations.

Thirdly, the fact that some young people will be more vulnerable than others to particular types of pressure must be borne in mind. In recent years a number of writers have referred to the possibility that the peer group only becomes important, and its influence therefore substantial, for a small group of teenagers who lack sufficient support and care from their families. Empey (1975) for example, in his discussion of delinquency, puts forward the view that a gap or 'vacuum' exists in the emotional life of certain adolescents as a result of inadequate parenting. This 'vacuum' is filled by the peer group, and the already vulnerable young person, lacking in self-confidence but badly needing to be accepted, becomes especially susceptible to peer group pressure.

The research carried out by Davies and Stacey (1972) and Aitken (1978) in Strathclyde on the drinking behaviour of young people illustrates one situation in which such a process might be operating.

This research showed, firstly, that a remarkably high proportion (82 per cent) started drinking within the home setting, a finding which accords well with the views of Akers (1970) and Kandel *et al.* (1978) mentioned earlier. However, the remaining 18 per cent reported that their drinking started outside the home, in parks, playgrounds and clubs, and in the company of their peers. Those in this group turned out to be the heaviest drinkers, to have poor relationships with their parents, and to have hostile attitudes to authority figures and to the older generation in general. Thus anti-social behaviour went hand in hand with alienation from the family and from the world of adults, and it is probable, in view of the way these young people started their drinking, that these adolescents would also be the ones who were most vulnerable to peer group pressure.

The last point to be considered here concerns a possible difference between the initiation into, and the maintenance of anti-social behaviour. It has been suggested that peer group influence may have a greater effect in the early stages of involvement in such behaviour, but may have increasingly less effect as the behaviour becomes more established. Kandel *et al.* (1978) take up this point. They refer to the opposing viewpoints in the literature, some of which stress the importance of psychological factors underlying drug use, while others concentrate on social factors. Kandel and her colleagues believe that both play their part, but at different stages in the process. Based on the results of their study they were able to show that what they called 'situational and interpersonal factors', i.e. type of school attended, the nature of the peer group, and the degree of family support, all played an important part during the stage at which the individual was likely to be initiated into the anti-social behaviour. However, 'intra-psychic factors', i.e. strengths and weaknesses of the personality, appeared to be more important in determining whether the young person would continue with and become more deeply involved in drug-related behaviour once it had already begun.

Apart from the mention of Empey's views, little reference has so far been made to delinquency. There are two reasons for this. In the first place this is a topic we will be considering in greater detail in the next chapter. However, it is also true to say that there is very little evidence available which relates specifically to the influence of the peer group on delinquent behaviour. In spite of this, though, all the points made so far refer just as well to delinquency as they do to drug or alcohol use. To take one example, both direct and indirect influences will operate as much where delinquency is concerned as with any other form of anti-social behaviour. Young people may, in a group, vandalize property, or steal a car, but this does not mean that influences stemming from the family context, or from the wider social setting, can be ignored in the explanations of such behaviour. If we are seeking to place the influence of the peer group in perspective one further point needs to be made. Findings of studies carried out by Conger *et al.* (1965) and by West and Farrington (1973) – of which more will be said later – indicate clearly that those who become delinquent during their teenage years may be distinguished from their peers at eight or ten years of age in terms of their behaviour in the classroom, attitudes to authority, and so on. Evidence of this nature underlines the fact that even if social factors, in the shape of peer group influences, are at work in causing anti-social behaviour in adolescence, psychological factors which have been in existence at least since middle childhood are likely to predispose the individual to be vulnerable to such influences.

It will be apparent from what has been said that the extent of the influence of the peer group on anti-social behaviour is difficult to estimate. Many factors have to be borne in mind. Clearly there is pressure within the peer group towards conformity, and in some groups expected behaviour will include involvement in drug or alcohol use, or in delinquent activities. Evidently some young people will be affected by such pressure, but what seems most striking is that peer group influence hardly ever appears to operate in isolation. Influence of this sort can only be exercised under certain circumstances, either where disinterested or non-existent parents leave a vacuum, or where they themselves provide models for anti-social behaviour. Where family influences are strong and pro-social, and where relationships in the home are good it seems highly unlikely that the peer group will be able to exert pressure upon individuals to act in an anti-social manner. It is on this note that we may turn to a consideration of a related topic known as the 'parent-peer' issue.

The parent-peer issue

The parent-peer issue essentially concerns the relative influence of each of these two reference groups in the life of the individual adolescent. This issue has obvious links with problems we have already discussed, such as conformity and the effect of the peer group on anti-social behaviour. It is also closely associated with the concept of the generation gap, considered in some detail in chapter 5. There we noted that although there are undoubtedly differences in taste between adults and young people, as well as disagreements over mundane domestic issues, such differences do not imply major dis-

crepancies where fundamental values are concerned. The stereotype
which carries with it a notion of a serious divergence of attitude and
belief between the generations has clouded the picture in many
respects, not least with regard to the issue of adolescent reference
groups. Thus, for example, it has commonly been assumed that an
inevitable consequence of increased involvement with the peer group
is a rejection of parental values. Clearly, however, this is not an
'either/or' situation, but one in which it is perfectly possible to
maintain respect for both reference groups.

An early study carried out in the USA by Bowerman and Kinch
(1959) illustrated this well. They were interested in changes in family
and peer orientation of children between the ages of ten and sixteen.
The subjects were classified on various types of orientation, as well
as on the extent they identified with one group or another. Thus, for
example, 'Normative Orientation' was defined as 'whose ideas were
most like those of the subject on a variety of topics', while in order to
assess 'Identification', subjects were asked whether family or friends
understood them better and whether when they grew up they would
rather be the kind of person their parents were or the kind they
thought their friends would be. Findings showed that 'Normative
Orientation' shifted dramatically from family to peer group over the
age span, with an especially strong swing between thirteen and
fourteen. However, the differences between age groups on the Identification measure, although in the same direction, were not nearly so
marked. These results, illustrated in table 6.1, indicate that there will
be a number of different dimensions of commitment to any reference
group, dimensions which do not necessarily show identical developmental patterns.

A study carried out by Brittain (1963) provided further corroboration for the view that orientation to one group or another was far
from being an all-or-none affair. In this study hypothetical situations
involving conflict between parent-peer expectations were presented
to the subjects, who were girls between the ages of fifteen and
seventeen. In each dilemma individuals were faced with a complex
choice where one course of action was favoured by parents and
another by peers, and the respondents were asked to indicate what
the girl would probably do. The results led Brittain to the conclusion
that whether the subject chose a course of action which conformed to
the parent's wishes or one that was in line with peer group pressures
depended primarily on the nature of the dilemma. This conclusion he
later formulated in terms of a 'situational hypothesis' (Brittain,
1968, 1969), which has been summarized by Larsen (1972a) as
follows:

Table 6.1 Percentage of children classified as having family or peer orientation by grade in school

	Grades						
	4th	5th	6th	7th	8th	9th	10th
Normative Orientation							
Family	82.2	64.6	69.8	51.9	33.0	42.4	30.4
Peer	11.9	23.2	18.1	34.3	52.2	41.2	50.6
Neutral	5.9	12.2	12.1	13.9	14.8	16.5	19.0
Identification							
Family	81.2	79.2	77.6	72.2	57.4	62.3	51.9
Peer	5.0	2.4	4.3	9.2	18.2	13.0	26.6
Neutral	13.8	18.3	18.1	18.5	24.3	24.7	21.5

(From C. E. Bowerman and J. W. Kinch (1959) *Social Forces*, 37.)

In this case the adolescent is said to follow the wishes of his parents rather than those of his peers when the context requires decisions that have futuristic implications. Conversely when the decision involves current status and identity needs, the adolescents opt for the wishes of their peers. Brittain's research has strongly supported the assumption that adolescents perceive peers and parents as competent guides in different areas. . . . (p. 84)

Brittain's 'situational hypothesis' was given additional impetus by the work of Lesser and Kandel (1969), whose findings led them to the conclusion that while, for certain values, peers may be more influential than parents, for other issues the reverse appears to be true. In their case they were concerned with educational plans and future life goals, and in order to assess the relative influence of parents and peers upon these future-oriented decisions they developed a measure of concordance both between adolescent and mother and between the adolescent and best friend. Results showed that there was strong concordance between the adolescent and both mother and best friend where educational goals were concerned, but that this concordance was significantly greater between adolescent and mother than it was between adolescent and best friend. As a result of these data the authors were left in little doubt that, in this domain at least, parents have a stronger influence than peers. Furthermore the majority of adolescents appeared from this study to hold views which were in agreement with both their mothers and their friends. As Lesser and Kandel put it: 'We take exception to the "hydraulic" view taken by many investigators regarding the relative influence of adults and peers which assumes that the greater the influence of the one, the less the influence of the other. Our data lead to another view: in critical areas, interactions with peers support the values of the parents' (1969, p. 222). Thus the authors not only support Brittain's hypothesis, but carry it a step further by underlining the interactive nature of parent and peer influence.

The work of Larsen (1972*b*) is also relevant in this context. He used the method of presenting subjects with hypothetical situations, but in addition introduced the further variable of 'parent-adolescent affect'. This he defined as 'the quality of parent-child relationships, as measured by parental interest and understanding, willingness to help, the number of family activities shared, and so on.' By considering this dimension of the situation he was able to show that parental influence was greater where 'parent-adolescent affect' was highest. In addition adolescents with high 'parent-adolescent affect' were less likely than those with low affect to see a need to differentiate between the influences of parents and peers, and furthermore the results indicated that 'parent-adolescent affect' had its greater effect on older teenagers. There were also quite considerable sex differences, with girls, especially fifteen- and eighteen-year-olds, being more affected by this variable than boys. Some of Larsen's findings are illustrated in figure 6.5.

From the foregoing it is clear that the so-called 'parent-peer' issue is a complex one, in which a number of factors may all play an important part. It seems probable that there are no simple solutions to questions concerning the relative influence of parents and peers, nor are there, at this stage, straightforward answers as to how adolescents resolve potential cross-pressures. In his textbook *Adolescence and Youth* (1977), John Conger describes five points which should be borne in mind when considering the parent-peer issue. In the first place he reminds us that there will usually be considerable overlap in values between parents and peers. In many areas there may be no conflict at all, with the values of the one group reinforcing rather than contradicting the values of the other. In this context it should perhaps be remembered that many teenagers will select precisely those friends whose values are congruent with those of their parents, a point underlined not only by Lesser and Kandel (1969), but more recently by Offer and Offer (1976). Secondly, Conger suggests that

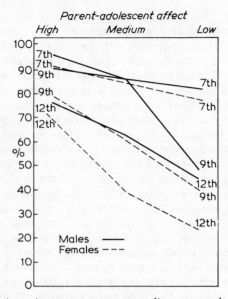

Figure 6.5   Orientation to parents according to grade level, parent-adolescent affect, and sex.
(From L. E. Larsen (1972*b*) *Pacific Sociological Review*, 34.)

in some areas parents will in any event experience some uncertainty, and in these spheres are likely to be quite willing to take their cues from the younger generation. Thirdly, it would clearly be erroneous to assume that either peer or parental values are all-embracing, extending to every area of decision making. In the large majority of families the opinions of parents will be of greater salience on some issues, while those of peers will be seen to be more relevant to a different set of problems. Fourthly, attention is drawn to the findings of a number of research projects which show that it is in situations where parental interest is lacking, or where the adolescent has no parental support to depend upon that commitment to peer group values is at its height. As we have already noted in this chapter, it is under such conditions that the peer group may be considered to be filling a vacuum rather than provoking conflict between parent and teenager. Finally, Conger argues that the need to conform to social pressures, whether they be from parents or peers, will vary from individual to individual. Personality, maturity and family structure, as well as other variables, all need to be considered, and these factors seem likely to be of far greater significance than the developmental

stage of the individual in determining the young person's relationships with both parents and peers.

To conclude, this chapter has considered a wide range of issues
concerning the role of friendship and the peer group. The importance
of age, sex and family background have been noted as factors which
affect friendship patterns, and conformity and the complex issue of the
power and direction of influence exercised by the peer group have been
discussed. We have seen that, as might be expected, teenagers differ
in their susceptibility to peer group pressure, and that conformity
varies as a result of age, personality, relationships with parents and
so on. A fundamental distinction has been drawn between the
influence of the peer group in such matters as dress and taste in music,
and its influence upon anti-social behaviour. In particular it has been
pointed out that peers only have a harmful effect under certain
conditions, and that it is quite erroneous to assume that the adolescent
peer group is normally a destructive force in society. We have also
noted that the very concept of a 'parent-peer issue' involves a false
dichotomy, since for most young people the two reference groups
reinforce rather than contradict each other. Where choices have to be
made, however, the majority of adolescents, contrary to expectations,
select parents rather than peers as final arbiters. This fact is well
illustrated in the interview material which follows, as is the ability of
most young people to see the role of the peer group in a sober and
realistic light. Its influence is neither denied nor exaggerated, and one
is left with the impression that a sense of proportion in this matter
is more likely to be achieved by young people than by many an
academic theorist.

Interview

As part of the interview two questions were asked concerning issues
related to the peer group. The first was:

> Do you feel you are sometimes under pressure from people of your
> age to do things that you would prefer not to do?

Jill (16 years): Not so much since I've been in the 6th form and have
been in a much smaller group, but with the 5th form, just the way
that you dress and that. Dressing like I am now wouldn't be quite
right, you know, they would like skirts and, you know, odd things
like that. Especially in the 5th form, that was one of the things they
expected you to follow, and if you didn't. . . . Eh, I don't like that
sort of thing. Not so much now, not since I joined the smaller
group in the 6th form, it's not too bad. I don't think I'd let them

anyway. How did it happen? I suppose at the time I felt out of it if I wasn't the same as them, but at the same time I felt well why should I be the same as them. But I was still, you know, with them, and I didn't like to go me own way. I do now though!

Elizabeth (17 years): Yeah, but I think that was mostly when you were younger. Because when you were younger you're more prone, I mean you're pressurized by your friends. In most cases you're more prone to go along with what they say just to make sure that you keep in that group, but now I think people are respecting people's values much more, and if there's something you don't want to do they take it, they take what you say.

Sarah (16 years): No. No. I just wouldn't do anything that I didn't want to do and that someone wanted me to do, you know I just wouldn't do it. I do mostly what I think is right, in some cases, that is, you know, but if a person wanted me to do something because they wanted that thing done, and I didn't want to do it, well I wouldn't do it.

Karen (15 years): Yes, like sort of under pressure from my friends to say 'Hello' and things like that. I mean, just put on a false act like everyone else – quick, put on your false act, you know, lost identity – do you know what I mean? I suppose if a friend wants me to go somewhere because they're with a fellow then I suppose I'll go. I'm really forced to go, but its my own decision to go as well, if you know what I mean. You sort of give in for her because she is your friend.

Harriett (16 years): Yes, but now I've sort of opted out of any of those sort of things. I've had a group of friends who've sort of done things that I wouldn't have done, but I opted out of that group, and, you know, found new friends, more mature friends perhaps who didn't sort of follow each other around like sheep.

Kevin (15 years): No, because I like doing things that people of my age do. I don't believe people are forced into doing things really. It's up to themselves if they want to do something, do it, and if they don't want to do it they don't have to.

Adam (17 years): Not so much. Well there is some. Not a great deal really. I suppose like in class, you know, there is a lot of talk and things like that, and if you want to get on and you're trying to work, and they're talking and they try to get you to join in with their conversation. . . . But I don't to a great extent.

Paul (17 years): Oh yeah, Well, me friends that have left school go out a lot more than I do, so they try and persuade me to get a job – to leave – but then you say 'Well I'm happy at school, I like it, and I'm not really bothered about going out as much as they do.' They seem to go out quite a lot, but you've got friends at school and that makes up for it. It's like they want you to go out when you've got some homework and things like that, but you've just got to face the fact that you've got the homework to do and get on with it.

The second question of relevance to the peer group was as follows:

If there was ever a clash between what your friends wanted you to do, and what your parents wanted you to do – which would you choose?

Harriett (16 years): What I wanted to do really. I'd be influenced by both, but in the end it would be very much what I wanted to do. What I thought was right or wrong really, and I think the influences would just come from both sides. I'm not easily swayed by either my parents or my friends, you know, I don't just follow the crowd really.

Jill (16 years): Probably me parents, they'd probably win, you know, I'd say first. Well I would discuss it with them, and ask them, and say what me friends had said, but they would probably be right anyway. And I would hope I would realize that, because with them being a lot older than me friends, and me friends, you know, they're just the same age as me, sometimes younger and they don't know what goes on, sort of thing. So it would probably be me parents.

Elizabeth (17 years): I think I'd have to weigh the matter up between myself and think 'What do I want to do?' I think what I would ask myself first is not what my mum or my dad or my friends want me to do, it's what I want to do, and what I think is right, and if what I think is right coincides with what my friends are saying, well then I'd take their side and that's it, but I don't think I'd take either side because they're my friends or because its my parents.

Valerie (17 years): It would depend on what it was really. If it was sort of going out and staying up late I think I'd probably come to a compromise so that I didn't stay out as late as me friends wanted to, but a bit later than me parents sort of thought was right.

Henry (16 years): Oh it depends what sort of thing it happens to be – do you mean something like going out? Eh, I think I'd go out with me mates I would, because the simple reason for that is they don't take me out that much, well me mum and dad hardly take me out at all, and I always go out with me mates because, well, I just go out with them.

Adam (17 years): Parents, I think, because they always want what's best for you. You know it could be that your friends want you to go somewhere and you parents don't think you should. I think I would agree with my parents and not go because they always want what's best. They're not trying to hinder you or anything like that.

Richard (15 years): I'd definitely do what my parents wanted me to because I owe them a lot really, and its just, well, it's expected really isn't it? Your parents come before your friends.

Paul (17 years): I think probably what me mother would choose in the end. Well, I'd talk to her and to me brother and sister. . . . Well, I suppose it would depend on what I thought as well. If I thought me friends were right, then I'd try and persuade me mum to say what she thought of it, but I would consider both opinions, both me friends and me mother, but I think I would more or less choose me mother's opinion because she would probably be right more than they would.

7

Adolescent sexuality

No study of adolescence would be complete without some consideration of the process of sexual maturation for, as we have seen in chapter 2, it is this process which forms the physiological background to many of the social and emotional changes which occur during the teenage years. Although the significance of sexual maturation has been recognized by many, from Freud onwards, who have written on the theme of adolescence, the volume of research on this topic has hardly matched its importance. Thus while there have been a number of surveys of sexual behaviour in adolescence, these have tended to concentrate on a limited range of issues: either on attitudes to sex, on sex education and the sources of initial sex information, or on the ages at which various types of sexual activity first occur. In contrast hardly anything is known of the consequences for adult life of different patterns of teenage sex, and in particular the effects of early premarital sexual experience on psychological maturation. Furthermore little information is available on topics such as sexual difficulties in adolescence, the choice of appropriate contraceptives, the psychological consequences of abortion, the problems of the handicapped adolescent, and so on.

It is very much to be hoped that in future more attention will be paid to these rather more practical issues, since it is this type of information which is most needed as a result of the fundamental changes in sexual attitudes which have occurred among young people over the last two decades. So far-reaching are these changes that they have led at least some commentators to talk of the development of a 'new sexual morality', which has significantly affected the behaviour of young people. In this chapter the origins of these changes of attitude will briefly be examined, and the results of the behaviour surveys which have been carried out will be discussed.

Attention will also be paid to some of the very real practical problems faced by teenagers as they come to terms with their sexual maturity, and in the last section the issue of sex education will be considered from a number of different points of view.

The 'new sexual morality'

There are few today who would disagree with the proposition that since the end of World War II fundamental changes have occurred in the attitudes of society generally towards sexual behaviour. It is these general changes which form an essential background to an understanding of adolescent sexual development. In the adult world extra-marital sex has become widely accepted, divorce is becoming more and more common, there is much greater tolerance of different types of sexual behaviour, homosexuality no longer needs to be invisible, advertisements, films and television bombard us all with sexual information, and the topic of sex is discussed openly and frequently. As part and parcel of all this, widely available contraception has had the effect of making possible a distinction between sex and procreation. These shifts in attitude, which are in some respects almost revolutionary, cannot fail to have had an effect on young people. Children growing up in a society cannot be insulated from what is happening to those of their parents' generation, and while it may be regretted by some, it is of course inevitable that such fundamental changes in adult behaviour will affect those just beginning their sexual lives.

Research evidence which is available, both in European countries and in the USA, indicates that young people are changing in their attitudes to sexual behaviour in ways which are very similar to adults. Essentially, if comparisons are drawn between the attitudes of adolescents today and those of adolescents twenty or thirty years ago, there seem to be three important differences. Firstly, young people today are more open about sexual matters, secondly, they see sexual behaviour as more a matter of private rather than public morality, and thirdly, there appears to be a growing sense of the importance of sex being associated with stable, long-term relationships. Let us consider these points in turn. In the first place, young people are more open about sexual matters. This in itself is obviously a reflection of the general frankness about sex in today's society. However, it is important to note that it is also associated with a need on the part of young people for greater opportunities for the discussion of sexual problems with adults, and for a greater availability of sex education in the widest sense of the term. This a topic to which we shall return later in the chapter.

Secondly, it is clear that young people believe sexual behaviour to be a matter of individual choice and belief, rather than of public morality. Thus present-day teenagers, it appears, are far less likely to condemn sexual minorities, or to make absolute judgements about what is right or wrong in individual cases. There has been a move among adolescents towards a moral stance which is more relative and less judgemental, with most believing that what is done in private is up to those concerned. Phrases such as 'doing your own thing' reflect this view, which is also associated with a growing distrust of the part played by official institutions, such as the Church, in determining moral values. Thirdly, today there is undoubtedly a belief in the importance of personal relationships where sexual behaviour is concerned. A common fear among adults is that greater sexual freedom will lead to greater promiscuity, yet all the evidence points in the opposite direction. Young people of the present generation it appears, far from sanctioning 'sex for fun', much prefer to view sexual activity as needing a framework of a relationship to give it meaning. Perhaps in this they have been influenced to some extent by the sight of their elders experiencing so much unhappiness in their own search for sexual fulfilment.

Evidence for these changes in attitude may be drawn from a wide range of sources. Firstly the interview material at the end of this chapter may be seen to contain reflections of almost all the attitudes mentioned. In the research literature Conger (1975) and Hoffman (1978) have summarized surveys of American youth, while Luckey and Nass (1969) review findings from various European countries. As far as the UK is concerned recent work reported by Schofield (1973) and Farrell (1978) amply demonstrates that adolescents in this country are undergoing similar changes to those experienced by teenagers in other parts of the world. Farrell's conclusion, following her survey into the attitudes of sixteen- to nineteen-year-olds, was that: 'The attitudes of the young people in this study to sex before marriage are in line with what has been described as the "widespread" view in this country – approval in the context of a stable relationship and if care is taken to avoid unwanted pregnancy' (p. 33).

How are changing attitudes reflected in behaviour?

While it seems clear that attitudes to sexual behaviour have changed radically over the last decade or so, we still have to ask to what extent these changes have led to changes in actual behaviour. Answers to this question are provided by the results of some of the surveys already mentioned, but before considering these a word of warning is in order. By the nature of things all the evidence which is available on the sexual behaviour of young people is derived either from interviews or from self-administered questionnaires. Not unnaturally researchers investing time and effort in the design and carrying out of such projects are often loath to dwell too much on the limitations of the methods involved. However, it must be evident that data derived in such a fashion are open to question on a number of counts.

Sexual behaviour is associated with a multitude of worries and anxieties; it is a matter of pre-occupation to most teenagers, it is certainly an extremely emotive topic, and most important, for many it represents a standard of evaluation against which to judge success or failure. Thus it seems highly unlikely that responses to interviews or questionnaires are going to reflect accurately real behaviour. In particular it should be borne in mind that for many boys sexual activity is a sign of achievement, and 'conquest' a matter for boasting. There is thus a strong possibility that reports of male sexual behaviour will tend to be exaggerated. On the other hand, for girls, sexual activity is not always a source of pride, and certainly in the past it may well have been true that female sexual behaviour was under-reported. Unfortunately it is extremely difficult to tell whether biases of this sort are operating, but some reservations at least need to be kept in mind in considering the available evidence.

As far as this research is concerned the recent review by Hoffman (1978) of the American studies provides a suitable starting point. She points out that the main evidence can be drawn from the work of Kinsey and his co-workers in the 1940s and 1950s and from the work of Kantner and Zelnick and the Finkels in the 1970s. A number of more circumscribed studies published between 1969 and 1975 fill in some of the gaps, and reference to these may be found in Hoffman's article. She notes that all these studies, including the major ones, are subject to the criticisms mentioned above, but, as she says: ' . . . while recognizing these limitations, this is still the best information we have' (1978, p. 27). In the research in the UK, to which we have already referred in the field of attitudes, Schofield (1965) and Farrell (1978) provide the two main sources of evidence on the sexual behaviour of young people.

We will first consider the evidence relating to girls, and we may begin with Kinsey (Kinsey et al., 1948; 1953). They found that by the age of seventeen years approximately 10 per cent of females had had sexual intercourse. At the age of twenty this figure had risen to 18 per cent of the population studied. Thirty years later Kantner and Zelnick (1972) found that 27 per cent of teenage girls had had intercourse by the age of seventeen and by their nineteenth year 46 per cent reported that they were sexually experienced. It will be noted that these figures represent an incidence of sexual intercourse among teenagers in the USA which has more than doubled in the period under review. In Great Britain comparisons can only be drawn between the early 1960s and 1976–7. Schofield's (1965) evidence indicated that 11 per cent of seventeen-year-old girls were sexually experienced, a figure which rose to 23 per cent by the age of nineteen. These results contrast markedly with those of Farrell (1978). She showed that for females, by the middle 1970s 39 per cent of seventeen-year-olds and 67 per cent of nineteen-year-olds had had sexual intercourse. Farrell's figures are illustrated in greater detail in table 7.1.

Table 7.1   Age of first sexual experience

Age of first experience	Males				Females				All
	Age at time of interview				Age at time of interview				
	16	17	18	19	16	17	18	19	
	%	%	%	%	%	%	%	%	%
Before 16	26	32	32	33	13	13	14	10	22
16	5	16	17	24	9	17	12	16	15
17	–	2	12	12	–	9	21	19	10
18	–	–	4	4	–	–	5	14	3
19	–	–	–	1	–	–	–	8	1
Refused	5	2	4	3	3	5	5	6	4
No experience	64	48	31	23	75	56	43	27	45
Number=100%	181	211	186	198	170	189	216	190	1,541

(From C. Farrell (1978) *My Mother Said*, Routledge & Kegan Paul.)

As far as males are concerned, Kinsey reported in the 1940s that 61 per cent had had intercourse by the age of seventeen, and 72 per cent by the age of twenty. When they first appeared these figures were greeted with some scepticism, especially in view of the very small number of girls reporting involvement in sexual activity! Kinsey explained the large differences by pointing out that most boys obtained their experience with prostitutes. With hindsight, however, it seems possible that bias in reporting may have played its part in obscuring accuracy. These conclusions are supported to some extent by the more recent work of Finkel and Finkel (1975), who showed that in the 1970s 69 per cent of seventeen-year-old boys had had sexual intercourse. This figure is more in line with the frequency of sexual activity reported by girls. Turning to Great Britain Schofield (1965) found that 25 per cent of seventeen-year-old males had had intercourse, a figure which increased to 37 per cent by the age of nineteen. Once again these data contrast sharply with the figures reported by Farrell and illustrated in table 7.1. In the 1970s it appears that 39 per cent of seventeen-year-old boys are sexually experienced, while 67 per cent of nineteen-year-olds have had intercourse. It is, of course, extremely difficult to assess the precise meaning of all these percentages. Even allowing for bias and some degree of inaccuracy, however, there can be little doubt that the findings reflect a marked increase in sexual activity over the years. Furthermore, there appears to be a greater change among girls and there are also some rather striking differences between the USA and Britain. American girls certainly give the impression, from these figures at least, of being sexually less experienced than British women, while with the boys it is the other way around. Some further data on the subject of transatlantic comparisons will be presented in a moment.

Conger (1975) makes a particular point of emphasizing the importance of taking into account individual differences when considering figures such as these. Apart from age, sex and nationality, variables such as social class, ethnic origin and cultural background will obviously play their part in determining sexual behaviour, and certainly the research evidence bears this out. Thus, for example, in the USA Kantner and Zelnick (1972) demonstrated a marked difference between black and white girls, with the average incidence of sexual intercourse being 23 per cent for the white girls in the sample, and 54 per cent for the blacks. Finkel and Finkel (1975) showed the same for males. In their study 75 per cent of black subjects had had intercourse while only 48 per cent of white boys were sexually experienced. Social class is another variable of obvious importance. For example, Farrell (1978) was able to show that working-class boys in Britain were more sexually experienced than middle-class boys, and Cooper (1975) reports studies in America which have found that the biggest relative changes, both in attitudes and in behaviour, have occurred among liberal white middle-class boys and girls.

As we have already noted, wider social groupings, such as nationality, also play their part in determining differences. In the study carried out by Luckey and Nass (1969) comparisons were drawn between students from universities in the USA, Great Britain, Germany, Norway and Canada. The results showed that in general North American students were more conservative in their attitudes and held more rigid stereotypes than their European counterparts. It may come as a surprise to some readers, however, to discover that where behaviour was concerned, it was the British students who appeared to be far and away more sexually experienced than students from any other country. Figures to illustrate these findings are shown in table 7.2, and a portion of the authors' summary runs as follows:

> While the investigators tried to construct patterns of sexual behaviour from the responses of men and women students indicating their degree of involvement in activities which range from light

Table 7.2 Percentage of males and females reporting respective sexual behaviours

Type of sexual behaviour	United States	Canada	England	Germany	Norway
Males					
Coitus	58.2	56.8	74.8	54.5	66.7
One-night affair involving coitus; didn't date person again	29.9	21.6	43.1	17.0	32.9
Females					
Coitus	43.2	35.3	62.8	59.4	53.6
One-night affair involving coitus; didn't date person again	7.2	5.9	33.7	4.2	12.5

(From E. B. Luckey and C. D. Nass (1969) *Journal of Marriage and the Family*, 59.)

embracing to coitus, it became obvious the English men and women more freely participate in a gamut of sexual activities, including more genital petting, more frequent coitus, more patronage of prostitution, more sado-masochistic practices, more one-night stands. They start petting and coitus at an earlier age, have more sexual partners, and report alcohol has been a factor in initial coital experience. (1969, p. 376)

It is certainly striking to see one's own country in international perspective, but the picture painted by these authors ought perhaps to be viewed with some reservations, especially since responses were obtained through a postal survey only. As far as the actual incidence of sexual intercourse is concerned, the figures are consistent with those reported by Kantner and Zelnick (1972), Finkel and Finkel (1975) and Farrell (1978), the only contradiction lying in the fact that Luckey and Nass's results cast some doubt on the greater sexual experience of the American male in comparison with his British counterpart.

Finally, in this section mention must be made of the alterations in contraceptive practice which have taken place in the last decade, for nothing illustrates more clearly than this the radical nature of the changes in the whole field of sexual behaviour which have affected young people. Schofield (1965) showed that in the early 1960s over half his population of teenagers only took precautions irregularly, if at all, and that of those who did the great majority used either the sheath (82 per cent) or withdrawal (31 per cent). He writes:

Our inquiries into the use of birth control methods among teenagers have shown that many boys are not using contraceptives and most girls who are having intercourse are at risk. This does not seem to be because teenagers have difficulty in obtaining contraceptives, but because social disapproval means that many of their sexual adventures are unpremeditated and therefore adequate precautions have not been taken beforehand; many of the teenagers are aware of the risks, but in these extemporary situations sexual desire may override an awareness of the possible consequences. (p. 251)

In contrast to this situation Farrell (1978) was able to report a major change. She showed that, in the main, in the 1970s sexually active young people were using methods of birth control, and only 8 per cent said that they had never taken any precautions. This small group of teenagers was predominantly working-class, and two out of every three were boys. However, according to Farrell, adolescents still appeared to be particularly at risk in the very early stages of their sexual experience, for only 54 per cent of the sample reported that they had used some method of birth control on the first occasion. Of particular interest are the changes that occur in the use of contraceptives with age and experience. The data in table 7.3 illustrate the way in which both boys and girls shift to more reliable methods as they get older or become more experienced.

Table 7.3   First and most recent methods of birth control used by age and sex

Methods*	16-year-olds		19-year-olds	
	First %	Most recent %	First %	Most recent %
Males				
Withdrawal	37	24	34	14
Sheath	57	65	57	34
Pill	2	6	7	52
Others	4	5	2	–
Number using birth control (= 100%)	49	49	137	137
% of sexually experienced young males who had never used any method	11		6	
Females				
Withdrawal	30	15	23	8
Sheath	61	45	53	22
Pill	6	36	19	67
Others	3	4	5	3
Number using birth control (= 100%)	33	33	120	120
% of sexually experienced young females who had never used any method	11		4	

* Percentages add to more than 100 because some had used more than one method (e.g. chemicals).

(From C. Farrell (1978) *My Mother Said*, Routledge & Kegan Paul.)

Implications of changing sexual behaviour

The evidence which has been presented so far, in spite of the methodological difficulties which may distort it to some extent, makes clear that adolescent values and attitudes, as well as sexual behaviour itself, are changing rapidly in today's society. Shifts in attitudes and behaviour of the order we have been discussing must inevitably have implications for adolescent development, as well as for personal adjustment. Not only do young people have to cope with their own maturational changes, but they also have to come to terms with a confusing inconsistency among adult views, and a lack of any clear standard or moral code of conduct. Such a situation hardly makes life for the teenager any easier. It would be reassuring if at least more adults in responsible positions showed an interest in these difficulties, and were more often seen developing ways and means of helping young people come to terms with problems associated with sexual behaviour. With rare exceptions, however, the boot is all too frequently on the other foot, with older people bemoaning the increased 'permissiveness' of the behaviour of their adolescent sons and daughters.

As has already been noted the major fear of most adults is that greater sexual freedom, associated in particular with the increased availability of the pill and the greater accessibility of abortion services for young people, will lead to more and more promiscuity. While promiscuity may be very difficult to define, it is the opinion of all social scientists who have investigated the reality of the situation that no such consequence has become apparent. Here is how Farrell (1978) summarized her findings:

> Although teenage sexual activity was not investigated in detail, there was little evidence of promiscuity. The majority of young people currently involved in a sexual relationship were having sex with someone they had been going out with for more than six months, and there was no evidence that the pill was encouraging casual relationships since most of the girls who were taking the pill at the time of the interview had known their partners for more than six months. . . . This overall picture of teenage use of birth control gives the lie to the image of careless and casual teenage sex often promoted by the media. Although there are gaps in birth control use particularly at the initial stages of sexual experience, the majority of teenagers held responsible attitudes to sex before marriage. (p. 219)

Figures on the number of abortions carried out in England and Wales over a five year period from 1973 to 1977 provide corroboration of this view. Thus greater promiscuity would be expected to lead to ever-increasing numbers of abortions, yet figures provided by the Family Planning Information Service, based in London, show that the numbers of abortions have remained steady over this period. These figures are set out in table 7.4.

Table 7.4   Information on pregnancy in young people resident in England and Wales

	1973	1974	1975	1976	1977	1978
Abortions to girls under 20	26,570	27,005	27,395	27,104	27,963	29,745
Of which abortions to girls under 16	3,090	3,243	3,526	3,412	3,592	3,317
Live births to girls under 20	73,300	68,700	63,500	57,900	54,400	55,900
Of which total illegitimate	20,700	21,000	20,500	19,900	20,010	21,700

(Derived from Fact Sheet No. 3 (1978), Family Planning Association Information Service.)

One fact which is often quoted as being indicative of increased promiscuity is the steadily growing incidence of venereal disease. While in some respects it is true that venereal disease is on the increase the situation is rather more complex than that statement implies. In the first place venereal disease is defined as syphilis, chancroid and gonorrhoea. Chancroid in Western societies is virtually unknown today, and syphilis figures are declining among women and remaining constant among men. Gonorrhoea, it is true, is increasing, but in England the rise in the numbers is hardly dramatic, as table 7.5 illustrates. Much greater increases have been charted in other countries, and there is no doubt that the problem must be seen as an international rather than a national one. According to most authorities, in European countries at least, a large proportion of the statistical increase in gonorrhoea figures can be accounted for by improved diagnostic techniques, better contact tracing, and the fact that the organisms involved are becoming drug resistant.

Table 7.5 Gonorrhoea figures for young people resident in England

	1971	1972	1973	1974	1975	1976
Males under 20	4,522	4,250	4,821	4,772	4,852	4,726
Females under 20	5,998	6,274	7,087	7,003	7,455	7,299
Total	10,510	10,524	11,908	11,775	12,307	12,025
Males under 16	129	109	151	118	107	126
Females under 16	400	420	458	460	445	511
Total	529	529	609	578	552	637

(Derived from Fact Sheet No. 3 (1978), Family Planning Association Information Service.)

The fact that promiscuity is not increasing to any great extent among young people is of great significance, and should not go unremarked by anyone interested in the lives of teenagers today. This is especially so in view of the pressures which operate in society, and which impinge on today's adolescents. Hershel Thornburg (1975) has coined the phrase 'social puberty' to describe the situation created by some of the more insidious of these pressures. In particular he draws attention to the heterosexual involvement which is thrust upon the pre-adolescent prior to physiological maturity. This occurs, he argues, as a result of the highly suggestive stimuli presented to young people, usually through the medium of television, but also in films, literature and pop music. Sex in this context is usually portrayed with a materialistic emphasis, and is often associated with the theme of immediate gratification. It is Thornburg's contention that young people are thus almost bullied into sexual activity by the social environment, long before they are mature or have reached puberty proper. Another closely related issue is that of peer pressure. For many teenagers a conflict exists between what they believe is right and what it appears many of their friends are doing. This is a theme already discussed in some detail in chapter 6, but it is especially acute in the area of sexual behaviour. It is just this sort of issue which needs sympathetic and informed support from adults most closely involved with young people.

In considering the difficulties faced by teenagers it should also be pointed out that the simple availability of contraceptive measures does not necessarily solve the problems associated with sexual activity. Some teenagers may, quite rightly, fear the biological consequences of the pill, while others, through shame or anxiety, may be unable to use the advisory medical services. In addition, there will be those whose contraceptive method has failed, and who therefore have to face the prospect of abortion, adoption of the child, or unintended marriage. While a few teenagers may say 'Now that science has given us the pill we no longer have to be worried about pregnancy. We just have to decide what is right' (Conger, 1973, p. 254), it would be a dangerous over-simplification to assume that the problems have gone away. As we have seen, in Britain a proportion of adolescents, particularly boys, still do not use contraception at all, and almost half do not do so on the first occasion. Yet even if there was a perfect contraceptive, used by all, there remains the most complex of all issues – what is right when it comes to sexual behaviour? It is to this problem that we shall undoubtedly turn to an increasing extent in the future, yet certainly today there are few obvious answers. It is for this reason that sex education ought to occupy a more and more important place in the socialization of young people.

Before closing this section on the implications of changes in sexual behaviour some mention needs to be made of current changes in the law, for it is through the legal apparatus that the most tangible evidence can be gained of a society's shift in attitudes. In the UK the 1969 Family Law Reform Act, which reduced the general age of majority from twenty-one to eighteen, states that a person of sixteen can give consent to surgical, medical or dental treatment on his or her own behalf without the consent of parents being obtained. The medical age of majority is thus set two years lower than the general age of majority of eighteen. Under the law in Britain, therefore, a person of sixteen is regarded as medically adult, having the right of professional secrecy and being able to decide what information, if any, should be passed to his or her parents. As far as teenagers under sixteen are concerned, it is for the individual doctor to decide whether to provide contraceptive advice and treatment. Voluntary bodies such as the Family Planning Association and the Brook Advisory Centres have been informed that a doctor who provides treatment or advice for a girl under sixteen is not, in the eyes of the law, 'aiding and abetting the offence of having unlawful sexual intercourse', so long as he or she acts in good faith in protecting the girl against the potentially harmful effects of intercourse.

While such an opinion may today appear perfectly reasonable and humane, it must be remembered that even fifteen or twenty years ago an attitude of this sort would have seemed almost revolutionary. In this context it is of interest to note the similarities in the legal changes which have taken place in Great Britain and the USA. As Hoffman (1978) points out, over the last few years regional decisions across the USA have given growing support to the notion that a person may be a minor in law but mature enough to take certain decisions without parental interference. Of the essence in this notion is the view that maturity and the capability of giving 'informed consent', rather than chronological age, are the primary determining factors in deciding when a minor should have rights of privacy and access to health care. Such a view has recently been embodied in a major constitutional ruling by the United States Supreme Court. In this case the Court was asked to rule on the constitutionality of a Missouri law which, in part, required parental consent for an abortion of a girl under sixteen. The Court invalidated the requirement stating:

> . . . the State may not impose a blanket provision requiring the consent of a parent . . . as a condition for abortion of an unmarried minor. The State does not have the constitutional authority to give a third party an absolute, and possibly arbitrary, veto over the decision of the physician and his patient to terminate the patient's pregnancy. Minors as well as adults are protected by the constitution and possess constitutional rights. Any independent interest the parent may have in the termination of the minor daughter's pregnancy is no more weighty than the right of privacy of the competent minor mature enough to have become pregnant. (Hoffman, 1978, p. 31)

As Hoffman points out, the significance of this decision can hardly be underestimated, for it reflects as clearly as any single statement can the growing acceptance in society of the right of the teenager to determine his or her own medical care, and by implication therefore, his or her own sexual behaviour.

Attitudinal changes of this sort lead one to speculate on the question of whether we will soon see further shifts of a similar kind, and whether the age of consent, at present sixteen in Britain, should be lowered still further. Farrell (1978) draws attention to this issue by pointing out that many British girls come to clinics for contraceptive advice on or around their sixteenth birthday, but very few come before this. Yet her findings show that today possibly as many as one in eight girls under sixteen are sexually experienced. These girls must, therefore, be particularly at risk of unwanted pregnancy, and it is surely reasonable, argues Farrell, to ask whether lowering the age of consent might not be worth it if it would encourage this group to seek reliable advice.

To summarize to this point, we have seen how changes in sexual behaviour have had implications throughout society. Of course it is impossible to determine how attitudes and behaviour interact, or to say which precedes the other. Do changes in the law, for example, encourage young people to gain sexual experience, or do these changes simply provide a legitimate framework for behaviour which is already occurring? No-one can say. Undoubtedly the availability of oral contraceptives has played as big a part as any in causing the changes, but other less tangible factors in society should not be underestimated. From the point of view of the teenager we have seen that, in spite of adult fears to the contrary, there is no evidence to support the view that promiscuity or casual sex is increasing among the young. However, the availability of contraception, while it may have reduced some problems, has in turn created others. Social pressures to gain sexual experience are hard to resist, and can be the cause of much personal conflict. The contraception available today is far from perfect, in spite of the myths which abound in films and literature, and many teenagers have to discover this for themselves the hard way. Finally, increased opportunities for sexual activity create moral and ethical dilemmas which are as complex and difficult to handle as any. It is because of this that good, informed sex education, which is not limited simply to the provision of biological facts, becomes so essential. It is to this issue that we now turn.

Sex education

All that has been said so far serves to underline the necessity for adequate sex education. Teenagers need the best possible preparation to enable them to cope well with their sexual development and to avoid the most obvious pitfalls. In this section we will consider some of the problems associated with sex education, and look at some of the ideas which are being used in schools to improve the traditional curriculum. Let us first, however, consider briefly the question of where most information on sexual matters comes from at the moment.

Many investigators have considered this question, and by and large the results of these studies are surprisingly consistent. In the USA, for example, Thornburg (1975) showed that among a large sample of teenagers from eleven different locations young people estimated that they obtained about 40 per cent of all their information from their peers, and another 40 per cent from school literature. Only about 15 per cent was believed to come from parents. Thornburg broke these figures down further to show that the source of information was linked closely with the content. Thus while 40–45 per cent of teenagers obtained information about menstruation from their mothers, only 9 per cent obtained information about contraception in this way. Schofield (1973) showed that in Britain over 60 per cent of both boys and girls obtained their information from friends, with both parents and teachers coming very low on the list. Interestingly Schofield also asked teenagers in his study how they would prefer to have found out about sex. 63 per cent of men and 50 per cent of women mentioned a teacher as their preferred source of information, and yet the actual numbers quoted in the report (based on research carried out in the 1960s) who were informed by teachers, were 5 per cent for boys and 8 per cent for girls.

To some extent the situation is changing, and there is evidence both from the USA and the UK that realistic sex education is becoming more widely available in schools, and that teachers are playing a more substantial part in the dissemination of sex information. In Farrell's (1978) survey she certainly found that more teachers than in the 1960s were acting as a source of information concerning sexual intercourse and reproduction. Figures to illustrate this will be found in table 7.6. However, the situation in Britain hardly seems to have improved as far as parents are concerned. Even in middle-class, better educated families only 12 per cent of boys and 25 per cent of girls receive information in the home, and these figures are substantially lower in working-class families. It may be, of course, that parents are not the best people to provide the information which is required in this context, and it must be remembered that sex education cannot any longer simply be a discussion of 'where babies come from'. It must now include information on contraception, venereal disease, abortion and so on, and perhaps it is not surprising that many parents feel loath to take on the task. This conclusion is to some extent supported by Farrell's work, for she reported that in her interviews with parents over 50 per cent of them felt that school rather than home was the most appropriate place for this type of learning to take place.

Schofield's (1973) results, referred to above, underline this point, since clearly many teenagers preferred to have this type of instruction away from home. The lesson to be learnt from these findings is undoubtedly that greater efforts should be concentrated on providing better programmes in school. Whatever the source of the sex information, however, and no matter whether it concerns inter-

Table 7.6 First source of information on sexual intercourse by sex and social class

Source	Male		Female		All
	Middle class	Working class	Middle class	Working class	
	%	%	%	%	%
Friends	48	51	37	34	43
Teachers	27	26	28	41	31
Parents	12	4	25	11	12
Books and media	16	14	19	18	17
Siblings	2	3	4	4	3
Other sources	9	12	5	6	7
Don't know/can't remember	6	6	6	6	6
Number = 100%*	310	431	289	427	1,556†

* Percentages add to more than 100% because some young people named more than one source.
† 41 boys and 58 girls included whose fathers' occupations were unclassified or armed forces.

(From C. Farrell (1978) *My Mother Said*, Routledge & Kegan Paul.)

course or venereal disease, parents cannot escape the fact that they too have a role to play. Although neither they nor their teenage children may wish them to act as primary teachers in this respect, attitudes in the home cannot fail to have a significant influence. In addition, it cannot be expected that any one agent, whether it be school, doctor, parent or friend, can fulfil all the needs of a teenager in this area. Thus whatever information is conveyed in school will need to be elaborated and re-examined subsequently if it is to be maximally useful and effective. It is by providing such opportunities that parents can, if they wish, play their part.

There are a number of writers (for example, Schofield, 1973; Cole, 1976) in the field of sex education who express a pessimistic view about the barriers hindering the development of what they see as adequate school programmes. In particular they mention a fear on the part of some teachers that more sex education will encourage casual sex or promiscuity, and the presence of 'old fashioned' attitudes of those who wish to teach a particular moral code, often linked with a religious view of love and marriage. While these issues may be germane in some quarters, it would seem that an undue concentration on such problems serves only to obscure the more fundamental issues which are relevant to all sex education, and which are shared by all teachers, no matter what their approach. Here one might bear in mind challenges such as providing the right information at the right time, making the material relevant not only to the bright and interested teenager, but to the slow learner as well, stimulating interest in parenthood, child development and so on as an essential part of sex education, and most important, giving young people the opportunity of exploring moral and ethical issues in an atmosphere which is both tolerant and supportive.

A number of educationalists have, in the last few years, been attempting to discover ways of achieving some of these goals, and a few examples may serve to illustrate the directions in which these people's thoughts are moving. Four approaches to sex education in the widest sense will be considered here. In the first example, the Health Education Council in Great Britain have used visual material concerning relationships and social situations to provoke discussion of this type of topic. In the second case Juhasz, an American doctor, has set out a chart which takes the adolescent through a process of sexual decision making. Laishley, a British social psychologist, has developed materials which encourage pupils to gain a greater understanding of themselves and of human relationships, and lastly Dalzell-Ward has put forward curriculum material for the study of parentcraft.

As sexual behaviour among young people has become a matter of social concern, teachers and others have looked for ways of incorporating into the curriculum topics which, without too much embarassment, can become the focus of group discussion. Bodies such as the Schools Council and the Health Education Council in Britain have produced materials which can be used with adolescents between the ages of twelve and eighteen. In general this material tends to consist of 'kits' of cards, stories or situations illustrating relevant issues likely to provoke interest among the age group concerned. One example from the Health Education Project 'Living Well' (McPhail, 1977) is shown in figure 7.1. This picture has the following set of questions attached to it:

1   Describe the attitude of the girl at the bus stop. What do you think she hopes will happen?
2   Why do you think she feels as she does?
3   Why do the women talking about her react as they do?

'It's no good saying anything. They always do
what they want.'

Figure 7.1   (From P. McPhail (1977) *And How Are We Feeling Today?*,
Health Education Project.)

4   Is this sort of conflict between the young and middle-aged
bound to happen? Give your reasons for thinking it is or is not.
5   Discuss with your friends how you feel about the cartoon.
A more direct, some might say too direct, approach to encouraging young people to think about sexual behaviour and its consequences is reflected in the work of an American, Ann Juhasz (1975).
She believes that by focusing on the decision making process she can
force teenagers to examine and face up to what can happen as a result
of sexual behaviour. In turn this, she argues, will help them acknowledge that their behaviour, and thus their future, is within their
own control – to see that they do have a choice in the matter. She
presents a model for sexual decision making, illustrated in figure 7.2,
which enables the teacher or counsellor to discuss with the group the
cumulative ramifications of any single decision in sexual behaviour.
The six questions on which this logical chain is based are as follows:
1   Intercourse or no intercourse?
2   Children or no children?
3   Birth control or no birth control?
4   Delivery or abortion?

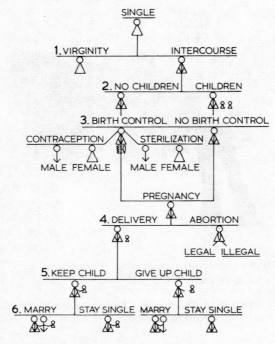

Figure 7.2   A model for sexual decision making.
(From A. M. Juhasz (1975) in *Studies in Adolescence*, ed.
Grinder, Collier-Macmillan.)

5   Keep the child or give it up?
6   Remain single or marry?
As Juhasz says:

> For each of the six questions in this chain, the adolescent should
> understand factors which could influence decisions. In addition,
> for each possible choice, he or she should be aware of the questions
> which will arise, the additional problems which must be faced, and
> the implications of subsequent actions. In other words a logical,
> systematic consideration of the knowns and unknowns is
> required. (p. 345)

For some this approach may simply be too cold-blooded, but what
more effective techniques are there to bring home to young people
the possible long-term consequences in their own lives of one single
act? It may be argued that the decision to have intercourse or not is

rarely a rational one, and that to consider it as part of a logical thought process is meaningless. This may well be true, but on the other hand the use of an effective contraceptive can, with help, be a rational decision. If sex education aims, as it must, to prevent unwanted pregnancy and unwanted marriage, then it is in contexts such as this that Juhasz's shock tactics may really help, encouraging teenagers to learn essential lessons about the consequences of their behaviour.

A rather more gentle, but no less thoughtful, approach is exemplified in Laishley's (1979) development of a Human Relations course. Here her aim was to enable teenagers to develop a deeper understanding of themselves and the problems they were likely to face in everyday living. In order to do this she designed materials which focused on four areas: person perception and judgement of character, issues of self-knowledge, the behaviour of individuals in groups, and personal development in relation to the events of adolescence such as sexual maturation. She relied heavily on participation in group discussion, and used aides such as a 'Who am I?' questionnaire, a check list of Self and Ideal Self, and a set of cards on which pleasant and unpleasant personality traits were depicted to encourage self-examination. Stories and visual material were used to illustrate common interpersonal situations, such as 'The problem of Carla and Andrew'. Here two teenagers were depicted who had just begun to date each other. Both are described as feeling that they fall short in some important respect, which they have judged by comparing themselves with other teenagers. As it happens this 'deficit' is of no concern to their partner, who admires the other for his/her good qualities. None the less these anxieties hinder the relationship. The group, having been presented with the problem, is then asked: 'What should Carla and Andrew do?' 'Are their worries reasonable?' 'How can they best cope with them?' and 'Is this a common problem?' Material of this sort, while not directly relevant to factual sex education, obviously acts as a background to the more traditional curriculum, and provides a basis for the more realistic sexual decision making discussed above.

Lastly, much the same can be said of Dalzell-Ward's (1975) suggestions for parentcraft to be included in health education programmes. He outlines a series of topics which he believes ought to be considered by teenagers which include: the cycle of deprivation, the involvement of boys and fathers in child-rearing, parental stress, the emotional needs of children, baby-sitting, the role of a substitute parent, and so on. He also suggests questions which might serve as background to a discussion, such as: 'How would you help a child of, say, two years to distinguish between right and wrong?' and 'A time comes when the young child shows signs of wanting to become independent. In what ways would you help it to achieve this aim with confidence?' Here again the stress is on focused group discussion, encouraging young people to think through issues directly relevant to their sexual behaviour and relationships with girlfriends or boyfriends before rather than after major life decisions are taken.

Clearly the four examples cited above are only a selection from the many which could have been chosen for discussion. Each of them, however, reflects a common belief: that sex education cannot any longer be limited to the provision of the biological facts of life. Greater sexual freedom for young people necessitates greater responsibility on the part of adults. In particular this responsibility should lead teachers, psychologists and others to provide the best possible preparation for the many problems and conflicts that adolescents will have to face as they mature sexually. As the interview material below indicates, while today's teenagers undoubtedly value the greater openness and freedom available to them, they are also very much alive to the dangers which can stem from such a situation. They are only too aware of the difficulties of controlling strong emotions, especially in a world which lacks any clearly defined guidelines of behaviour, and thus they are able to put the case for appropriate sex education better than any adult.

Naturally, it should not be assumed that all problems will evaporate as a result of good sex education. Some have even pointed out (for example, Schofield, 1973) that research into the effects of sex education finds that there is very little tangible evidence to show for it. This is an argument, however, which can really have very little weight. Perhaps research to date has not been as effective as it might. Perhaps sex education itself has not, in the past, been all that one might have wished. It remains a fact that anything which prepares young people for potentially troublesome areas of their future, and does so in time to prevent difficulties, must be beneficial. Thus self-knowledge, an understanding of sexual decision making, a recognition of the consequences of sexual behaviour and a knowledge of parenthood and what it entails, are all integral aspects of the intellectual equipment needed to grow up today. The more this material can be incorporated into education, the greater chance young people will have of avoiding crises and of retaining control over their own lives.

Interview

Two questions were asked which are relevant to the issues we have been considering in this chapter. Firstly:

As far as having a boyfriend/girlfriend is concerned, what do you think are the problems that people of your age have to face?

Elizabeth (17 years): I think boyfriends are one big problem. Well, it's difficult to say why really, but I mean they can try and change your views in a very subtle way. 'Oh, if you liked me enough you'd do this.' It's really frustrating you know, you have your own values and views, and I don't see why my values and my views should be changed by someone else however much you like them. You know what I mean, and this can clash sometimes.

Jill (16 years): Ah, well, you know, parents. The parents wouldn't turn round and say 'I don't like him, you can't go out with him.' You know, things like that, but if they did I don't know what I would do. I don't know if I would say 'Ah well, get lost, I'm going out with him.' I don't think I would stop seeing him if I loved him enough, but parents is one problem. Money is another, just little things, you know, you're not allowed to go out, you have to stay in, just little things.

Harriett (16 years): Well, my problems are problems in general. Well, I'm very lucky really because my boyfriend is a very good friend to me, and I think a lot of girls see boyfriends as, you know, just somebody they see at 8 o'clock on a certain night. But my boyfriend's very much a platonic friend as well and I find it a lot easier. I don't know, I've never really had any of the sort of classic boyfriend problems really.

Sarah (16 years): Well, at this age personally I don't think it's very important to have a steady boyfriend. O.K., so enjoy yourself at a party, but I don't really approve of, you know, having a steady boyfriend because I don't think at this age it would lead anywhere. Well, personally I believe that if I have a steady boyfriend it will be to get married eventually, and I just don't think of such things at this age. Too young.

Karen (15 years): I don't know, I'm very different from everyone I think – you've got a very different person here. I told you I hate that sort of funny relationship, and I'm quite happy just to sort of . . . I like more to get to know people mentally you know. I'm not into physical relationships really, I don't know why, must be something wrong with me. I think everyone matures at different heights, and sometimes you think 'Good God' you must be sort of abnormal, but sometimes I think to myself, you know, does it matter? What about my friends? Well, I don't know if any of my friends have ever sort of been put into a position that it's either sex or nothing – I've never known any of my friends being put in that position, but there is sort of the problem of getting carried away which has happened to a few of my friends, and I think that's really just about it.

Kevin (15 years): Problems? Well, being shy to take a girl out. There isn't many places you can take a girlfriend out though. You can't go and see some of the films you want to see, you can't go out for a drink, half the time you can't get into a restaurant that's open – they won't allow younger people in, you know, because they think they're going to run off, you know, when they've had the meal. There just isn't a lot of places to go.

Adam (17 years): Well, if you're working for your O levels or A levels, and if you've got a girlfriend you've got responsibilities towards them as well. And you can't do your work fully, you know, your attention isn't directly on your work, and you know, they could interfere. Like, if you're doing your homework and you get a 'phone call or something. The major problem is it draws you away from your work when you should be working.

Richard (15 years): Well, I mean sometimes you might get too involved, you know, really early, and that's one thing, if you get too involved with a girl at this age, then that does bring hardship to you really.

Paul (17 years): Staying on at school you mean? Well, there's money problems I suppose. I suppose some boys think that they've got to get money to take their girlfriends out, but then I suppose it would depend on the girl or whether you knew her well enough or not. It would be different if the girlfriend was at school as well. If she was at school then she would probably understand more than somebody who had left.

The second question asked was as follows:

It is often said that we live in a permissive society today, with young people having more sexual freedom than they ever did. Do you think this is true?

Elizabeth (17 years): To a certain extent yes, I think it is true. But even so the sexual stigma is still there very very strongly. It's still very strong. What do I mean? Well, if a girl sleeps with more than two people she gets labelled, and that is still a very very strong thing. It's not only with older people either, but with your friends as well, because it's usually in some cases your friends that label you.

Jill (16 years): Well the laws are still the same, you know, for drugs and things. Sex? I don't think it's that free you know. Well, I don't know, they go out a lot more I suppose, so if you don't tell your parents where you are you can be doing whatever you like. But then pressure of homework and things like that is a lot more than it was, so it's not the 'swinging 70s' I wouldn't say!

Karen (15 years): Yes, I think so because now everyone sort of comes out and talks about it but before it was never ever uttered. Now because it's more out in the open, and you get tons of thousands of magazines about it, and all this sort of thing, it's so commercialized in fact that it doesn't seem as much as it used to be – it's lost its magic I think mainly. Do I think it's made things more difficult? No, easier, I would have thought. Yes easier because it's not as if you're in the dark about anything – it's all been brought to light.

Kevin (15 years): Well, yeah, it's much more open nowadays you know, and young people can do what they want to. It's up to them really, as long as they realize what the consequences are, and they realize what could happen. I mean there's some kids, you know, who just haven't got a clue. Do I think it makes things more difficult nowadays? Well, I think it's a good thing to be more open, to be more open with your parents about sexual activities, you know. I mean I can go in and tell me mum – like some people call it a dirty joke – but I don't look at it as a dirty joke. So it's easier.

Adam (17 years): Yes, I think so. You always hear parents talking about what it was like fifty years ago for the teenagers of those times and they always say: 'Things weren't like they are today', it has changed a great deal. Has it made things more difficult? Yes and no. It's got its drawbacks as well as its advantages. The idea of younger people having a say, that's alright, but the law could be that much stricter I think, there's much more leniency than what I think there should be.

Richard (15 years): I suppose it is actually, isn't it? I mean you see someone on the corner sort of 'at it', that wouldn't ever have happened before, would it?

Henry (16 years): Oh yeah, that's right. I think it's ridiculous now what goes on in schools, even in schools is bad enough. I think teachers are a bit too tight on it. I mean you can't even walk around school with an arm round a girl – not that you obviously want to anyway – but I don't know, some of the things that I've heard of going on in schools, well, I wouldn't like to say. Everything's going on in schools that you can imagine. How about outside school? Well, I think it's up to people what they want to do out of school really. But I think younger people ought to be told more about it, because in school we don't get told that much, we don't.

8

Turmoil and treatment

'Storm and stress'

The phrase 'storm and stress' has a long history as a description of adolescence. Plato and other Greek writers held a view of youth as a time of marked emotional upheaval, Shakespeare described Elizabethan teenagers as spending their time doing little more than 'wronging the ancientry' and the idea of turmoil following the years of puberty has been an integral feature of all modern theories of adolescence. As Muuss (1975) points out, it was G. Stanley Hall who, at the beginning of this century, borrowed the phrase 'Sturm und Drang' from the history of German literature and first applied it to the psychology of adolescence. The phrase was originally used to describe the writings of authors such as Goethe and Schiller who, in the early eighteenth century, were members of a literary movement committed to a revolution against the old order, and to idealism, passion and suffering. Hall (1904) saw the emotional life of the young adolescent as being not at all dissimilar. He wrote: 'The teens are emotionally unstable and pathic. It is a natural impulse to experience hot and perfervid psychic states, and the whole is characterized by emotionalism. We see here the instability and fluctuations now so characteristic. The emotions develop by contrast and reaction into the opposite' (Vol. 2, pp. 74–5).

As was indicated in chapter 1 both major present-day theories of adolescence – the psychoanalytic and the sociological – incorporate similar notions. While their explanations for the phenomenon of adolescent turmoil may be different, both theories are united in the view that, as Anna Freud expressed it: '. . . adolescence is by its nature an interruption of peaceful growth.' However, we have already noted that other similar theoretical concepts, such as 'identity crisis' and 'the generation gap' have received little support from empirical studies of adolescence. In these areas research evidence does not appear to accord with theory, and it may reasonably be asked whether the same can be said where 'storm and stress' is concerned.

Unfortunately a problem immediately arises as to definition. The phrase 'storm and stress' is used in the literature in widely varying contexts, and it is impossible to be precise about its meaning. While it is taken by some to refer specifically to psychiatric disorder, as manifested in a clinic or hospital, the phrase is used by others to refer to anti-social conduct, to feelings of misery or depression, or even simply to a subjective sense that, as one of the teenagers in the interview material at the end of the chapter expresses it: 'you feel you're being battered from all sides.' In addition there is considerable overlap between the notion of storm and stress and other aspects of adolescent turmoil, such as conflict with parents, self-image disturbance, and so on. 'Storm and stress' is often used to mean something very similar to identity crisis or the generation gap, and thus it is perhaps the most ambiguous concept of all in the literature on adolescence.

In view of this anyone attempting to assess the validity of the notion of 'storm and stress' should proceed with caution. Furthermore what little hard evidence there is available relates primarily to psychiatric disorder, and we still know very little about the adolescent's more subjective experiences of stress or turmoil. This should be borne in mind in the subsequent discussion. In this chapter questions concerning the prevalence and nature of psychiatric disorder in the teenage years will be considered and, in addition, some attention will be paid to three particular types of problem – delinquency, suicide and eating disorders. The reader will of course recognize that this is not a psychiatric textbook, and it will not therefore be possible to give a comprehensive account of the range of psychiatric conditions seen in young people. For this purpose reference may be made to Howells (1971) or Rutter and Hersov (1977). Nonetheless these three problem areas have been chosen as illustrative of widely diverse types of difficulty expressed by young people. A consideration of these problems will provide an opportunity for a discussion of some of the issues surrounding the psychological treatment of adolescents, and will also allow us to pay some attention to the vexed problem of the recognition and identification of psychiatric disorder in this age group.

Psychiatric disorder

Two separate questions may be considered. In the first place theories of adolescence see this period as one of 'storm and stress', and thus it is reasonable to ask whether such a phenomenon is associated with an increased rate of psychiatric disorder. While it must be recognized that 'storm and stress' and psychiatric disorder are not necessarily synonymous, clearly the prevalence of psychiatric disturbance is of considerable interest in this context. If adolescence really is a 'problem stage' in development, however that is defined, at least some increase in psychiatric disorder may be expected. The second question concerns the nature of psychiatric disturbance. Is this the same as that found in childhood, or in adulthood, or are most of the difficulties manifested during this period unique to adolescence? Again if the theories are correct one would anticipate that teenage problems have some special features and, furthermore, that the nature of these problems might cast an important light on the adolescent process itself.

As far as rates of disturbance are concerned, it is hardly surprising to find that these vary according to the type of population investigated. There is however a reasonable extent of agreement in the limited number of studies which have been carried out. Studies of exclusively urban populations (for example, Leslie, 1974) report rates as high as 17 per cent or 19 per cent, while investigations which have been carried out in rural areas (for example, Lavik, 1977) show that only about 8 per cent of the teenage population manifest psychiatric disturbance. Other studies report rates of disturbance which vary between these two extremes. What is most important about these results is the fact that this level of prevalence is very similar to that found in child or adult populations. Rutter *et al*. (1976) provide important evidence in support of this conclusion, for they were able to make comparisons between the rates found in a fourteen-year-old group, and the rates found in the same children when they were ten. In addition, they looked at the prevalence of psychiatric disorder among the parents of these young people, and allowing for some under-estimation because of the fact that information on the adults, particularly the fathers, was only gathered incidentally, they were able to show remarkable similarities across age groups. These figures are illustrated in table 8.1. Thus it appears unlikely that in the adolescent population there is a higher level of psychiatric disturbance than in other age groups, although undoubtedly further investigation is necessary. In particular it should be noted that most studies have concentrated on the younger

Table 8.1   Prevalence of psychiatric disorder by age

| | Ages | | |
	10 years	*14 years*	*Adult (Parent)*
Male	12.7% (*n* = 55)	13.2% (*n* = 91)	7.6% (*n* = 250)
Female	10.9% (*n* = 46)	12.5% (*n* = 88)	11.9% (*n* = 270)

In each case *n* refers to the total sample from the general population who were interviewed in order to determine the proportion with psychiatric disorder.

(From M. Rutter *et al.* (1976) *Journal of Child Psychology and Psychiatry*, 17.)

adolescent, usually on thirteen- or fourteen-year-olds, and far less is known about psychiatric disturbance among older teenagers. Studies of this population would appear to be a high priority.

The second question to be considered is whether the nature of psychological disorder changes in the adolescent years. It may be that while prevalence in the general population does not increase at adolescence, the problems themselves are of a different type, being more severe, more difficult to treat, or following a different course. In their recent review of adolescent disorders Graham and Rutter (1977) consider this issue, and by comparing child and adolescent psychiatric problems, come to the following conclusions. Firstly, they believe that depression, anxiety and other emotional disorders become very much more common in adolescence. Secondly, they point to the altered sex ratio in those presenting psychiatric problems. While in childhood disorders are much more likely to be found in boys than in girls, during the teenage years the ratio becomes more equal. Thirdly, there are important changes in the incidence of the less common psychiatric problems. Thus, for example, schizophrenia and other psychotic conditions, obsessional-compulsive states and suicide attempts – all very rare in childhood – become gradually more manifest as reflections of psychiatric disorder in adolescence. Finally, Graham and Rutter mention the fact that among teenagers severe family discord is less frequently an associated factor of psychiatric disturbance than it is in childhood.

Conclusions such as these are, in general, supported by research findings. For example, Framrose (1975) reviewed the first seventy admissions to an adolescent in-patient unit in Scotland, and showed that two-thirds of the patients were diagnosed as having a 'developmental crisis'. While the author describes this as a 'rather non-specific diagnosis' it is apparent from the results presented that the most common symptoms were anxiety and depression. Other symptoms seen in these patients included phobic states, delinquency, learning difficulties and somatic complaints. Woodmansey (1969) also reviewed a series of seventy patients, in this case adolescents at a child guidance clinic. He showed that of the seventy cases by far the greatest proportion – approximately 35 per cent – expressed anxiety, often accompanied by physical symptoms such as headaches, fainting fits, stomach pains and so on. Other commonly occurring problems were depression, sometimes with suicidal thoughts or fantasies, delinquency, and what the author called 'current friction', i.e. relationship difficulties in the home. In addition to studies such as these work carried out in the USA comes to much the same conclusions. Reports by Rosen et al. (1965), Masterson (1967) and Offer (1969) all indicate a gradual increase in the incidence of psychotic disorders, the common occurrence of anxiety states and depression, and the association between conflict with parents and other psychiatric problems.

Rutter et al. (1976) also stressed the central position of depression in the constellation of adolescent disorders. Here findings showed that while 20 per cent of boys and 23 per cent of girls reported on a questionnaire that they often felt miserable or depressed, a further 21 per cent of boys and 25 per cent of girls agreed at interview with the statement that: 'they sometimes felt miserable or unhappy to the extent that they were tearful or wanted to get away from it all.' Thus almost half of the total sample were experiencing some form of mild depression. Not surprisingly, many such feelings went unnoticed by the adults in the immediate environment. Nonetheless, Rutter and his colleagues lay some emphasis on these results, pointing out that this is the closest they got to finding evidence of general 'adolescent turmoil'. Unfortunately it is difficult to know whether a similar level of depression might not be found in an adult population, but in this context note should be taken of the interviews at the end of the chapter. Such material serves to underline the significance of depressive feelings in a group of relatively well-adjusted young people, as well as providing some support for Rutter et al.'s conclusions.

To recapitulate, rates of psychiatric disorder do not appear to show a marked increase in adolescence, although this deduction must remain a somewhat tentative one until further studies have been carried out among older teenagers. Secondly, as Graham and Rutter indicate in their review, adolescent disorders are clearly different in a number of respects from those found in younger children. However, they are not fundamentally dissimilar from those which might be found in a young adult population. The nature of the problems presented reflect the fact that adolescence is a transitional period, with disorders coming closer and closer in pattern to those manifested in adulthood. In addition, teenage problems do not appear to follow a different course from that seen in an older age group; in other words problems do not last longer, nor are they necessarily any more severe. Lastly, the prognosis for different psychiatric conditions is much the same in adolescence as at any other time; whether the individual improves or not will depend on the nature of the disorder, and not on the age of the patient.

From what has been said it may be concluded that psychiatric disorders in adolescence, although somewhat different from those occurring in childhood, are not at all dissimilar from those observed among adults. However, there are obviously some types of problem behaviour which are, if not unique to the adolescent stage, at least more common during the teenage years than at any other period. Many of these typically adolescent problems tend to be in the realm of social behaviour, and delinquency is the example which springs most readily to mind. In addition, though, there are other forms of problem behaviour which may not come to the notice of a psychiatric clinic, but which are more often dealt with by youth workers, teachers, social workers and school counsellors. For instance, drug problems, eating disorders, depression, refusal to go to school, and difficulty in settling to a job, are all manifestations of difficulties in the adolescent process of adjustment. While it is not possible to deal with all these issues in this short chapter, three rather different aspects of problem behaviour will be considered.

Delinquency

In comparison with all other problems of adolescence, juvenile delinquency is both the most common and the most likely to create concern on the part of governments, professional agencies and the man in the street. Technically, the term is used in Great Britain to describe behaviour of those under the age of seventeen which is punishable by law. In fact, delinquency is frequently used in a much wider sense to mean any anti-social behaviour on the part of young people. Studies are limited by the fact that criminal behaviour only becomes apparent once the individual is apprehended. Thus all the statistics available are generally considered to be underestimates of the true dimensions of the problem. Nevertheless, they are striking enough. To take two examples, in West and Farrington's (1977) most recent book they report that 30.8 per cent of the working-class London boys whom they first interviewed at the age of eight had had at least one conviction by the time the majority of them had reached the age of twenty-one. In the USA, the delinquency rate has risen from approximately 20 per 1,000 head of the population in 1957 to 35 per 1,000 in 1974 (Conger, 1977). These figures give some indication of the extent of the problem, although it should be noted that rates vary widely depending on the population studied, and that there are a number of important variables to be taken into account.

Maliphant (1979) gives a breakdown of the types of offences of all those under the age of seventeen found guilty or cautioned for indictable offences in England and Wales in the year 1974. These figures show that by far the most common offences concern theft and the handling of stolen goods. Fifty-five per cent of the boys and 82 per cent of the girls who came before the courts fell into this category. Thirty-six per cent of the boys were involved in the more serious crimes of burglary or criminal damage, while this only applied to 10 per cent of the girls. It is interesting to note that in terms of actual numbers 144,238 boys and 29,372 girls were involved, a ratio of approximately 5:1. According to Conger (1977), however, the trend in the USA indicates that an increasing number of girls are receiving convictions, and West (1977) points to the beginning of a similar process in Great Britain.

One of the difficulties facing any commentator on delinquency is that there are clearly many types of offender, and to discuss all delinquents as if they were the same obviously represents a serious over-simplification of the problem. Yet the classification of delinquents into different categories is far from easy. Maliphant (1979) makes the point that to differentiate delinquents according to the offence they have committed makes little sense, especially since few habitually commit similar offences. Furthermore, there is little to be gained by attempting a classification according to sentence, since attitudes amongst judges and magistrates vary widely. Perhaps the most realistic classification is one related to re-conviction rates. In the UK approximately 50 per cent of delinquents do not offend again after their first court appearance, and there is strong evidence to suggest that there are substantial differences between first offenders and those who come before the courts more than once. West and Farrington (1977) have indicated that personality factors differenti- ate between the two types of delinquent, and other writers (for example, Gold, 1970) support this view. Writers have also drawn attention to possible social class differences between the two groups, pointing out that delinquents from middle-class backgrounds are more likely to be once-only offenders. Another distinction which is sometimes drawn is one between the 'sociologic' and the 'individual' delinquent (Conger, 1977). According to this view, the former type is 'largely moulded by the community and home forces more or less consciously in opposition to the whole other social world'. In other words, anti-social behaviour for such people is 'the norm', the police and the forces of law and order are perceived as legitimate opponents in a necessary struggle for survival, and criminal behaviour is believed to be an integral part of a deprived working-class way of life. In contrast to this pattern the 'individual' delinquent is more likely to have a home background which is either middle-class or unlikely to condone anti-social behaviour, and he is, therefore, frequently at odds with his parents, liable to suffer from some form of emotional difficulty, or to come from a family in which there is marked disrup- tion or parental disharmony.

Much recent work in this field, and in particular that carried out by sociologists, has tended to focus on what are known as the ecological factors associated with delinquency. Thus it is well known that areas which have high rates of delinquency are likely to be urban environments with poor housing, a declining population, a lack of recreational facilities, high unemployment and so on. It also appears that in spite of social changes, these high delinquency areas remain the same over considerable periods of time. For example, Maliphant (1979) quotes studies which have reported highly significant correla- tions over a period of thirty years for rates of delinquency in the same city areas, in spite of major alterations in population and distribution of urban resources over this time span. Naturally, findings such as these raise as many questions as they answer, and we are no closer to knowing whether deprived environments attract families whose members are likely to be involved in criminal behaviour or whether such behaviour is actually facilitated by poor environments.

One topic of special interest to the sociologists and ecologists has been the relation between school and delinquency. In Great Britain it was Michael Power (1967) who first drew attention to the possibility that secondary schools might have differing rates of delinquency, even when their pupils came from identical 'social backgrounds'. As might be imagined, such a heretical suggestion created a furore among head teachers, but more recent work (for example, Gath *et al.*, 1975; Reynolds *et al.*, 1976) has provided substantial support for Power's findings. In an article entitled 'The Delinquent School' Reynolds (1976) compared delinquency rates of nine secondary schools in South Wales, all of which drew upon a homogeneous working-class population. He showed that while one school had 10.5 per cent of its boys officially registered as delinquent, another averaged only 3.8 per cent. Reynolds also reported on attendance rates, which ranged from 89.1 per cent to 77.2 per cent, and on levels of academic achievement within the schools. His findings showed a clear relation between these three indices – for example, poor attendance was associated with a high delinquency rate and low academic performance – as well as a striking consistency over the years, for the relative performance of the schools remained largely unchanged between 1966 and 1972. As Reynolds wrote: 'The effective schools continued to be effective.' Table 8.2 indicates the relation between the three indices. Although as part of the study Reynolds investigated a number of other factors, such as staff turnover, which might possibly contribute to the morale and effectiveness of the school, he readily admits that little is known of exactly what it is within the

Table 8.2   Secondary modern school performance, academic years 1966–7 to 1972–3

School	Delinquency	Attendance	Academic attainment
	%	%	%
A	10.5	79.9	34.8
B	8.6	78.3	26.5
C	8.3	84.3	21.5
D	8.1	77.2	8.4
E	7.4	89.1	30.4
F	7.2	81.3	18.5
G	5.2	87.0	37.9
H	4.5	88.5	52.7
I	3.8	83.6	36.5

Note: Delinquency is defined as first offenders per annum.
(From D. Reynolds *et al.* (1976) *New Society*.)

schools which creates the critical difference. In spite of this, however, studies such as these cannot be ignored. As Michael Power has said, whatever the explanation, it seems probable that some schools are actually preventing a proportion of their pupils – potential delinquents – from becoming involved in criminal activities, while others are providing an environment which encourages delinquent behaviour outside the school boundary.

A criticism which is sometimes levelled at the social approach to delinquency is that although it may succeed in identifying relevant factors in society at large, it cannot solve the problem of why, within one homogeneous social group, some young people will become delinquent, while others will not. For answers to that question it is necessary to turn to research on family background and personality development. The area is an extensive one and cannot adequately be covered here. Interested readers are referred to Cooper (1977), West (1977) and Maliphant (1979). Two points may, however, be noted. Firstly, it is probably one of the most frequently documented findings in child psychology that there is a relation between delinquency and disrupted family background. Such factors as divorced parents, violence in the home, absentee fathers, early mother-child separation, and so on, are all known to be associated with anti-social behaviour among teenagers. However, what is less well-known is that in recent years a number of studies have indicated that the relation between family background and delinquency is not as simple as has hitherto been assumed. Thus, for example, it now seems more probable that it is the emotional conflicts within the home which are linked with delinquent behaviour, rather than the actual fact of parental separation, loss of father figure, or whatever it is. Recent research (for example, Rutter, 1971; West and Farrington, 1973; Power et al., 1974) has indicated that simple indices of family circumstances are less closely associated with teenage delinquency than are more sensitive indicators of emotional climate within the home.

One other issue of note is the prediction of delinquency from childhood behaviour. Glueck and Glueck (1950, 1960) have championed the view that it is possible, even during the pre-school years, to differentiate between those who are and those who are not likely to come into conflict with the law during adolescence. Perhaps the most impressive work to substantiate a similar, although somewhat modified, view is that of Conger and his colleagues (1965, 1966), who carried out a large-scale longitudinal study of children between the ages of six and eighteen in Colorado. Their findings showed that already by the ages of seven and eight future delinquents appeared to their teachers to be less friendly, less responsible, more impulsive, and more antagonistic towards authority. They were less liked and accepted by their peers, while in their schoolwork they were more easily distracted and had greater difficulty maintaining attention and completing tasks. These differences persisted as the children got older and, in addition, other features became apparent. For example, by the ages of ten and eleven inconsistent academic performance among the future delinquents became more marked, while in middle adolescence poor peer relationships, refusal to accept responsibility, and continual clashes with authority distinguished the delinquent group from others in the study. At all ages delinquents tended to have predominantly negative self-concepts, to see themselves as useless and worthless in comparison with their contemporaries, and to have very little liking or respect for themselves. In the UK West and Farrington (1973) have more recently carried out a longitudinal study in which they found that by the ages of eight to ten future delinquents could be differentiated from others in a similar way.

Studies such as these are important for a number of reasons. In the first place, they indicate only too clearly the way in which adolescent delinquent behaviour has its antecedents in earlier stages of childhood. This certainly provides a counterbalance to those who argue that much delinquent behaviour results solely from adolescent frustrations or difficulties. Findings of this nature are also important because they highlight what is likely to be a vicious circle in the school career of many problem children. They do less well, and are less popular in the early years. They themselves learn to expect unpopularity and failure. This in turn leads to anxiety, frustration and even worse performance, and thus the vicious circle is set in motion. In addition to this, such children rapidly become 'labelled' by teachers in the manner described by David Hargreaves and his colleagues (1975), and are in this way almost helped towards deviance by a mixture of the self-fulfilling prophecy and rejection by the teaching staff.

It may seem to some that the findings of Conger *et al.* and West and Farrington are incompatible with the view of those who ascribe an important role to the school itself. On second glance, however, the two approaches are far from contradictory. Power, Reynolds and others are simply arguing that some schools are more likely to foster delinquent behaviour than others. That is not to say that the school alone causes delinquency. Clearly, as we have seen in the previous chapter, there are a multitude of influences which determine anti-social behaviour, and personality and family background are in all probability likely to play a larger part than institutions and environment. Nevertheless, up to now one of the major faults in all social science research investigating a phenomenon such as delinquency has been to over-simplify. Thus it is a welcome trend in this field to find writers acknowledging the multiplicity of factors at work in the determination of something as complex as delinquent behaviour. The next step for those involved in research will be to look at the ways in which factors so far identified interact one with the other.

Suicide

As everyone who has written on this topic has pointed out, the occurrence of suicide in an adolescent is something which creates a special anxiety and distress in adults. A sense of waste, the wish to have been able to foresee the tragedy, and the guilt of those who might have been able to prevent such an irrevocable act, although in evidence following any successful suicide attempt, tend to be especially acute when it is a young person who has taken his or her own life. Andre Haim, a French psychoanalyst writing about adolescent suicide goes further. He states:

> The attitude of the adult is further complicated by the fact that he uses the image of the adolescent to defend himself against death. . . . The intensity of the adolescent's impulses makes him the symbol of the life instinct almost in its pure state. . . . In order to forget that death exists within every man . . . the adult uses the image of the adolescent as a representative of reality, freshness, love of life. . . . (1974, p. 42)

Be that as it may, there can be few more upsetting things than to have known well a young person for whom death was the only solution to the problems of growing up.

In the literature on suicide in individuals under the age of fifteen the study carried out by Shaffer (1974) is probably the most thorough to date, certainly in the UK. Shaffer investigated all childhood suicides in England and Wales over a seven-year period, 1962–9. He found that there were no deaths at all from this cause below the age of twelve, but that in the twelve to fourteen year age range such deaths gradually increased in number. As in the adult population, twice as many boys as girls committed suicide successfully, and among this group who took their own lives there were more tall children and more of superior intelligence than would have been expected, which implies an accelerated degree of both conceptual and physical maturity among such individuals. The study showed that the most common precipitating situation before the suicidal act was one in which the young person knew that the parents were to be told of some type of anti-social behaviour or loss of face which had taken place away from the home. Actual disputes within the home were relatively rare as precipitating events. It is a sobering fact that Shaffer noted previous suicidal behaviour in 40 per cent of those who did take their own lives, and he further pointed out that, as a result of the difficulty in gathering information of this nature, such a figure may well be an underestimate. Finally, it was shown that the extent of experience of suicide among those who actually took their own lives was very much greater than it was among those in the normal population. Many had relatives or contemporaries at school who had been involved in suicidal behaviour, and those who did not have models of this sort were often found to have been reading books with suicidal content, or to have indulged in suicidal fantasies of one type or another. The effect of modelling on suicidal behaviour has also been stressed by other writers such as Kreitman *et al.* (1970).

It is clear from a large number of studies of older adolescents that suicide rates increase sharply after the age of fifteen. In addition, some studies have shown that since the 1950s actual numbers of suicides per head of the population have increased among those in the adolescent age range. Conger (1977) reports that in the US the adolescent suicide rate has nearly trebled in the two decades from 1954–74, in comparison with the adult rate which has stayed relatively constant. This is a point also stressed by Bronfenbrenner (1974), in his article entitled 'The Origins of Alienation'. However, data prepared by the DHSS in the United Kingdom indicate a rather different picture for British adolescents. As may be seen from figure 8.1 there has hardly been any overall change among the fifteen to nineteen year age group between 1960 and 1974. In spite of this difference between the two countries, in both the USA and the UK actual suicides among older adolescents, as with Shaffer's younger group, are more common among boys, while attempted suicides are more common among girls. A study carried out in New South Wales, Australia (Kraus, 1975), reiterated this point by showing that among all suicide attempts 14.7 per cent were successful in boys between the ages of ten and nineteen, while only 2.9 per cent were successful among girls of the same age. Morgan *et al.* (1975), studying attempted suicides in Bristol in the years 1972–3, showed that among the fifteen to twenty year age group, for every 100,000 of the population, there were 166 suicide attempts by boys as compared with 660 by girls, representing quite a substantial difference.

Evidently statistics of this sort, while valuable as background

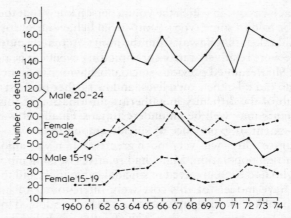

Figure 8.1   Death by suicide or self-inflicted injury 1960–74.
(From M. Tyler (1978) *Advisory and Counselling Services for Young People*, HMSO.)

information, do not give much of a picture of the actual behaviour of a suicidal adolescent. In a useful book on the subject Jacobs (1971) describes four likely stages in the development of suicidal behaviour:

1   A long-standing history of problems.
2   A period of 'escalation' of problems.
3   The progressive failure of available techniques for coping with old and increasing new problems, which leads the adolescent to a progressive social isolation from important relationships.
4   The final phase, characterized by a chain reaction dissolution of any meaningful social relationships in the weeks and days preceding the suicide attempt.

Such an outline may seem perhaps a little too glib, and it is unlikely that many teenagers will actually show such a clearly delineated and progressive breakdown. Shaffer (1974), in the study already discussed, showed that in almost all cases there was a pre-cipitating event, but only too frequently it was not possible, without the aid of hindsight, to see its potentially critical significance for the individual concerned. Furthermore, while Shaffer's study underlined the role of family disturbance and earlier stressful events, in very few cases was there a deterioration of relationships which could have been charted in the manner suggested by Jacobs. In this context it is important, as Conger (1977) and many other writers point out, to dispel the myth that those who talk about committing suicide will never do it. While it is obviously exceptionally difficult to predict suicidal behaviour, it is worth remembering that communications of any sort which may represent pleas for help ought not to be disregarded. Teenagers who talk openly about suicide should not be ignored, even if all that is done is to take seriously their distress or need for attention. Conger (1977) himself suggests four warning signs which might serve to alert any concerned adult:

1   The continuing presence of a depressed mood, eating and sleeping disturbances, or declining school performance.
2   Gradual social withdrawal and increasing isolation from others.
3   Breakdowns in communication with parents or other important persons in the adolescent's life.
4   A history of previous suicidal attempts or involvement in accidents.

Thus it will be apparent that Conger places the emphasis on behavioural indices of disturbance in mood or relationships; the issues raised by such an approach will be examined at the end of the chapter. Valuable though these indicators may be, however, it remains a sad but inescapable fact that in many cases it is quite impossible to predict or prevent individuals from taking their own lives. It is worth remembering that where such a situation has occurred, the professionals involved have just as much of a responsibility to the surviving parents, siblings and close friends, and this refocusing of concern can be a constructive way of coping with the feelings of guilt and inadequacy which are almost always aroused by a teenage suicide.

Eating disorders

In view of the marked physical changes which occur at puberty, and the consequent concern with self and body image which was discussed in chapters 2 and 3, it is not surprising to find that many young people become pre-occupied with problems of weight and diet. Eating disorders have been selected for discussion, therefore, as an issue having more general relevance than the topics of suicide and delinquency, although of course such disorders can in some cases be severe enough to warrant medical or psychiatric attention. In this section we will consider both obesity and excessive weight loss, sometimes known as anorexia nervosa. Before we do so, however, it is important to point out that any precise definition of these conditions is bound to run into difficulties. An individual's weight is determined by many factors, and can only be judged in relation to his or her height, weights in the rest of the family, past nutritional and medical history, and so on. In addition, the period of adolescence frequently brings with it marked weight variations, as the individual adjusts to the hormonal changes taking place in the body. Furthermore, social pressures play their part, and it is not uncommon for teenagers, especially girls, to go through stages of intense weight and figure consciousness, during which the intake of every calorie is watched. Others, on the contrary, may have bouts of over-eating, gorging themselves on snacks as well as large meals, and stating, to the despair of those around them, that they are continually hungry. These relatively normal variations in diet make it extremely difficult at times for parents to determine what constitutes serious weight gain or loss, and a medical opinion may sometimes be necessary in such situations.

While obesity has been recognized as a medical problem for some considerable time it is only recently that serious attention has been paid to the psychological factors involved in excessive over-eating. Obesity is clearly a complex problem, and as Graham (1977) points out, it is unlikely to occur in isolation and is commonly associated with a range of other difficulties. In addition, no one single cause is likely to be responsible. Chisholm (1978) indicates a number of possible reasons which may underlie obesity in adolescence. In the first place, many young people with eating disorders show an impairment in their ability to recognize internal hunger cues. Thus while most people are able to judge whether they have had enough to eat as a result of physiological feedback, obese individuals either ignore or misinterpret such signals. Schachter (1968) designed a simple laboratory experiment to demonstrate this. He had two groups of subjects, an obese and a normal group, whom he invited to take part in a study of taste. Half of each group were fed before the experiment began. In the experiment itself, subjects were presented with five different types of food, and told they could eat as much as they liked in order to be able to describe adequately the tastes in each. In the control group, those who had eaten beforehand ate very little in the experiment proper, while in the obese group those whose stomachs were already full ate as much and sometimes more, than those whose stomachs were empty.

A second factor thought to underlie obesity is a disturbance in the sense of self-control. Obese individuals are frequently those who lack a sense of personal autonomy, and feel that they are being managed by others. Thus it is only in their eating behaviour that they are able to express their own wishes and needs. Conger (1977) describes a number of experiments which have shown obese adolescents to be passive or timid, eager to please, tolerant of abuse, and willing to accept other people's negative views of themselves. Thirdly, a number of writers have drawn attention to the fact that over-eating may be a reactive phenomenon as, for example, in those who have suffered some psychological trauma or loss. Under such conditions eating may represent a compensation for loss, and may be used by the individual to reduce depression or emotional emptiness. Finally, it needs to be borne in mind that one reason for over-eating may be to do with its effect on the individual's body image. To be fat, and therefore not good-looking, can be a defence against sexual attractiveness or popularity. It can also be a useful way of resisting parental aspirations, such as social success for girls or achievement on the sports field for boys, which the adolescent wishes to reject without direct confrontation. Lastly, for the especially vulnerable young person, it can be a means of ensuring the rejection which he or she fears, and yet is driven to seek as a confirmation of a negative self-image and poor self-esteem.

Where weight loss is concerned, somewhat different considerations apply. Many young people, particularly girls, are likely to be affected by the stress placed on the necessity for having a slim figure in present day society. What might seem to parents like an excessive concern with weight is probably not at all unusual, and teenagers who eat very little for short periods are not necessarily suffering from the condition known as anorexia nervosa. This condition occurs infrequently, and can in the main be recognized by an abnormal pre-occupation with the need to be thin combined with serious weight loss. Tolstrup's description is as follows:

> Anorexia nervosa can be defined as a disease characterized by a severe loss of weight which is caused by the patient deliberately restricting food intake. There is a considerable loss of weight as a consequence. The patients also show faulty perceptions of their own body image, unusual eating habits, unusual interest in their own food intake and the intake of others, and a considerable increase in bodily activity. (1975, p. 75)

The condition rarely occurs before puberty, and is very much more common in females. Amenorrhoea is a usual accompanying symptom. This is a disorder which, unlike obesity, has received considerable attention in the literature, partly as a result of the severity of the condition in some cases. Much research has been carried out, both in the UK and in the USA (for example, Crisp et al., 1976; Bruch, 1974a), and many theories have been postulated in an attempt to explain such a phenomenon. However, it is almost always extremely hard to judge exactly what lies behind such apparently irrational behaviour as self-starvation. Most commentators believe that the condition is associated with a disturbance in psycho-sexual development, an important element of which is an irrational fear of sexuality and of normal maturation. Thus, for girls, eating may be associated with sexuality either as a result of primitive ideas about oral conception (food-stomach-babies growing), or because of the link between a shapely female figure and sexual attractiveness. In this latter situation to be thin represents a denial of femininity.

Bruch (1974b), while agreeing with formulations such as these, also points to two other critical features. In the first place, she believes that young people in this condition are involved in a desperate fight for self-determination. As she puts it: '. . . anorexics struggle against feeling enslaved, exploited and not being permitted to lead a life of their own. They would rather starve than continue a life of accommodation. In this blind search for a sense of identity and selfhood they will not accept anything that their parents or the world around them has to offer' (p. 250). In relation to this it is important to note her view that many teenagers who develop anorexia will be found to have been 'model' children, conforming to parental expectations and showing no signs of atypical development. Bruch concludes that, among other things, it is precisely this 'too good' orientation which leads to difficulties in the establishment of an individual identity in adolescence. She also underlines the importance of a distortion in body image as a feature of anorexia nervosa. Patients with this condition often appear unable to judge what is normal or abnormal as far as body size and weight are concerned, and frequently deny vehemently that there is anything wrong with their own emaciated appearance. Finally, nothing has been said so far, either in relation to obesity or anorexia, concerning the symbolic meaning of food. It must be self-evident that where individuals show disorders of eating behaviour, these are highly likely to be linked with their own idiosyncratic fantasies about food and what it represents. Undoubtedly the meaning ascribed by each individual, often at an unconscious level, to meals and to the process of eating will play its part as one aspect of the problem, although rarely will this be a sufficient explanation for a serious condition such as anorexia.

There is general agreement among writers that the treatment of teenagers with eating disorders is a difficult and delicate process. Chisholm (1978) has reviewed treatment programmes for obese adolescents, while Tolstrup (1975) has done the same for anorexics. Both writers make the point that the multiplicity of causes usually underlying such conditions means that rarely will any one single treatment approach be sufficient. A combination of different types of treatment is thus often necessary, associated with a flexible approach on the part of the doctor or psychologist. Having said this we may now turn to a consideration of the various types of treatment available.

'Why bother – we're all fat.'

Figure 8.2 (From P. McPhail (1977) *And How Are We Feeling Today?*, Health Education Project.)

Psychological treatment

Treatment of adolescents, it is generally felt, is a more demanding process than is usually the case with younger children or adults. There are a number of reasons for this. In the first place teenagers, especially those in the younger age range, frequently appear resentful or unco-operative. This may simply be a reflection of their present relationships with adults; they may feel put upon, resistant to the idea of help, or angry because they have been dragged to the clinic by someone else. Secondly, the course of treatment seldom runs smoothly – at one moment the adolescent may be expressing black depression, at the next elated optimism; today the therapist may be the only person who really understands, tomorrow he or she may be the most unsympathetic person in the whole world. This inconsistent behaviour, and the violent mood swings which accompany it, are a common characteristic of work with disturbed adolescents, and can

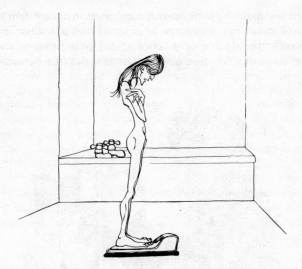

'Oh God, I've put on two pounds again!'

Figure 8.3   (From P. McPhail (1977) *And How Are We Feeling Today?*, Health Education Project.)

lead not surprisingly to a sense of bewilderment and exasperation on the part of the adult involved. Anthony (1974) describes involvement in adolescent therapy as being similar to 'running next to an express train'.

A further problem faced more commonly by those working with adolescents than those working with any other age group is the threat of acting-out behaviour. The knowledge that if things do go badly the teenager may take an overdose, get pregnant, leave home, steal a car, or whatever, are possibilities that hang over the head of the therapist, and lead to the sensation of continually walking on a tightrope. Finally, there is almost always the critical issue to face – is this individual to be treated as a child or as an adult? Such a question may sound simple, but all too often it is just this dilemma which makes treatment so problematic, for it enables the teenager to place the therapist in the classical 'no win' situation. Whichever side the adult chooses will be the wrong one, and it is only with considerable experience that the therapist learns to find the delicate balance which admits of both possibilities. In spite of all these pitfalls there is no doubt that work with disturbed adolescents can be extremely rewarding, particularly if, as Conger (1977) puts it: 'One's definition of reward is the adolescent's ultimate psychological growth and improved chances of leading a reasonably effective existence' (p. 624). Obviously there are many different types of treatment facility available for teenagers. As far as psychiatric services are concerned, these range from the structured in-patient unit for seriously disturbed adolescents, usually attached to a hospital, to the unstructured walk-in or consultation centre, and it is with these facilities that we shall be primarily concerned. However, adolescents with problems do not always reach the psychiatric services, and it must be recognized that many such young people will be found in various types of special school, in community homes, in assessment centres and so on. A consideration of these provisions is unfortunately beyond the scope of this chapter. Here we will look first at the structured in-patient unit.

Framrose (1975) describes the work of the Young People's Unit in Edinburgh:

> The Unit provides fifteen beds for adolescents of both sexes between the ages of fourteen and twenty. The Unit is run on fairly permissive, democratic lines. The adolescents attend daily small group psychotherapy sessions of an hour and a quarter with the psychiatrists, and also community meetings with the nurses. At one of these meetings they organize a rota of domestic chores in the house and the allocation of evening passes. *Ad hoc* meetings can be convened by staff or patients in times of crisis. In the afternoons the adolescents are required to attend local school or to obtain part-time employment. There are weekly psycho-drama sessions. The youngsters go home at weekends and join with their parents in multiple-family groups once a week. While the emphasis is towards a psycho-therapeutic understanding of individual and family difficulties, constant stress is also placed on appropriate maturational progress, often involving techniques of direct confrontation from staff or other patients. Firm limits are set on time-keeping and on 'acting out' behaviour, but as far as possible the staff try to use the democratic atmosphere to enable the adolescents to set limits for themselves. There is a high staff-patient ratio, with eight nurses as well as a full-time social worker and three psychiatrists who also have out-patient commitments. (p. 381)

Situated at Hill End in Hertfordshire a not dissimilar Unit is described by Bruggen *et al.* (1973). While it would seem that in Edinburgh the main focus of the work is on the maturational tasks of adolescence, at Hill End a particularly strong emphasis is placed on the reason for admission. Thus many of the resources of the Unit are concentrated on family meetings which occur before the teenager is admitted, in order to define the problem in terms which are understood by all concerned. In addition, the staff aim to create a contract between themselves and the family, which emphasizes the shared nature of the problem, and defines the changes required before discharge can take place. The authors explain:

> During the period of admission, which gives the family a break to recuperate, the Unit's professional skills are offered to help them develop a better understanding of themselves, particularly those aspects which make separation necessary. Work is directed towards reunion. It is argued that by admitting adolescents only while families or institutions cannot cope, or by supporting them with offers to do so in the future should the need arise, the adolescent's long term placement is maintained. Important emotional ties are not broken, but merely interrupted when absolutely necessary. (p. 328)

In-patient units are rare, and are obviously only able to cater for a small minority of disturbed adolescents. More common is treatment offered in an out-patient setting, either in a child guidance clinic or in a social work context. In settings such as these a recent development has been a greatly increased use of family therapy, that is, involvement of all members of the family in the treatment process. Reviews of this type of therapy may be found in Minuchin (1973, 1974), Skynner (1976) and Bruggen and Davies (1977). As the latter authors make clear, however, family therapy is not one single type of treatment, but rather a range of techniques and approaches, all of which share the common belief that the greater the involvement of family members, the more effective the process is likely to be. Minuchin et al.'s (1973) work in Philadelphia with anorexic teenagers illustrates these points. First he combines a behavioural and a family approach. Thus, initially a 'contract' will be worked out between the therapist and the individual adolescent in which increasing rewards (for example, access to television) may be gained by progress in eating and weight gain. In addition to this, however, family sessions are held in which the therapist concentrates on the behaviour of all members, and focuses on the maladaptive relationships in the home setting. In order to do this techniques will be borrowed from many sources, including psychotherapy and Gestalt therapy, and individuals will be required to take part in role-playing and other active group exercises.

While family therapy is being used fairly widely today with adolescent patients, it would be wrong to give the impression that all treatment runs along these lines. As Rutter (1975) points out, it is an approach which is only appropriate in certain circumstances. Thus, for example, if parents are about to separate or the teenager is about to leave home there would be little point in attempting family therapy. Furthermore, it is not usually the best form of treatment when the predominant feelings in the family are ones of rejection and hostility towards the young person, without any compensatory warmth or tolerance. In addition to these considerations a number of therapists prefer to work with teenagers on their own, and of course for many older adolescents treatment in the family setting would in any event be inappropriate. Where work is likely to be carried out on an individual basis some form of psychotherapy is the most commonly used approach.

According to Irene Josselyn (1952, 1971) individual psychotherapy with adolescents is most frequently directed towards finding new, more adaptive and less self-defeating ways of handling current problems and of relating to others. Other important goals include the elimination of unnecessary fears and conflicts, and the achievement of a greater integration of the individual's needs with the demands of reality. In order to do this the therapist will be most likely to note and interpret distortions in the adolescent's reactions to people and events in everyday life, as well as distortions in the young person's relationship with the therapist. Rutter (1975) has noted that, in comparison with earlier types of intensive psychoanalytic treatment, psychotherapy today is more likely to focus primarily on the present here-and-now situation, to pay greater attention to conscious rather than unconscious conflict, to place greater reliance on the therapist–teenager relationship as the main treatment agent, and to curtail the length of treatment by setting specific goals rather than having an open-ended contract.

Hilde Bruch's work with young people suffering from eating disorders provides an excellent illustration of this modern approach. She writes:

> Disappointing treatment results led to my re-evaluation of these patients' needs, and I felt it necessary to examine the question of to what extent the traditional model had failed to fulfil them. In spite of gaining insight some basic disturbance in their approach to life remained beclouded and untouched, or was even reinforced in the traditional psychoanalytic setting, where the patient expresses his secret thoughts and feelings, and the analyst interprets their unconscious meanings. This represents in a painful way a repeti-

tion of the significant interaction between patient and parents, where 'mother always knew how I felt', with the implication that they themselves do not know how they feel. 'Interpretation' to such a patient may mean the devastating re-experience of being told what he feels and thinks, confirming his sense of inadequacy, and thus interfering with his developing true self-awareness and trust in his own psychological faculties.

Under a fact-finding, non-interpretive approach, seemingly unanalysable patients who were filled to the brim with useless, though not necessarily incorrect, knowledge of psychodynamics, began to change and improve. This was achieved by paying minute attention to the discrepancies in a patient's recall of his past, and to the way he misperceived or misinterpreted current events, often responding to them in an inappropriate way. Hiding behind expressions like 'compulsive eating' or 'food addiction' patients will uncover, when held to a detailed examination of the when, where, who and how, real or fantasized difficulties and emotional stresses of which they had been completely unaware. . . . For many this close collaborative work with the therapist is a new type of experience, his being listened to, and not being told by someone else what he 'really' feels or means, is important because his own contributions are being treated as worthwhile. (1974b, pp. 336–7)

A term which has in recent years become popular to describe a more non-directive, non-interpretative approach is counselling. In particular it is this approach which is usually taken in the more informal treatment settings mentioned earlier, such as the walk-in or consultation centres (Laufer, 1975; Nichtern, 1978). These are designed specifically to encourage young people, often hesitant or sceptical, to make use of adult resources, and in order to do this they are usually situated in an accessible place away from an institutional framework, they stay open at weekends and in the evenings, and perhaps most important, they do not require the young person to have an appointment in order to be seen by a counsellor. Nichtern (1978) describes vividly the work and problems of one such facility, a 'store front clinic' in New York, and he makes the point that those who refer themselves to centres of this sort are likely to differ in a number of ways from those whose referral is 'arranged' by school, parents, or the juvenile courts. A description of the counselling movement in Great Britain is provided by Tyler (1978), who charts the growth of this type of service from 1961, when the Young People's Consultation Centre was set up in Hampstead in London. Today, as she points out, there are a wide range of agencies, both statutory and voluntary, as well as a professional organization, the National Association of Young People's Counselling and Advisory Services (NAYPCAS).

It is important to remember, however, that an increase in the availability of informal treatment and advice centres does not necessarily provide the solution to all adolescent difficulties. Even when the teenager has crossed the threshold and arrived at the reception desk there are still a multitude of problems to be faced, as Noonan (1975) points out. In her discussion of the counselling process she describes three major hurdles which have to be surmounted if the teenager is to be helped. In the first place his or her initial distrust of the counsellor has to be overcome, as has the adolescent's fear of acknowledging the existence of real problems. Noonan quotes some typical opening statements made to her as illustrative of the sort of attitudes and resistances met in this type of work.

> 'My sister got some help from your service, so I was interested to hear what you would find wrong with me. Probably nothing, which will show her.'
>
> 'My mother sent me because you would tell me what job I want.'
>
> 'I get headaches. My GP made this appointment. You won't be able to do anything, but I never refuse anything, so I came along.'
>
> 'I don't particularly want counselling, there is no specific problem. But I *had* to come because I don't enjoy anything I *have* to do.'
>
> 'I am an acid casualty. I have had two deep experiences with LSD and have not come back together again. I need time and a place to get back together. But what is the point? – it makes me sick to see all the violence in the world, and the way people exploit each other. How do *you* survive in a psychotic society?'
>
> 'You will probably think it is silly, but I can't communicate with people.'

A second issue concerns the question of who shall do the work and take the main responsibility for treatment progress. Is it the adult who should be able to 'make the young person better', or is it the teenager – now mature enough to accept personal responsibility – who should be able to use the resources of the counsellor to help him or herself? The third issue is about change. All too frequently the young person's realization that improvement must involve a change in personality or behaviour leads to serious anxiety and resistance. This is because in the adolescent context change means growing up, and growing up can represent not only upheaval but also the loss of childhood supports and relationships. To be successful, as Noonan points out, counselling with adolescents has to acknowledge and in some way come to terms with each of these problems if it is not simply to perpetuate old life styles and maladaptive solutions to conflict.

To conclude this chapter something needs to be said about the recognition of disorder. We have already noted Graham and Rutter's (1977) point that psychiatric problems in adolescence have a similar prognosis to those which occur at other times. This may be relevant once the disorder is recognized, but does not touch on the problem of how to decide whether features of behaviour such as depression, refusal to go to school, or heavy drinking are simply transient signs of an adolescent 'hang up', or whether they are symptoms of a more serious disturbance. As Conger says:

> Differential diagnosis in adolescence is often a difficult task. . . . On the one hand it is essential to avoid over-emphasizing the importance of symptoms that may prove transitory. On the other hand it is equally essential to avoid dismissing the warning signs of significant and potentially chronic disturbance as 'situational disturbance of adolescence'. (1977, p. 596)

Difficult though this task may be, teachers, youth workers and others are frequently faced with such dilemmas, and so it is important to consider the guidelines that do exist. Laufer (1975), in a small book entitled *Adolescent Disturbance and Breakdown*, suggests a number of 'danger signs in development', which he phrases in the form of questions. Some examples of these are:

1   Is the adolescent able to feel that his actions are determined by himself rather than by somebody or something outside of himself?
2   Is there any interference in the adolescent's ability to judge and distinguish other people's reactions from the creations of his own mind?
3   Is the pull back to forms of behaviour common in childhood so strong that there is the danger of giving up the effort or a wish to adopt more adult behaviour?
4   Does the adolescent have the ability to express or experience appropriate feelings or is there a marked discrepancy between an event and the way in which he reacts to it?

While suggestions such as these may be useful to the extent that they indicate areas of functioning which might reflect pathology, they provide little guidance on when to seek professional advice. If the intention is to provide advice for adults who are concerned about teenage problems, it would seem more realistic to take a pragmatic view. Conger's suggestions concerning suicidal behaviour which were mentioned earlier focus on observable behaviour, and avoid any attempt to become involved in psychiatric classification. Rutter (1975) makes a similar point when he writes that it is not enough to consider abnormality in purely statistical terms, i.e. how many symptoms does the individual complain of, how frequently does a particular symptom occur, but that it is also necessary to consider how far the abnormality is associated with impairment. He defines impairment as having four characteristics: the degree of suffering for the individual; the extent of the social restriction imposed as a result of the problem; the amount of interference with normal development; and the effects of the problem on others.

It is, in the author's view, an approach of this sort which is likely to be most helpful. If adults need to know to what extent adolescent difficulties should be taken seriously, they must ask themselves how much disturbance is being caused either in the teenager or to the adults involved. They should attempt to assess to what extent the problem or symptom is interfering with the young person's normal life; for example, has school work suffered? Has a fifteen-year-old boy given up all sports and leisure activities? Has a previously sociable girl lost all her friends? Questions of this sort will aid the adult in focusing on impairment, and assessing for themselves the degree to which individuals are affected. Thus adults should seek help when the teenager is distressed beyond the point where parent or teacher can provide assistance, when the adults themselves are in distress, or when the young person's life style has been obviously distorted. It is these indications which provide the clearest danger signs, and it will, therefore, prove in the long run more useful to concentrate on them rather than to attempt to understand the complexities of psychiatric diagnosis. Naturally, not all problems can be avoided or foreseen, no matter how experienced the individuals concerned. Nevertheless there are many situations in which informed adults can help in a constructive fashion by obtaining appropriate assistance. These guidelines should be useful in such circumstances.

Conclusion

In this chapter an attempt has been made to cover a number of issues relevant to the emotional problems of adolescence. We have seen that rates of psychiatric disorder are no higher during this period than at any other time, although the evidence for this is derived primarily from work with younger adolescents. We have also noted that the nature of psychiatric disturbance among young people is not radically different from that found in adulthood, and the prognosis for the various types of condition is also much the same as at other periods. We have briefly discussed three areas of problem behaviour – not all of which could be described as psychiatric disorders – and have paid some attention to types of treatment and to the recognition of serious disturbance.

At an early point in the chapter mention was made of the concept of 'storm and stress'. Clearly such a concept is not synonymous with psychiatric disorder. However, it has to be acknowledged that the hard evidence which is available stems primarily from studies which have a psychiatric orientation (for example, Offer, 1969; Rutter *et al.*, 1976). These tend broadly to the conclusion that adolescence cannot be considered as 'an interruption of peaceful growth', if by this is meant that for the majority the teenage years represent a stage of life characterized by pathology of emotion or behaviour. Evidently a minority manifest problem behaviour – the extent of delinquency bears witness to this – and in addition we cannot rule out the possibility that during adolescence there is an increase in subjective experiences of stress. In fact the interview material below provides support for this notion, but it must be recognized that such inner experience is unlikely to spill over into overt behaviour.

In general, the great majority of adolescents cope well with the problems of adjustment inherent in the transitional period between puberty and adulthood. In saying this one would not in any way wish to underestimate the degree of distress experienced by some young people. However, especial emphasis needs to be laid on the conclusion that adolescence itself is not a handicapping psychiatric condition. This may seem obvious to some, but it is not always accepted by those who are most influential in determining public opinion. In addition, it is a conclusion which could have important implications for research. Once it is acknowledged that the majority of adolescents cope reasonably well, then attention can be turned to the urgent task of learning more about the minority who are vulnerable and who are likely to find the pressures inherent in the adolescent process too great. Our major concern in the future must be to identify this minority, and to devise ways of intervening with them at the earliest possible moment.

Interview

The question relevant to the topics covered in this chapter was phrased as follows:

> People say adolescence is a time of 'storm and stress', a time of turmoil. Have you ever heard this phrase? From your own experience would you agree with it?

Sarah (16 years): That's definitely true because I've been depressed, you know, loads of times with no reason at all. It's just the slightest thing, really, that upsets me, you know: like going back to this boyfriend business again, I think that boys . . . they really do help get a girl really depressed, because the slightest thing you think: 'Oh God, that's it!', and it really does depress you, you know. I get really depressed about things like that, and sometimes I think, well, life's just not worth living any more – it really depresses me. I definitely agree with what you said.

Elizabeth (17 years): I think it's true in the sense that it's a time when you go through a lot of depression – I don't know why, but you do – and I certainly feel that sometimes. In that sense yes, I think it's true, and there's a constant battle within yourself and you have so many pressures from outside, pressures from school and parents and your friends, and you have to battle with all these pressures and from that you have to say: 'whatever all these are trying to tell me I have to think – what do I want to do?' In some cases you find that what you really want doesn't matter, it doesn't come into it, even though everybody thinks they're doing what's right for you and doing what's in your interest. You want to do what you think's right – even if it's wrong – you know that it's what you chose to do so whatever happens it's your fault – I'd rather that – in some cases do something and if it's wrong then I know it's me – I chose to do it.

Valerie (17 years): It's just that you're being battered from all sides – you know – different people saying 'Do this' 'Do that', and different pressures all over. Do I agree with it? Well, maybe from the school point of view – maybe it's work – but that's your own choice if you want to go on you're going to have to stand up to that pressure – just to get on with it. I suppose from families as well, as you're growing up maybe certain concepts are changing – and you're changing – and they just want to keep you as you were when you were about three. I suppose that it's that some people just can't stand up to the pressures. At school there's a few girls that have just left, and one, she just got so nervous she just had to leave – she couldn't take an exam. And at home I think it's the same thing – some of them just pack up and leave to get out of it all.

Karen (15 years): I think I make problems for myself. If I hadn't got any I'd make them. Say someone says something – it's nothing to them – but I really think about it and analyse it and turn it over and make a problem out of it, and sort of it really means a lot to me. . . . Also I think with all this sort of blooming work for your O levels it's really depressing. And then you get all these teachers saying: 'Now what are you going to do afterwards?' 'Are you going to do this, and that, and that . . .?' And then your parents . . . , and you're being lectured at from all sides. I'm not going to over-exert myself for these exams. I'll do as much as I do, and what'll happen later in life . . . I'll think I could have worked harder, but then everyone does. I'll do what I can, and get what I can, and take the consequences for it, and it's none of their business what happens.

Paul (17 years): I haven't heard that one before, but I can quite clearly see what it means. Well yes, I think you want to do drastic things sometimes. Sometimes leave school when you're disillusioned with it – or just any other thing. I suppose it passes over – just phases you go through I suppose. I suppose you're not sure what you want, you're always asking yourself questions. You're just going through a lot of uncertainty I think, you just don't know what you want to do, but I suppose I'll get over that, I suppose everybody will.

Henry (16 years): No, not really. Do I know what it means? Well like you're under a strain and all that. I think that's really only when it comes up to leaving school and all that. Perhaps if you've got family worries at home, but otherwise there's not much I can think of. Money – well, not money really because there's nothing round here to spend it on.

Stephen (16 years): Yes definitely. Especially I found last year after revising and sitting my exams, and before I got the results there was a period when I felt empty in myself, and very depressed, and I didn't want to go out anywhere. One night I ended up going to bed really early, which is unusual for me, and my mother came in to see what was wrong and I almost ended up in tears. But you know I find I can talk to my parents, especially when I'm really down in the dumps, and that sort of makes all the difference. When it does happen it's sort of quite a strong mood though, although other people don't think it is. They don't believe you're going through a depression, but you do, definitely, and I'm not just the only one.

9
Conclusion: a new theoretical approach

It was stated at the outset that the intention in this book was to consider, first, two major theoretical approaches, and then subsequently the empirical evidence which has accumulated on a range of topics within the field of adolescent psychology. This having been done it is now possible to turn our attention to the question of the extent to which the theories have been corroborated or weakened by this empirical evidence. At this stage this is, to some extent, a rhetorical question, for throughout the preceding chapters concern has been expressed on a number of occasions over the limitations of theories of adolescence, and the need for a new theoretical approach has been implicit in much of what has been said. Let us now look more closely at the basis for this contention.

As was noted in the introductory chapter, while the two major theories differ in many respects, they are united in the view that adolescence is a stressful period in human development. According to the psychoanalytic position the reason for this is to be found in the upsurge of instinctual forces which occurs as a result of puberty. These forces are said to cause a disturbance in the psychic balance, which is believed to lead in turn to regression, ambivalence and non-conformity. In addition some form of identity crisis is to be expected among older adolescents. As far as the sociologists are concerned there are a number of factors related to the young person's position in society which may be assumed to result in stress of one sort or another. In the first place, adolescence is a period of both role transition and role conflict. Also, increasing age segregation means less opportunity for young people to be in contact with adult models, making the transition to maturity and the assumption of adult roles more problematic. Furthermore it is argued that teenagers are exposed to a variety of conflicting agents of socialization, with educational institutions, the peer group, the mass media and political institutions all pulling in different directions. Finally teenagers are often seen as reflecting divisions within society itself. Their position is that of the 'marginal man' – being a member of various groups, but belonging to none. Thus they may be said to have an affinity with both conservative and radical forces, owing allegiance to both, but in reality, occupying the battle zone between the two.

In this book the results of a large amount of research have been considered. How does it bear on these theoretical notions? Broadly speaking, as we have noted in the individual chapters, research provides little support for current theories, and fails to substantiate much of what both psychoanalysts and sociologists appear to believe. To take some examples, while there is certainly some change in the self-concept, there is no evidence to show that any but a small minority experience a serious identity crisis. In most cases relationships with parents are positive and constructive, and young people, by and large, do not reject adult values in favour of those espoused by the peer group. In fact, in most situations peer group values appear to be consistent with those of important adults, rather than in conflict with them. Fears of promiscuity among the young are not borne out by the research findings, nor do studies support the belief that the peer group encourages anti-social behaviour, unless other factors are also present. Lastly there is no evidence to suggest that during the adolescent years there is a higher level of psychopathology than at other times. While a lot still needs to be learnt about the mental health of young people, almost all the results which have become available so far indicate that, although a small minority may show disturbance, the great majority of teenagers seem to cope well and to show no undue signs of turmoil or stress.

Support for this contention may be found in every major study of adolescence which has appeared in recent years. In summarizing the findings which emerged from an extended study of the psychological development of young people in the USA, David Offer – a psychiatrist – had this to say about the concept of 'storm and stress':

The transitional period of adolescence does present the adolescent with a special burden, a challenge, and an opportunity. He has to individualize, build up confidence in himself and his abilities, make important decisions concerning his future, and free himself of his earlier attachments to his parents. Our observations have led us to conclude that the majority of the teenagers in our sample coped with these tasks successfully. They lack the turmoil of the disturbed adolescent precisely because their ego is strong enough to withstand the pressures. . . . It seems to us that someone might eventually raise an objection concerning our subjects that, because of their low level of turmoil, they are cases of arrested development. Certain investigators who have also observed the low level of turmoil in a large number of adolescents have interpreted their findings somewhat differently than we have. . . . Implicitly these investigators have adopted the position that lack of turmoil is a bad prognostic sign and must necessarily prevent the adolescent from developing into a mature adult. All our data, including the psychological testing, point in the opposite direction. The adolescents not only adjusted well; they were also in touch with their feelings and developed meaningful relationships with significant others. (1969, p. 184)

Lest it be thought that such conclusions apply only to the North American continent, the following paragraph is taken from the final chapter of a book by Denise Kandel and Gerald Lesser (1972), entitled *Youth in Two Worlds*. In this study the authors were able to make comparisons between large samples of both Danish and American teenagers, concentrating particularly on home and school life, and the relations between the two. Here is how they bring their book to a close:

American and Danish adolescents are surprisingly close to their parents; they tend not to rebel against authority; they often share with parents goals and aspirations for their future role in society. Whether in quality of family life or personal aspirations for adolescents' future role in society, the findings of this study fail to support the notion of an extensive gap between parents and their adolescent children. (p. 184)

There would appear to be a sharp divergence of opinion, therefore, between what have been called the 'classical' and 'empirical' points of view (Coleman, 1978; 1979). Beliefs about adolescence which stem from theory (the 'classical' view) do not in general accord with the results of research (the 'empirical' view). We need now to consider some of the reasons for this state of affairs. Firstly, as many writers have pointed out, psychoanalysts and psychiatrists see a selected population. Their experience of adolescence is based primarily upon the individuals they meet in clinics or hospitals. Such experience is bound to encourage a somewhat one-sided perspective in which turmoil or disturbance is over-represented. For sociologists, on the other hand, the problem is often to disentangle concepts of 'youth' or 'the youth movement' from notions about young people themselves. As a number of commentators have observed, youth is frequently seen by sociologists as being in the forefront of social change. Youth is, as it were, the advance party where innovation or alteration in the values of society are concerned. From this position it is but a short step to use youth as a metaphor for social change, and thus to confuse radical forces in society with the beliefs of ordinary young people (cf. Hall and Jefferson, 1976).

A third possible reason for the divergence of viewpoint is that certain adolescent behaviours, such as vandalism, drug-taking, hooliganism and so on, are extremely threatening to adults. The few who are involved in such activities, therefore, attain undue prominence in the public eye. The mass media unfortunately play an important part in this process by publicizing sensational behaviour, thus making it appear very much more common than it is in reality. One only has to consider critically the image of the teenager portrayed week after week on the television to understand how, for many adults, the minority come to be representative of all young people. All three tendencies mentioned so far lead to an exaggerated view of the amount of turmoil which may be expected during adolescence, and thus serve to widen the gap between research and theory.

One other factor needs to be considered in this context. In general, psychologists responsible for large-scale surveys have tended to neglect the possibility that individual adolescents may be either unwilling or unable to reveal their innermost feelings. Much depends on the way the study is carried out, but it is important to remember how very difficult it is for anyone, let alone a shy, resentful and anxious teenager, to share fears, worries or conflicts with a strange interviewer. Inhibition of this sort may well result in a bias on the part of those writing from the empirical point of view, and cause an underestimation of the degree of stress experienced by young people. Problems of method, therefore, may also be playing their part in widening the gap between theory and research, not by exaggerating the amount of inner turmoil, but by doing just the opposite, namely, causing research workers to miss the more subtle indications of emotional tension. The divergence of opinion referred to earlier can thus be seen to be the result of a number of factors. The fault cannot be said to lie exclusively with one side or the other. Both methods and theories have their weaknesses, and we may now consider some of the ways in which these might be corrected.

Where methodology is concerned there have, it is true, been many improvements. In the early years when theories of adolescence were first being formulated, evidence was gathered in a haphazard fashion from school playground, clinic or street corner. During the last thirty years, however, there has been an almost complete transformation in the social sciences, with a quite remarkable growth in the systematic collection of information. Yet there still are far-reaching difficulties. One which we have already touched on is the problem of being able to get close enough to the young person's subjective, personal world so as to circumvent the possibility that responses to an interview will simply reflect what he or she considers to be socially acceptable answers. Some have attempted to get around this by using projective tests, involving techniques such as incomplete sentences, or picture-story methods where the individual is required to tell a story about what might be happening in pictures chosen for their relevance to adolescent development. In this way researchers (for example, Douvan and Adelson, 1966; Eppel and Eppel, 1966; Coleman, 1974) have tried to encourage adolescents to express aspects of their inner experience, and examples of such an approach are to be found at various stages throughout this book. This strategy has been successful to some extent, but it has in turn raised further problems, such as those relating to the scoring and interpretation of the material.

A further difficulty concerns the need to observe behaviour 'as it happens', in order that studies do not have to rely exclusively on reports after the event. We have already considered one side of this particular issue in our discussion of the distinction between moral thought and moral action. Thus it may be all very well to obtain responses to hypothetical situations, but these may bear little relation to what happens in overt behaviour. As a result of this dilemma there is an obvious need for some method which allows adults to observe directly a phenomenon such as peer group interaction. It is in response to this need that the sociological method of 'participant observation' has become more popular. This is an approach which has obvious limitations, in particular the high likelihood of personal involvement on the part of the research worker, as well as problems concerning the reliability of the observations. None the less there appears to be not only a growing awareness of the advantages of such an approach (Schaffer and Hargreaves, 1978), but also a determination on the part of some writers to grapple with the weaknesses inherent in the method (for example Butters, 1976).

A third problem which cannot be ignored concerns the developmental nature of adolescence. This is not a static but a dynamic period in the life cycle; the young person is growing and changing throughout this stage, and the design of research projects should take this fact into account. Unfortunately, however, the great majority of studies focus on one age only, and those that are aware of the necessity of comparing age groups almost always use a cross-sectional design. While everyone acknowledges the necessity for more longitudinal research, involving the study of individuals over time, few have the resources or the commitment necessary to plan and carry out research which could last six or more years. Longitudinal studies have a further disadvantage, in addition to the length of time involved. This is a tendency to confuse maturational with social change. If, for example, a study is planned which follows a group of twelve-year-olds through until they are eighteen, it may not always be possible to distinguish variation which is due to the growth process from changes which have occurred in society during the six-year period of the study. In an attempt to find a solution to these problems Nesselroade and Baltes (1974) have proposed the use of short-term longitudinal studies, a suggestion which has received considerable attention in the last few years. Studies of this sort would take place over relatively short periods of time, and involve overlapping cohorts. As an example three age groups might be selected – say eleven-, thirteen- and fifteen-year-olds – and each of these groups would be followed for three years. In this way both adolescent maturation and social change can be investigated in the same study, and in addition information can be obtained on a six-year age range in a period of three years. A hypothetical design is illustrated in figure 9.1.

We have now looked at some of the methodological problems which have hampered studies of the teenage years. However, current theories also have serious limitations. In particular we have noted that both psychoanalytic and sociological theories are based primarily on the development of atypical young people. Furthermore, such theories have been extremely slow to take account of empirical evidence which has become available. Obviously these two theories have some value, and it would be wrong to leave the impression that neither are any longer relevant. Perhaps the most important contribution made by these theories is that they have provided the foundation for an understanding of young people with serious problems and a greater knowledge of those who belong to minority or deviant groups. In this respect the two major theories have much to offer. However it must be recognized that today they are inadequate as a basis for an understanding of the development of the great majority of young people. The most fundamental conclusion of the review carried out in this book is that adolescence needs a theory, not of abnormality, but of normality. Any viable theoretical viewpoint put forward today must not only incorporate the results of empirical studies, but must also acknowledge the fact that, although for some young

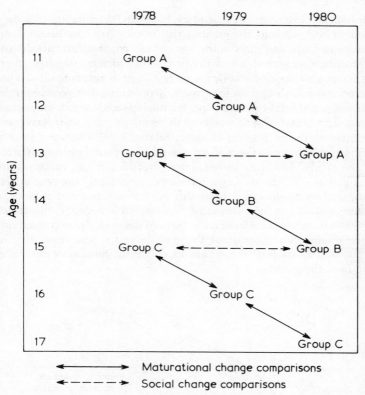

Figure 9.1   Hypothetical design for a short-term longitudinal study.

people adolescence may be a difficult time, for the majority it is a period of relative stability. None the less, there is general agreement that during the teenage years major adaptation has to occur. The transition between childhood and adulthood cannot be achieved without substantial adjustments of both a psychological and social nature; and yet most young people appear to cope without undue stress. How do they do so?

It is this contradiction between the amount of overall change experienced, and the relative health and resilience of the individuals involved in such change, which now requires some consideration. In earlier papers (Coleman, 1974; 1978; 1979) the author has outlined a 'focal' theory of adolescence, in the hope that this will go some way towards resolving such a contradiction. Before this is explained, however, it will be necessary to sketch briefly the background to this theory. The theory grew out of the results of a study of normal adolescent development, a study which has been mentioned on a number of occasions throughout this book. To recapitulate, large groups of boys and girls at the ages of eleven, thirteen, fifteen and seventeen were given a set of identical tests which elicited from them attitudes and opinions about a wide range of relationships. Thus material was included on self-image, being alone, heterosexual relationships, parental relationships, friendships and large group situations. The material was analysed in terms of the constructive and negative elements present in these relationship situations, and in terms of the common themes expressed by the young people involved in the study. Findings showed that attitudes to all relationships changed as a function of age, but more importantly the results also indicated that concerns about different issues reached a peak at different stages in the adolescent process. This finding is illustrated for boys in figure 9.2 where it can be seen that simply by considering three of the most important themes, there are peak ages for the expression of each of these various concerns. Similar results were obtained for girls.

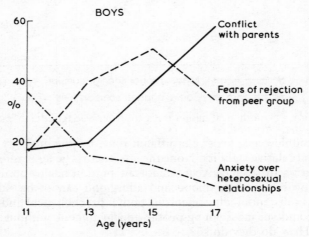

Figure 9.2   Peak ages for the expression of different themes.
(From J. C. Coleman (1974) *Relationships in Adolescence*, Routledge & Kegan Paul.)

It was this finding that led to the formulation of a 'focal' theory. The theory proposes that at different ages particular sorts of relationship patterns come into focus, in the sense of being most prominent, but that no pattern is specific to one age only. Thus the patterns overlap, different issues come into focus at different times, but simply because an issue is not the most prominent feature of an age, does not mean that it may not be critical for some individuals. These ideas, in association with empirical findings such as those illustrated in figure 9.2, combine to suggest a symbolic model of adolescent development where each curve represents a different issue or relationship. This is portrayed in figure 9.3.

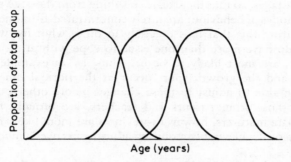

Figure 9.3   Focal theory. Each curve represents a different issue or relationship.
(From J. C. Coleman (1974) *Relationships in Adolescence*, Routledge & Kegan Paul.)

In many ways such a notion is not dissimilar from any traditional stage theory. However, it carries with it a very much more flexible view of development, and therefore differs from stage theory in three important respects. In the first place, the resolution of one issue is not seen as the *sine qua non* for tackling the next. In fact it is clearly envisaged that a minority of individuals will find themselves facing more than one issue at the same time. Secondly, the theory does not assume the existence of fixed boundaries between stages and, therefore, issues are not necessarily linked to a particular age or developmental level. Finally, there is nothing immutable about the sequence involved. In our culture it appears that individuals are more likely to face certain issues in the early stages of adolescence, and different issues at other stages, but the 'focal' theory is not dependent on a fixed sequence, and it would be of very great interest to examine other cultures in the light of this theory of development. It is the author's belief that the 'focal' theory of adolescent development may provide a clue to the resolution of the apparent contradiction between the amount of adjustment required during adolescence on the one hand, and the relatively successful adaptation among the general population on the other. If adolescents have to adjust to so much potentially stressful change, and at the same time pass through this stage of their life with relative stability, as the 'empirical' view indicates, how do they do it? The answer which is suggested by the 'focal' theory is that they cope by dealing with one issue at a time. They spread the process of adaptation over a span of years, attempting to resolve first one issue, and then the next. Different problems, different relationship issues come into focus and are tackled at different stages, so that the stresses resulting from the need to adapt to new modes of behaviour are rarely concentrated all at one time. It follows from this that it is precisely in those who, for whatever reason, do have more than one issue to cope with at a time that problems are most likely to occur. Thus, as an example, where puberty and the growth spurt occur at the normal time individuals are able to adjust to these changes before other pressures, such as those from parents and teachers, are brought to bear. For the late maturers, however, pressures are more likely to occur simultaneously, inevitably requiring adjustments over a much wider area.

The 'focal' theory is only one of a number of possible ways of conceptualizing adolescent development, but it has two particular advantages. Firstly it is based directly on empirical evidence, and secondly, it goes at least some way towards reconciling the apparent contradiction between the amount of adaptation required during the transitional process, and the ability of most young people to cope successfully with the pressures inherent in this process. Such a theory evidently needs further testing, and it is to be hoped that others may be stimulated to build upon what has been said here. Without a firm base in theory there can be no significant advance in our understanding of the adolescent years, and therefore concentration on the relation between theory and research must rank as a high priority in future work.

During the course of this book a number of topics have been highlighted which, like theoretical issues, need additional clarification. The development of the self-concept during adolescence is one such area. Other obvious examples are the extent of inner turmoil and the prevalence of psychiatric disorder among older teenagers, the development of attitudes to authority, the growth of moral and political ideas, conflicts surrounding sex-role identity, and some aspects of the role of the peer group. In our review of the literature it has become apparent that all these are issues about which far too little is known. Yet our overall conclusion must be that enormous strides have been taken in the psychology of adolescence during the last two decades. A wide range of research has been carried out, and perhaps most important, this research has enabled us to comprehend more clearly the needs of young people in our society.

As a conclusion let us briefly consider some of the most obvious of these needs. It has been stated that empirical research has led to a greater understanding of the needs of adolescents. To justify this statement it is necessary to consider some examples. Among those which might have been included here, the following stand out:

1   Contrary to expectations, adolescents do have a need for adults to exercise their authority, so long as this is kept within reasonable limits. Studies of different types of power structure within the home have shown that a permissive environment is no more preferable to young people than an authoritarian one. In general teenagers adjust best in situations where they are able to play some part in the decision making process, but where adults are not afraid to make rules and to ensure that these are respected.

2   Young people have a need to participate as much as possible in the adult world, and especially in the world of work. Research demonstrates that the fewer the opportunities for adolescent involvement in the activities of the older generation, and the lower the level of parental concern, the less well motivated and the more vulnerable to peer group pressure the teenager will be.

3   Adolescents have a strong need to be seen as individuals, and not to be handicapped by stereotypes of what 'youth' is believed to represent. Work carried out by the Eppels, among others, leads inevitably to this conclusion, and thus it may be supposed that the more care adults take to treat teenagers as real people rather than as members of a movement, the more rewarding their relationships with them are likely to be.

4   We have noted the relatively low proportion of young people who reach the level of formal operational thought. While we know little of why this should be so, one possibility which suggests itself is that adults still spend too little time encouraging thought among adolescents. This is what is needed, but although many adults are aware of the roles they are able to play in facilitating social relationships, it seems probable that very few outside the school setting have much faith in the contribution they can make to the young person's intellectual development.

5   Teenagers quite clearly feel a need for more help with their developing sexuality. This fact emerges unequivocally from the studies we have considered, and hopefully both teachers and psychologists can be persuaded to take a greater interest not only in sex education, but in what may be more generally called 'social education'.

6   Young people need to be given every opportunity to become involved in peer group activities. Studies show that other teenagers have an invaluable role to play in providing both the support and context necessary for the learning of new social skills. The peer group is only harmful where family influences are absent, and in most cases parents and friends act together as mutually reinforcing agents of socialization.

7   Lastly it needs to be recognized that there are stresses inherent in the transitional process, but so long as major adjustments can be dealt with one at a time most young people have the resources necessary to cope. The 'focal' theory would suggest that adults can help most by recognizing the importance of a phased adjustment, and by not expecting maturity to be achieved in all areas simultaneously.

Some, reading this, may feel that the emphasis is being placed too heavily on the responsibilities of adults. This has certainly not been the intention. Obviously teenagers have responsibilities too, not the least of which is to remember that adults are real people with real needs and that they will respond better when treated as individuals rather than as stereotypes of a particular generation. In addition we should not forget that there are times when nothing the adult does can ever be right. Adolescent non-conformity, for example, can lead to unpredictable or simply impossible behaviour, and under such circumstances there are rarely any easy solutions. Nevertheless at this point what needs to be stressed above all else is that major advances have occurred in this field of psychology. Theories highlighting adolescence as a 'problem stage' have been placed in a more realistic perspective. Information is now available which makes it possible to understand more clearly the needs of young people. Finally, the psychology of adolescence, although still seriously limited in some respects, has shown that it has a substantial contribution to make to society.

Appendix: interview

1 What sort of things do you like doing in your spare time?
2 It is said that during adolescence there is a change in the way people think, that they are able to think in more abstract terms. An example might be that it becomes easier to see both sides of an argument. Have you noticed this?
3 Another thing which is said to change is the way people decide what is right and wrong. Have you noticed a change in yourself as far as this is concerned?
4 Now a phrase that is often used when talking about teenagers is 'the generation gap'. You know what is meant by that? Do you think there is any truth in it?
5 Obviously parents are very important for adolescents – what do you think are the most important things parents ought to provide?
6 To continue this, would you say either of your parents have provided an example for how you want to be when you are older?
7 It's a well known fact that teenagers are becoming physically mature at a younger age these days. Do you think this makes things more difficult for young people of today?
8 In early adolescence – usually around eleven or twelve – people experience something called the growth spurt, when their bodies change and grow very quickly. Do you remember this? How did you feel at the time?
9 Another thing that's said to change at adolescence is the way young people think about themselves. It's said that adolescence can be a time of worries and identity problems, with young people asking themselves the question 'Who am I?' Does this ring any bells for you?

10   How about the question 'Who will I become?'. 'Who will I be in the future?'.

11   Now friends are often very important for teenagers. Why do you think this is so?

12   If there was ever a clash between what your friends wanted you to do, and what your parents wanted you to do – which would you choose?

13   Do you feel that you are sometimes under pressure from people of your age to do things that you would prefer not to do?

14   It is often said that we live in a permissive society today, with young people having much more sexual freedom that they ever did. Do you think this is true?

15   As far as having boyfriends/girlfriends is concerned, what do you think are the problems that people of your age have to face?

16   People say adolescence is a time of 'storm and stress', a time of turmoil. Have you ever heard of this phrase? From your own experience would you agree with it?

17   Looking back over the last few years, has there been a time when you felt things were really going badly?

18   Now, finally, what do you think is the best thing that has happened to you in the last few years?

Bibliography

Adelson, J. (1970) What generation gap? *New York Times Magazine*, 18 January, 10.

Adelson, J. (1971) The political imagination of the young adolescent. *Daedalus*, Fall, 1013–50.

Adelson, J. and O'Neill, R. (1966) The development of political thought in adolescence. *Journal of Personality and Social Psychology*, 4, 295–308.

Aitken, P. P. (1978) *Ten- to Fourteen-Year-olds and Alcohol*, vol. 3, London: HMSO.

Akers, R. L. (1970) Teenage drinking and drug abuse. In E. D. Evans (ed.) *Adolescence: Readings in Behaviour and Development*, New York: Dryden Press.

Anderson, J. E. (1939) The development of social behaviour. *The American Journal of Sociology*, 44, 839–57.

Anthony, E. J. (1974) Psychotherapy of adolescence. In G. Caplan (ed.) *American Handbook of Psychiatry*, vol. 2, New York: Basic Books.

Baittle, B. and Offer, D. (1971) On the nature of male adolescent rebellion. In F. C. Feinstein, P. Giovacchini, A. Miller (eds) *Annals of Adolescent Psychiatry*, New York: Basic Books.

Bandura, A. (1972) The stormy decade: fact or fiction? In D. Rogers (ed.) *Issues in Adolescent Psychology* (2nd edn), New York: Appleton-Century-Crofts.

Bandura, A. and Walters, R. H. (1959) *Adolescent Aggression: A Study of the Influence of Child Training Practices and Family Interrelations*, New York: Ronald Press.

Baruch, G. K. (1972) Maternal influences upon college women's attitudes toward women and work. *Developmental Psychology*, 6, 32–7.

Baumrind, D. (1968) Authoritarian versus authoritative parental control. *Adolescence*, 3, 255–72.

Baumrind, D. (1975) Early socialization and adolescent competence. In S. E. Dragastin and G. Elder (eds) *Adolescence in the Life Cycle*, New York: John Wiley.

Bayley, N. and Schaefer, E. S. (1960) Maternal behaviour and personality development data from the Berkeley Growth Study. *Psychiatric Research Reports*, 13, 155–73.

Bee, H. (1975) *The Developing Child*, New York: Harper & Row.

Bell, A. P. (1969) Role modelling of fathers in adolescence and young adulthood. *Journal of Counselling Psychology*, 16, 30–5.

Benedict, R. (1938) Continuities and discontinuities in cultural conditioning. *Psychiatry*, 1, 161–7.

Bengston, V. L. (1970) The generation gap. *Youth and Society*, 2, (1), 7–32.

Bigelow, B. J. and La Gaipa, J. J. (1975) Children's written descriptions of friendship. *Developmental Psychology*, 4, 178–81.

Biller, H. B. and Bahm, R. M. (1971) Father absence, perceived maternal behaviour, and masculinity of self-concept among junior high school boys. *Developmental Psychology*, 4, 178–81.

Blos, P. (1962) *On Adolescence*, London: Collier-Macmillan.

Blos, P. (1967) The second individuation process of adolescence. *Psychoanalytic Study of the Child*, 22, 162–86.

Bowerman, C. E. and Bahr, S. J. (1973) Conjugal power and adolescent identification with parents. *Sociometry*, 36, 366–77.

Bowerman, C. E. and Kinch, J. W. (1959) Changes in family and peer orientation of children between the fourth and tenth grades. *Social Forces*, 37, 206–11.

Brim, O. G. (1965) Adolescent personality as self-other systems. *Journal of Marriage and the Family*, 27, 156–62.

Brittain, C. V. (1963) Adolescent choices and parent-peer cross pressures. *American Sociological Review*, 28, 385–91.

Brittain, C. V. (1968) An exploration of the bases of peer-compliance and parent-compliance in adolescence. *Adolescence*, 2, 445–58.

Brittain, C. V. (1969) A comparison of rural and urban adolescence with respect to peer versus parent compliance. *Adolescence*, 13, 59–68.

Bronfenbrenner, U. (1974) The origins of alienation. *Scientific American*, 231, 53–61.

Bronson, G. A. (1959) Identity diffusion in late adolescence. *Journal of Abnormal and Social Psychology*, 59, 414–17.

Bruch, H. (1947a) Eating disturbances in adolescence. In G. Caplan (ed.) *American Handbook of Psychiatry*, vol. 2, New York: Basic Books.

Bruch, H. (1974b) *Eating Disorders: Obesity, Anorexia Nervosa, and the person within*, London: Routledge & Kegan Paul.

Bruggen, P. and Davies, G. (1977) Family therapy in adolescent psychiatry. *British Journal of Psychiatry*, 131, 433–47.

Bruggen, P., Byng-Hall, J. and Pitt-Aiken, T. (1973) The reason for admission as a focus of work for an adolescent unit. *British Journal of Psychiatry*, 122, 319–30.

Buck, C. and Stavraky, K. (1967) The relationship between age of menarche and age of marriage among child-bearing women. *Human Biology*, 39, 93–102.

Butters, S. (1976) The logic of enquiry of participant observation. In S. Hall and T. Jefferson (eds) *Resistance through Rituals*, London: Hutchinson.

Campbell, J. D. (1964) Peer relations in childhood. In M. L. Hoffman and L. W. Hoffman (eds) *A Review of Child Development*, vol. 1, New York: Russell Sage Foundation.

Carlsmith, L. (1964) Effects of early father absence on scholastic aptitude. *Harvard Educational Review*, 34, 3–21.

Carlson, R. (1965) Stability and change in the adolescent's self-image. *Child Development*, 36, 659–66.

Cavior, N. and Dokecki, P. R. (1973) Physical attractiveness, perceived attitude similarity, and academic achievement as contributors to inter-personal attraction among adolescents. *Developmental Psychology*, 9, 44–54.

Chisholm, D. (1978) Obesity in adolescence. *Journal of Adolescence*, 1, 177–94.

Clausen, J. A. (1975) The social meaning of differential physical and sexual maturation. In S. Dragastin and G. Elder (eds) *Adolescence in the Life Cycle*, New York: John Wiley.

Cloutier, R. and Goldschmid, M. (1976) Individual differences in the development of formal reasoning. *Child Development*, 47, 1097–102.

Cockram, L. and Beloff, H. (1978) *Rehearsing to be Adults*, Leicester: National Youth Bureau.

Cole, M. (1976) What about a new approach to sex education? In S. Crown (ed.) *Psycho-sexual problems*, New York and London: Academic Press.

Coleman, J. C. (1974) *Relationships in Adolescence*, Boston and London: Routledge & Kegan Paul.

Coleman, J. C. (1978) Current contradictions in adolescent theory. *Journal of Youth and Adolescence*, 7, 1–12.

Coleman, J. C. (1979) Current views of the adolescent process. In J. C. Coleman (ed.) *The School Years*, London: Methuen.

Coleman, J. C. and Zajicek, E. (1980) Adolescent attitudes to authority. *Adolescence*, in press.

Coleman, J. C., George, R. and Holt, G. (1977) Adolescents and their parents: a study of attitudes. *Journal of Genetic Psychology*, 130, 239–45.

Coleman, J. C., Herzberg, J. and Morris, M. (1977) Identity in adolescence: present and future self-concepts. *Journal of Youth and Adolescence*, 6, 63–75.

Coleman, J. S. (1960) The adolescent sub-culture and academic achievement. *American Journal of Sociology*, 65, 337–47.

Coleman, J. S. (1961) *The Adolescent Society*, New York: The Free Press.

Conger, J. J. (1973) *Adolescence and Youth* (1st edn), New York: Harper & Row.

Conger, J. J. (1975) Sexual attitudes and behaviour of contemporary adolescents. In J. J. Conger (ed.) *Contemporary Issues in Adolescent Development*, New York: Harper & Row.

Conger, J. J. (1977) *Adolescence and Youth* (2nd edn), New York: Harper & Row.

Conger, J. J. and Miller, W. C. (1966) *Personality, Social Class and Delinquency*, New York: John Wiley.

Conger, J. J., Miller, W. C. and Walsmith, C. (1965) Antecedents of delinquency: personality, social class and intelligence. In P. H. Mussen, J. J. Conger and J. Kagan (eds) *Readings in Child Development and Personality*, New York: Harper & Row.

Connell, W. F., Stroobant, R. E. and Sinclair, K. E. (1975) *Twelve to Twenty: Studies of City Youth*, Sydney: Hicks & Sons.

Costanzo, P. R. (1970) Conformity development as a function of self-blame. *Journal of Personality and Social Psychology*, 13, 366–74.

Costanzo, P. R. and Shaw, M. E. (1966) Conformity as a function of age level. *Child Development*, 37, 967–75.

Crain, W. C. and Crain, E. F. (1974) The growth of political ideas and their expression among young activists. *Journal of Youth and Adolescence*, 3, 105–33.

Crisp, A. H., Palmer, R. L. and Kalucy, R. S. (1976) How common is anorexia nervosa? A prevalence study. *British Journal of Psychiatry*, 128, 549–54.

Dalzell-Ward, A. J. (1975) *A Textbook of Health Education*, London: Tavistock.

Davies, B. (1977) Attitudes toward school among early and late maturing adolescent girls. *Journal of Genetic Psychology*, 131, 261–6.

Davies, J. and Stacey, B. (1972) *Teenagers and Alcohol*, vol. 2, London: HMSO.

Douvan, E. (1979) Sex role learning. In J. C. Coleman (ed.) *The School Years*, London: Methuen.

Douvan, E. and Adelson, J. (1966) *The Adolescent Experience*, New York: John Wiley.

Douvan, E. and Gold, M. (1966) Modal patterns in American adolescence. In M. C. Hoffman and L. W. Hoffman (eds) *Review of Child Development Research*, vol. 2, New York: Russell Sage Foundation.

Dulit, E. (1972) Adolescent thinking à la Piaget: the formal stage. *Journal of Youth and Adolescence*, 1, 281–301.

Elder, G. H. (1963) Parental power legitimation and its effects on the adolescent. *Sociometry*, 26, 50–65.

Elder, G. H. (1968) Adolescent socialization and development. In E. Borgatta and W. Lambert (eds) *Handbook of Personality Theory and Research*, Chicago: Rand McNally.

Elder, G. H. (1975) Adolescence in the life cycle: an introduction. In S. E. Dragastin and G. H. Elder (eds) *Adolescence in the Life Cycle*, New York: John Wiley.

Elkind, D. (1966) Conceptual orientation shifts in children and adolescents. *Child Development*, 37, 493–8.

Elkind, D. (1967) Egocentrism in adolescence. *Child Development*, 38, 1025–34.

Emler, M. P., Heather, N. and Winton, M. (1978) Delinquency and the development of moral reasoning. *British Journal of Social and Clinical Psychology*, 17, 325–31.

Empey, L. T. (1975) Delinquency theory and recent research. In R. E. Grinder (ed.) *Studies in Adolescence* (3rd edn), London: Collier-Macmillan.

Engel, M. (1959) The stability of the self-concept in adolescence. *Journal of Abnormal and Social Psychology*, 58, 211–15.

Eppel, E. M. and Eppel, M. (1966) *Adolescence and Morality*, London: Routledge & Kegan Paul.

Erikson, E. (1963) *Childhood and Society*, Harmondsworth: Penguin.

Erikson, E. (1968) *Identity, Youth and Crisis*, London: Faber.

Erikson, E. (1969) The problem of ego-identity. In M. Gold and E. Douvan (eds) *Adolescent Development: Readings in Research and Theory*. Boston: Allyn & Bacon.

Eveleth, P. and Tanner, J. (1977) *World Wide Variation in Human Growth*, Cambridge: CUP.

Farrell, C. (1978) *My Mother Said*, London: Routledge & Kegan Paul.

Faust, M. (1960) Developmental maturity as a detriment in prestige of adolescent girls. *Child Development*, 31, 173–84.

Feshbach, N. and Sones, G. (1971) Sex differences in adolescent reactions towards newcomers. *Developmental Psychology*, 4, 381–6.

Finkel, M. L. and Finkel, D. J. (1975) Sexual and contraceptive knowledge, attitudes and behaviour of male adolescents. *Family Planning Perspectives*, 7, 256–62.

Fodor, E. M. (1972) Delinquency and susceptibility to social influence among adolescents as a function of level of moral judgement. *Journal of Social Psychology*, 86, 257–60.

Fodor, E. M. (1973) Moral development and parent behaviour antecedents in adolescent psychopaths. *Journal of Genetic Psychology*, 122, 37–43.

Fogelman, K. (1976) *Britain's Sixteen-Year-Olds*, London: National Children's Bureau.

Framrose, R. (1975) The first seventy admissions to an adolescent unit. *British Journal of Psychiatry*, 126, 380–99.

Fransella, F. and Frost, K. (1977) *On Being a Woman*, London: Tavistock.

Freud, A. (1937) *The Ego and the Mechanisms of Defence*, London: Hogarth Press.

Gath, D., Cooper, D., Gattoni, F. and Rockett, D. (1975) Child guidance and delinquency in a London borough. *Institute of Psychiatry, Maudsley Monograph*, 24, Oxford: OUP.

Glueck, S. and Glueck, E. (1950) *Unravelling Delinquency*, Oxford: OUP.

Glueck, S. and Glueck, E. (1960) *Predicting Delinquency and Crime*, Boston: Harvard University Press.

Gold, M. (1970) *Delinquent Behaviour in an American City*, Monterey, Calif.: Brooks/Cole Publishing Co.

Graham, P. (1977) Psychosomatic relationships. In M. Rutter and L. Hersov (eds) *Child Psychiatry: Modern Approaches*, Oxford: Blackwell Scientific Publications.

Graham, P. and Rutter, M. (1977) Adolescent disorders. In M. Rutter and L. Hersov (eds) *Child Psychiatry: Modern Approaches*, Oxford: Blackwell Scientific Publications.

Gronlund, N. E. and Anderson, L. (1957) Personaiity characteristics of socially accepted, socially neglected and socially rejected junior high school pupils. *Educational Administration and Supervision*, 43, 329–38.

Gunderson, E. K. (1956) Body size, self-evaluation and military effectiveness. *Journal of Personality and Social Psychology*, 2, 902–6.

Haim, A. (1974) *Adolescent Suicide*, London: Tavistock.

Hall, G. S. (1904) *Adolescence: its Psychology and its Relations to Physiology, Anthropology, Sociology, Sex, Crime, Religion and Education*, vols 1 and 2, New York: D. Appleton.

Hall, S. and Jefferson, T. (1976) *Resistance Through Rituals*, London: Hutchinson.

Hargreaves, D. H., Hester, F. and Mellor, S. (1975) *Deviance in Classrooms*, London: Routledge & Kegan Paul.

Harvey, O. J. and Rutherford, J. (1960) Status in the informal group. *Child Development*, 31, 377–85.

Hetherington, E. M. (1966) Effects of paternal absence on sex-typed behaviours in Negro and white pre-adolescent males. *Journal of Personality and Social Psychology*, 4, 87–91.

Hetherington, E. M. (1972) Effects of father absence on personality development in adolescent daughters. *Developmental Psychology*, 7, 313–26.

Hoffman, A. D. (1978) Legal and social implications of adolescent sexual behaviour. *Journal of Adolescence*, 1, 25–34.

Hogan, R. (1975) The structure of moral character and the explanation of moral action. *Journal of Youth and Adolescence*, 4, 1–15.

Horowitz, H. (1967) Predictions of adolescent popularity and rejection from achievement and interest tests. *Journal of Educational Psychology*, 58, 170–4.

Horrocks, J. E. and Buker, M. (1951) A study of the friendship fluctuations of pre-adolescents. *Journal of Genetic Psychology*, 78, 131–44.

Horrocks, J. E. and Thompson, G. G. (1946) A study of the friendship fluctuations of rural boys and girls. *Journal of Genetic Psychology*, 69, 189–98.

Howard, L. P. (1960) Identity conflicts in adolescent girls. *Smith College Studies of Social Work*, 31, 1–24.

Howells, J. G. (ed.) (1971) *Modern Perspectives in Adolescent Psychiatry*, Edinburgh: Oliver & Boyd.

Hutt, C. (1979) Sex role differentiation in social development. In H. McGurk (ed.) *Issues in Childhood Social Development*, London: Methuen.

Inhelder, B. and Piaget, J. (1958) *The Growth of Logical Thinking*, London: Routledge & Kegan Paul.

Iscoe, I., Williams, M. and Harvey, J. (1963) Modification of children's judgements by a simulated group technique. *Child Development*, 34, 963–78.

Jacobs, J. (1971) *Adolescent Suicide*, New York: John Wiley.

Jones, M. C. (1957) The later careers of boys who were early or late maturing. *Child Development*, 28, 113–28.

Jones, M. C. (1958) The study of socialization patterns at the high school level. *Journal of Genetic Psychology*, 93, 87–111.

Jones, M. C. and Bayley, N. (1950) Physical maturing among boys as related to behaviour. *Journal of Educational Psychology*, 41, 129–48.

Josselyn, I. M. (1952) *The Adolescent and His World*, New York: Family Service Association.

Josselyn, I. M. (1971) *Adolescence*, New York: Harper & Row.

Jourard, F. M. and Secord, S. F. (1955) Body-cathexis and the ideal female figure. *Journal of Abnormal and Social Psychology*, 50, 243–6.

Juhasz, A. M. (1975) Sexual decision making: the crux of the adolescent problem. In R. E. Grinder (ed.) *Studies in Adolescence* (3rd edn), London: Collier-Macmillan.

Kandel, D. B. and Lesser, G. S. (1972) *Youth in Two Worlds*, London: Jossey-Bass.

Kandel, D. B., Kessler, R. C. and Margulies, R. Z. (1978) Antecedents of adolescent initiation into stages of drug use. *Journal of Youth and Adolescence*, 7, 13–40.

Kantner, J. F. and Zelnick, M. (1972) Sexual experience of young unmarried women in the United States. *Family Planning Perspectives*, 4, 9–16.

Katchadourian, H. (1977) *The Biology of Adolescence*, San Francisco: Freeman.

Katz, P. and Zigler, E. (1967) Self-image disparity: a developmental approach. *Journal of Personality and Social Psychology*, 5, 186–95.

Kinsey, A. C., Pomeroy, W. B. and Martin, C. E. (1948) *Sexual Behaviour in the Human Male*, Philadelphia: W. B. Saunders.

Kinsey, A. C., Pomeroy, W. B., Martin, C. E. and Gebhard, P. H. (1953) *Sexual Behaviour in the Human Female*, Philadelphia: W. B. Saunders.

Koch, H. L. (1957) The relation in young children between characteristics of their playmates and certain attributes of their siblings. *Child Development*, 28, 175–202.

Kohen-Raz, R. (1974) Physiological maturation and mental growth at pre-adolescence and puberty. *Journal of Child Psychology and Psychiatry*, 15, 199–214.

Kohlberg, L. (1964) The development of moral character and moral ideology. In M. L. Hoffman and L. W. Hoffman (eds) *Review of Child Development Research*, vol. 1, New York: Russell Sage Foundation.

Kohlberg, L. (1969) *Stages in the Development of Moral Thought and Action*, New York: Holt, Rinehart & Winston.

Kohlberg, L. and Gilligan, T. F. (1971) The adolescent as philosopher: the discovery of the self in a post-conventional world. *Daedalus*, 100, 1051–6.

Kraus, J. (1975) Suicidal behaviour in New South Wales. *British Journal of Psychiatry*, 126, 313–18.

Kreitman, N., Smith, P. and Tan, E. (1970) Attempted suicide as language: an empirical study. *British Journal of Psychiatry*, 116, 465–73.

Kuhlen, R. G. and Lee, B. J. (1943) Personality characteristics and social acceptability in adolescence. *Journal of Educational Psychology*, 34, 321–40.

Laishley, J. (1979) The human relations course. In G. Verma and C. Bagley (eds) *Race Relations and Education*, London: Macmillan.

Landsbaum, J. and Willis, R. (1971) Conformity in early and late adolescence. *Developmental Psychology*, 4, 334–7.

Langford, P. E. and George, S. (1971) Intellectual and moral development in adolescence. *British Journal of Educational Psychology*, 45, 330–2.

Larsen, L. E. (1972a) The influence of parents and peers during adolescence: the situation hypothesis revisited. *Journal of Marriage and the Family*, 34, 67–74.

Larsen, L. E. (1972b) The relative influence of parent-adolescent affect in predicting the salience hierarchy among youth. *Pacific Sociological Review*, 15, 83–102.

Laufer, M. (1975) *Adolescent Disturbance and Breakdown*, Harmondsworth: Penguin.

Lavik, N. (1977) Urban-rural differences in rates of disorder. In P. Graham (ed.) *Epidemiological Approaches in Child Psychiatry*, New York and London: Academic Press.

Lerner, R. and Karabenick, S. (1974) Physical attractiveness, body attitudes, and self-concept in late adolescents. *Journal of Youth and Adolescence*, 3, 7–16.

Leslie, S. (1974) Psychiatric disorder in the young adolescents of an industrial town. *British Journal of Psychiatry*, 125, 113–24.

Lesser, G. S. and Kandel, D. B. (1969) Parental and peer influences on educational plans of adolescents. *American Sociological Review*, 34, 213–23.

Lewis, M. and Rosenblum, L. (1975) *Friendship and Peer Relations*, New York: John Wiley.

Luckey, E. B. and Nass, C. D. (1969) A comparison of sexual attitudes and behaviour of an international sample. *Journal of Marriage and the Family*, 31, 364–70.

Lynn, D. B. and Sawrey, W. L. (1959) The effects of father absence on Norwegian boys and girls. *Journal of Abnormal and Social Psychology*, 59, 258–62.

Maccoby, E. and Jacklin, C. (1975) *The Psychology of Sex Differences*, Oxford: OUP.

McCord, J., McCord, W. and Thurber, E. (1962) Some effects of paternal absence on male children. *Journal of Abnormal and Social Psychology*, 54, 361–9.

McGeorge, C. (1974) Situational variation in levels of moral judgement. *British Journal of Educational Psychology*, 44, 116–22.

McPhail, P. (1977) *And How Are We Feeling Today?* Health Education Council Project, Cambridge: CUP.

Maliphant, R. (1979) Juvenile delinquency. In J. C. Coleman (ed.) *The School Years*, London: Methuen.

Marcia, J. E. (1966) Development and validation of ego-identity status. *Journal of Personality and Social Psychology*, 3, 551–8.

Marcia, J. E. (1967) Ego identity status: relationships to change in self-esteem, general adjustment and authoritarianism. *Journal of Personality*, 35, 118–33.

Marcia, J. E. and Friedman, M. L. (1970) Ego identity status in college women. *Journal of Personality*, 38, 249–63.

Marshall, W. A. and Tanner, J. M. (1970) Variations in the pattern of pubertal change in boys. *Archives of Disease in Childhood*, 45, 13.

Masterson, J. (1967) *The Pychiatric Dilemma of Adolescence*, Boston: Little, Brown.

Matteson, D. R. (1975) *Adolescence Today: Sex Roles and the Search for Identity*, Homewood, Illinois: Dorsey.

Matteson, D. R. (1977) Exploration and commitment: sex differences and methodological problems in the use of identity status categories. *Journal of Youth and Adolescence*, 6, 353–74.

Meredith, H. (1963) Changes in the stature and body weight of North American boys during the last eighty years. In L. Lipsitt and C. Spiker (eds) *Advances in Child Development and Behaviour*, vol. 1, New York and London: Academic Press.

Miller, K. and Coleman, J. C. (1980) Attitudes to the future as a function of age, sex and school leaving age. In preparation.

Minuchin, S. (1974) *Families and Family Therapy*, London: Tavistock.

Minuchin, S., Baker, L. and Liebman, R. (1973) Anorexia nervosa: successful application of a family therapy approach. Paper presented to the American Paediatric Society, San Francisco, quoted in J. J. Conger (ed.) (1977) *Adolescence and Youth*, New York: Harper & Row.

Monge, R. H. (1973) Developmental trends in factors of the adolescent self-concept. *Developmental Psychology*, 8, 382–93.

Montagna, W. and Sadler, W. A. (eds) (1974) *Reproductive Behavior*, New York: Plenum.

Morgan, H. G., Pocock, G. and Pottle, S. (1975) The urban distribution of non-fatal deliberate self-harm. *British Journal of Psychiatry*, 126, 319–28.

Musgrove, F. (1964) *Youth and the Social Order*, London: Routledge & Kegan Paul.

Mussen, P. H. (1962) Long term consequences of masculinity of interest in adolescence. *Journal of Consulting Psychology*, 26, 435–40.

Mussen, P. H. and Jones, M. (1957) Self conceptions, motivations and interpersonal attitudes of late and early maturing boys. *Child Development*, 28, 243–56.

Mussen, P. H., Conger, J. J. and Kagan, J. (1974) *Child Development and Personality* (4th edn), New York: Harper & Row.

Mussen, P. H., Young, H. V., Gaddini, R. and Morante, L. (1963) The influence of father/son relationships on adolescent personality and attitudes. *Journal of Child Psychology and Psychiatry*, 4, 3–16.

Muuss, R. E. (1970) Adolescent development and the secular trend. *Adolescence*, 5, 267–84.

Muuss, R. E. (1975) *Theories of Adolescence* (3rd edn), New York: Random House.

Neimark, E. D. (1975) Intellectual development during adolescence. In F. D. Horowitz (ed.) *Review of Child Development Research*, vol. 4, Chicago: University of Chicago Press.

Nesselroade, J. R. and Baltes, P. B. (1974) Adolescent personality: development and historical change. *Monograph for the Society of Research in Child Development*, 39, (Serial No. 154) 1–80.

Nichtern, S. (1978) The walk-in clinic. *Journal of Adolescence*, 1, 55–60.

Noonan, E. (1975) Counselling with adolescents. Paper presented to the British Psychological Society Annual Conference at Nottingham.

Offer, D. (1969) *The Psychological World of the Teenager*, New York: Basic Books.

Offer, D. and Offer, J. B. (1976) *From Teenage to Young Manhood*, New York: Basic Books.

Peck, R. F. (1958) Family patterns correlated with adolescent personality structure. *Journal of Abnormal and Social Psychology*, 47, 347–50.

Peel, E. A. (1971) *The Nature of Adolescent Judgement*, London: Staples Press.

Peel, E. A. and de Silva, W. A. (1972) Some aspects of higher level learning processes during adolescence. In W. D. Wall and V. P. Varma (eds) *Advances in Educational Psychology*, vol. 1, London: University of London Press.

Piaget, J. (1932) *The Moral Judgement of the Child*, London: Routledge and Kegan Paul.

Piaget, J. (1972) Intellectual evolution from adolescence to adulthood. *Human Development*, 15, 1–12.

Piers, E. V. and Harris, D. B. (1964) Age and other correlates of self-concept in children. *Journal of Educational Psychology*, 55, 91–5.

Plant, M. (1975) *Drugtakers in an English Town*, London: Tavistock.

Poppleton, P. and Brown, P. (1966) The secular trend in puberty: has stability been achieved? *British Journal of Educational Psychology*, 36, 95–100.

Powell, M. (1955) Age and sex differences in degree of conflict within certain areas of psychological adjustment. *Psychological Monographs*, 69, 387.

Power, M. J. (1967) Delinquent schools. *New Society*, 19 October.

Power, M. J., Benn, R. and Morris, J. (1974) Neighbourhood, school, and juveniles before the courts. *British Journal of Criminology*, 12, 11–112.

Rest, J., Turiel, E. and Kohlberg, L. (1969) Level of moral judgement as a determinant of preference and comprehension of moral judgements made by others. *Journal of Personality*, 37, 225–52.

Reynolds, D. (1976) The delinquent school. In M. Hammersley and P. Woods (eds) *The Process of Schooling*, London: Routledge & Kegan Paul with the Open University.

Reynolds, D., Jones, D. and St Ledger, S. (1976) Schools do make a difference. *New Society*, 29 July.

Root, N. (1957) A neurosis in adolescence. *Psychoanalytic Study of the Child*, 12, 320–34.

Rosen, B., Bahn, A., Shelow, R. and Bower, E. (1965) Adolescent patients served in outpatient psychiatric clinics. *American Journal of Public Health*, 55, 1563–77.

Rosen, G. and Ross, A. (1968) Relationship of body image to self-concept. *Journal of Consulting and Clinical Psychology*, 32, 100.

Rosenberg, M. (1965) *Society and the Adolescent Self-image*. Princeton, NJ: Princeton University Press.

Rosenberg, M. (1975) The dissonant context and the adolescent self-concept. In S. Dragastin and G. Elder (eds) *Adolescence and the Life Cycle*, New York: John Wiley.

Rutter, M. (1971) Parent-child separation: psychological effects on the children. *Journal of Child Psychology and Psychiatry*, 12, 233–60.

Rutter, M. (1975) *Helping Troubled Children*, Harmondsworth: Penguin.

Rutter, M. and Hersov, L. (eds) (1977) *Child Psychiatry: Modern Approaches*, Oxford: Blackwell Scientific Publications.

Rutter, M., Tizard, J. and Whitmore, K. (1970) *Education, Health and Behaviour*, London: Longman.

Rutter, M., Graham, P., Chadwick, O. and Yule, W. (1976) Adolescent turmoil: fact or fiction? *Journal of Child Psychology and Psychiatry*, 17, 35–56.

Salmon, P. (1979) The role of the peer group. In J. C. Coleman (ed.) *The School Years*, London: Methuen.

Schachter, S. (1959) *The Psychology of Affiliation*, Stanford, Calif.: Stanford University Press.

Schachter, S. (1968) Obesity and eating. *Science*, 161, 751–6.

Schaffer, H. R. and Hargreaves, D. (1978) Young people in society: A research initiative by the SSRC. *Bulletin British Psychological Society*, 31, 91–4.

Schofield, M. (1965) *The Sexual Behaviour of Young People*, London: Longman.

Schofield, M. (1973) *The Sexual Behaviour of Young Adults*, London: Allen Lane.

Secord, P. F. and Jourard, F. M. (1953) The appraisal of body cathexis. *Journal of Consulting Psychology*, 17, 343–7.

Shaffer, D. (1974) Suicide in childhood and early adolescence. *Journal of Child Psychology and Psychiatry*, 15, 275–92.

Sharpe, S. (1974) *Just Like a Girl*, Harmondsworth: Penguin.

Shayer, M. and Wylam, H. (1978) The distribution of Piagetian stages of thinking in British middle and secondary school children: II. *British Journal of Educational Psychology*, 48, 62–70.

Shayer, M., Kuchemann, D. E. and Wylam, H. (1976) The distribution of Piagetian stages of thinking in British middle and secondary school children. *British Journal of Educational Psychology*, 46, 164–73.

Simmons, R. and Rosenberg, F. (1975) Sex, sex-roles and self-image. *Journal of Youth and Adolescence*, 4, 229–58.

Simmons, R., Rosenberg, F. and Rosenberg, M. (1973) Disturbance in the self-image of adolescents. *American Sociological Review*, 38, 553–68. Reprinted in J. J. Conger (ed.) (1975) *Contemporary Issues in Adolescent Development*, New York: Harper & Row.

Skynner, R. (1976) *One Flesh; Separate Persons*, London: Constable.

Smith, D. M. (1978) Social class differences in adult attitudes to youth. *Journal of Adolescence*, 1, 147–54.

Tanner, J. M. (1962) *Growth at Adolescence*, Oxford: Blackwell Scientific Publications.

Tanner, J. M. (1970) Physical growth. In P. H. Mussen (ed.) *Carmichael's Manual of Child Psychology*, vol. 2, New York: John Wiley.

Tanner, J. M. (1973) Growing up. *Scientific American*, 229, 35–42.

Tanner, J. M. (1978) *Foetus into Man*, London: Open Books.

Tanner, J. M., Whitehouse, R. H. and Takaishi, M. (1966) Standards from birth to maturing for height, weight, height velocity and weight velocity: British children. *Archives of Disease in Childhood*, 41, 455–71.

Thomas, E. J. (1968) Role theory, personality and the individual. In E. F. Borgatta and W. Lambert (eds) *Handbook of Personality Theory and Research*, Chicago: Rand-McNally.

Thompson, G. G. and Horrocks, J. E. (1947) A study of the friendship fluctuations of urban boys and girls. *Journal of Genetic Psychology*, 70, 53–63.

Thornburg, H. D. (1975) Adolescent sources of initial sex information. In R. E. Grinder (ed.) *Studies in Adolescence* (3rd edn), London: Collier-Macmillan.

Toder, N. L. and Marcia, J. E. (1973) Ego identity status and response to conformity pressure in college women. *Journal of Personality and Social Psychology*, 26, 287–94.

Tolstrup, K. (1975) Treatment for anorexia nervosa in children. *Journal of Child Psychology and Psychiatry*, 16, 75–8.

Tomé, H. R. (1972) *Le moi et l'autre dans la conscience de l'adolescence*, Paris: Delachaux & Niestle.

Tomlinson-Keasey, C. and Keasey, C. B. (1974) The mediating role of cognitive development in moral judgement. *Child Development*, 45, 291–8.

Tuma, E. and Livson, N. (1960) Family, socio-economic status and adolescent attitudes to authority. *Child Development*, 31, 387–99.

Turiel, E. (1969) Developmental processes in the child's moral thinking. In P. H. Mussen, J. Langer and M. Covington (eds) *Trends and Issues in Developmental Psychology*, New York: Holt, Rinehart & Winston.

Turiel, E. (1974) Conflict and transition in adolescent moral development. *Child Development*, 45, 14–29.

Turiel, E. and Rothman, G. R. (1972) The influence of reasoning on behavioural choices at different stages of moral development. *Child Development*, 43, 741–56.

Tyler, M. (1978) *Advisory and Counselling Services for Young People*, DHSS Research Report No. 1, London: HMSO.

Waterman, A. S. and Waterman, C. K. (1971) A longitudinal study of changes in ego identity status during the freshman year in college. *Developmental Psychology*, 5, 167–73.

Waterman, A. S. and Waterman, C. K. (1972) Relationship between freshman ego identity status and subsequent academic behaviour. *Developmental Psychology*, 6, 179.

Waterman, A. S., Geary, P. S. and Waterman, C. K. (1974) Longitudinal study in changes of ego identity status from the freshman to the senior year at college. *Developmental Psychology*, 10, 387–92.

Weinreich, H. (1978) Sex role socialization. In J. Chetwynd and O. Hartnett (eds) *The Sex Role System*, London: Routledge & Kegan Paul.

Weinreich, P. (1979) Ethnicity and adolescent identity conflicts. In S. Khan (ed.) *Minority Families in Britain*, London: Macmillan.

Weinreich-Haste, H. (1979) Moral development. In J. C. Coleman (ed.) *The School Years*. London: Methuen.

West, D. (1977) Delinquency. In M. Rutter and L. Hersov (eds) *Child Psychiatry: Modern Approaches*, Oxford: Blackwell Scientific Publications.

West, D. and Farrington, D. (1973) *Who Becomes Delinquent?* London: Heinemann.

West, D. and Farrington, D. (1977) *The Delinquent Way of Life*, London: Heinemann.

Wheeler, D. K. (1961) Popularity among adolescents in Western Australia and in the United States of America. *The School Review*, 49, 67–81.

Woodmansey, A. (1969) The common factor in problems of adolescence. *British Journal of Medical Psychology*, 42, 353–70.

Name index

Adelson, J., 38, 39, 49, 66, 67, 77, 82, 83, 92, 93, 94, 95, 97, 98, 99, 181, 191, 195
Aitken, P. P., 110, 191
Akers, R. L., 108, 111, 191
Anderson, J. E., 91, 191
Anderson, L., 100, 196
Anthony, E. J., 166, 191

Bagley, C., 199
Bahm, R. M., 96, 192
Bahn, A., 203
Bahr, S. J., 73, 74, 192
Baittle, B., 5, 191
Baker, L., 201
Baltes, P. B., 182, 201
Bandura, A., 66, 191
Baruch, G. K., 78, 191
Baumrind, D., 9, 73, 74, 192
Bayley, N., 18, 98, 101, 192, 198
Bee, H., 57, 192
Bell, A. P., 78, 192
Beloff, H., 57, 193
Benedict, R., 8, 192
Bengston, V. L., 66, 192
Benn, R., 202
Bigelow, B. J., 93, 192
Biller, H. B., 96, 192
Blos, P., 3, 6, 192
Borgatta, E., 195, 204
Bower, E., 203
Bowerman, C. E., 73, 74, 113, 114, 192

Brim, O. G., 9, 192
Brittain, C. V., 113, 114, 115, 192
Bronfenbrenner, U., 10, 90, 159, 192
Bronson, G. A., 55, 192
Brown, P., 20, 202
Bruch, H., 163, 164, 169, 192
Bruggen, P., 167, 168, 193
Buck, C., 19, 193
Buker, M., 91, 197
Butters, S., 181, 193
Byng-Hall, J., 193

Campbell, J. D., 102, 193
Caplan, G., 191, 192
Carlsmith, L., 79, 193
Carlson, R., 45, 60, 193
Cavior, N., 103, 193
Chadwick, O., 203
Chetwynd, J., 205
Chisholm, D., 162, 164, 193
Clausen, J. A., 17, 193
Cloutier, R., 30, 193
Cockram, L., 57, 193
Cole, M., 137, 193
Coleman, J. C., 49, 50, 60, 69, 70, 71, 82, 83, 84, 85, 93, 94, 95, 96, 106, 107, 179, 181, 183, 184, 185, 193, 194, 195, 200, 201, 203, 205
Coleman, J. S., 66, 100, 101, 102, 103, 194
Conger, J. J., 20, 21, 22, 26, 35, 40,

Subject index